Basic Christian Faith

By C. Donald Cole

Have I Committed the Unpardonable Sin? (And Other Questions You've Wanted to Ask About the Christian Faith)

Abraham, God's Man of Faith

I Believe

Christian Perspectives on Controversial Issues

Basic Christian Faith

C. Donald Cole

CROSSWAY BOOKS • WESTCHESTER, ILLINOIS
A Division of Good News Publishers

Biblical quotations, unless otherwise indicated, are taken from *Holy Bible: New International Version,* copyright © 1978 by the New York International Bible Society. Used by permission of Zondervan Bible Publishers.

Front cover design by Lane T. Dennis

First printing, 1985

Printed in the United States of America

Library of Congress Catalog Card Number 84-72008

ISBN 0-89107-338-8

Contents

Publisher's Introduction

Christians in every age need a clear understanding of the central doctrines of biblical faith. C. Donald Cole, radio pastor of Moody Bible Institute, shares in this book helpful discussion of God's purpose for man, biblical authority, the significance of Christ's Incarnation, and many other important teachings of the Holy Scriptures.

We heartily commend this resource for individual or group study.

"Do your best to present yourself to God as one approved, a workman who does not need to be ashamed and who correctly handles the word of truth," for "All Scripture is God-breathed and is useful for teaching, rebuking, correcting and training in righteousness, so that the man of God may be thoroughly equipped for every good work" (2 Timothy 2:15; 3:16, 17).

1

The Purpose of Man

A great Scottish theologian of the nineteenth century said, "If an assembly of philosophers had been convened at [ancient] Athens to compose a catechism of religion and morals for the youth of Greece, to a certainty it would have opened with, 'What is the chief end of man?' " Modern writers may say that human existence is as meaningless as that of a slug or a lemming, but the ancients knew better. As Alexander Whyte said, "Almost all the dialogues and discussions of the fathers of moral philosophy revolve around this supreme and everlasting question, What is the final cause and chief end of man?"[1]

There are many ends or purposes of life. Some, though subordinate to man's chief end, are nonetheless legitimate. For example, it is required of Christian men that they provide for their families. They get jobs and work at them in order to feed and clothe their wives, children, and anyone else for whose welfare they are responsible. Paul says that we ought to "make it [our] ambition to lead a quiet life, to mind [our] own business and to work with [our] hands."[2]

But what is the primary purpose of man, his purpose above all other purposes? If we look carefully at Scripture we will find that the primary purpose of man is to glorify God.

Glorifying God

But what does it mean to glorify God? For many years in my early life I never really thought about it, though I was a Christian. *Glorify* was, for me, a strictly religious term, with a rather vague meaning.

An ordinary dictionary may help us understand the verb *to glorify:* "to shed radiance or splendor on; to make glorious by presentation in a favorable light; to magnify in worship."[3] Combined, those definitions suggest that to glorify God means to magnify the Lord by declaring what he is like.

It should be obvious that whether we declare what we think he is like or not, we cannot change his divine nature. "I am who I am," God told Moses.[4] God is the eternally self-existent One. What he really is and what he is perceived to be are not always the same.

In its deepest sense, glory is God manifested; it is something which God already has, and we can neither add to nor subtract from it. When John said of Christ, "We have seen his glory,"[5] he meant that he and the other disciples saw in Christ a manifestation of the Second Person of the triune God. The divine glory is God's own nature as he reveals it to us.

But how can *we* glorify God? The answer lies in a second use of the word *glory*.

To Glorify God Is to Tell of His Greatness Glory also is related to reputation, which is the character commonly imputed to a person. Glory is a reputation for goodness, wisdom, righteousness, and other exalted qualities. Now we begin to see how we can glorify God. We cannot alter his character or change the glory which he already has in himself, but we can improve or worsen his reputation. This is what David had in mind when he said at the dedication of the Temple choir:

> Sing to the Lord, all the earth;
> proclaim his salvation day after day.
> Declare his glory among the nations,
> his marvelous deeds among all peoples.[6]

It is also what the psalmist had in mind when he wrote, "Ascribe to the Lord, O families of nations, ascribe to the Lord glory and strength."[7]

When we glorify God, we do not make him different. What we do is enhance his reputation, somewhat in the sense of the Nineteenth Psalm, which begins with these familiar words: "The heavens declare the glory of God; the skies proclaim the work of his hands." I say "somewhat" because there is a difference. From a poet's point of view, the heavens are talking; they are telling of the glory of God. Actually, of course, the starry heavens just exist; but that very existence reveals something about God. To the extent that he is revealed or made manifest, he is glorified. We, of course, are able to talk about God, and to the extent that what we say about him is true, we glorify him.

Even our own existence, like that of the heavens, reveals something about God. The prophet Isaiah quotes God as referring to "everyone who is called by my name, whom I created for my glory, whom I formed and made."[8] Another translation reads, "These are my own people, and I created them to bring me glory."[9] That may be the best explanation we can find for the divine decision to create mankind. If the existence of planets that rotate flawlessly in their orbits tells of the glory of God, how much more does the existence of rational beings made in his own image![10]

The trouble is, from the beginning men and women in great numbers have behaved as if the universe could be explained by a Big Bang or some other mechanical, nonsupernatural act, and the existence of mankind by evolutionary processes. They have been unwilling (and still are unwilling) to give God credit for having created either the universe or life itself.

Millions of people throughout history have acknowledged God, of course, but the most God-conscious person who ever lived has glorified him imperfectly. The one exception was Jesus Christ, who, as every Christian knows, was more than a man.

How did Christ glorify God? He himself explains. In a prayer offered to his Father shortly before proceeding to the Garden of Gethsemane, and from there to Calvary, Jesus said, "I have brought you glory on earth."[11] What did he do to justify that claim? He consistently manifested the moral nature of God. Thinking about those things much later, the Apostle John wrote, "No one has ever seen God, but God the only Son, who is at the Father's side, has made him known."[12] John was remembering Jesus' evidences of deity, including the absolute perfection of a man without sin. Christ revealed the nature of God, and in that way glorified God.

Jesus further revealed the glory of God by finishing the work the Father gave him to do. Never before was God's glory more perfectly revealed than at Calvary. There God manifested his love by becoming our substitute, in the person of his beloved Son. The Father sent the Son to be the Savior of the world; and in the Son's atoning death God was glorified.

To Glorify God Is to Obey Him Glorifying God means more than enhancing his reputation. To glorify God also means to honor him, to give him his due. What is his due? What is owed him? The only complete answer, of course, would be "everything." But among the specific things we owe, one of the most important is our obedience.

A familiar passage makes clear the connection between obeying and glorifying God. "Flee from sexual immorality," Paul tells the Corinthians and all Christians. He then reminds us that because we are Christ's, our bodies are temples of the Holy Spirit, who is in each one of us. We are not our own; we are not free to live according to the dictates of normal human appetites or desires. We belong to God, who bought us with a price, the price of Christ's blood. Paul concludes, "Therefore honor God with your body."[13]

How do we honor, or glorify, God with our bodies? In light of what Paul says in the passage just cited, the least we can do is obey his law that restricts sexual activity to marriage. That is what Paul intended by the two imperatives: "flee sexual immorality" *and* "honor [or glorify] God with your body." Those are by no means the only biblical demands with reference to our bodies, but they are a starting-place. In our times, obedience to God's standard of sexual purity is a key test of a believer's desire to glorify God with his body.

Recognizing and Enjoying God's Goodness

Another primary purpose of man is simply to recognize and enjoy the Lord's goodness. The devil's first trick was to raise questions in Eve's mind about the goodness of God. He wanted Eve to believe that the Lord was depriving her of something good and pleasant; and he succeeded. Paul says that "Eve was deceived by the serpent's cunning,"[14] so that she was "quite deceived."[15] She completely swallowed his lie. Everyone knows what happened next. Adam and Eve disobeyed God, and thereby brought the fall of man, the effects of which it is the business of history to record and of theology to explain.

For our purposes, we are interested only in one aspect of the Fall: the persistence of the notion that God is the Great Inhibitor, that he requires an obedience which, of necessity, makes people miserable, or at least less happy than they would be if he were not involved in their lives. That is what many, if not most, people think—when they think of God at all.

The idea of obedience to God is rather easy to understand, though for many it is not easy to accept. The idea of enjoying God, however, seems hard even for many Christians to understand. We may greatly enjoy God's blessings and thank him for them without really enjoying *him*.

One of the most beautiful passages in the Psalms is the last verse of Psalm 16: "You have made known to me the path of life; you will fill me with joy in your presence, with eternal pleasures at your right hand." As for the Gospels, who is not familiar with some of our Lord's last words to his friends? "I have told you this," he said, "so that my joy may be in you and that your joy may be complete."[16] A few minutes later Jesus prayed to his Father, and in his prayer he reveals the source of his boundless joy—his relationship with his Father. He prayed aloud so that his friends could hear what he was saying to his Father: "I say these things while I am still in the world, so that they may have the full measure of my joy within them."[17]

If there were no other testimonies to the possibility of joy in God, or at least joy in his presence, those should suffice. But there are others. Take Psalm 43, a prayer directed to God and also a meditation:

> Send forth your light and your truth,
> let them guide me;
> let them bring me to your holy mountain,
> to the place where you dwell.
> Then will I go to the altar of God,
> to God, my joy and my delight.
> I will praise you with the harp,
> O God, my God. (vv. 3, 4)

In a concluding word, the psalmist exhorts himself:

> Why are you downcast, O my soul?
> Why so disturbed within me?
> Put your hope in God,
> for I will yet praise him,
> my Savior and my God. (v. 5)

The psalmist makes clear the connection between his exceeding joy and God's character. God not only sends out light and truth, but he is also our Savior and God. The psalmist rejoiced in God because of who God is and what God does for those who trust in him. God is not the Great Inhibitor; he is the Great Giver and the Great Helper.

Often it seems harder to enjoy God than to glorify him. It is harder because praise and obedience, by which we glorify God, are superficially possible even when our heart is not in them. It is therefore easy to think we are glorifying God when we are not. But who can *enjoy* God, or enjoy anyone or anything else, if his heart is not in it?

To enjoy God is to have joy in him. If the dictionary's definition of joy as "deeper-rooted than delight, more radiant or demonstrative than gladness" is correct (and it is), how many Christians really enjoy God? It is a troubling question. It troubles *me* very much, especially in view of Paul's repeated imperative: "Rejoice in the Lord always. I will say it again: Rejoice!"[18] A biblical imperative (i.e., command) implies the ability, whether natural or God-given, to comply. This particular passage in God's Word *commands* us to have joy in the Lord and to be radiant. The implication is clear: because God commands Christians to enjoy him, we *can* enjoy him.

It is easy to "explain" our failure to delight in God. We can come up with several problems so-called, but they all boil down to a single problem—the problem of sin. Sin raises barriers between God and us as sinning people, and on our part it generates hostility. The prophet Isaiah says, "Your iniquities have separated you from your God."[19] Offenders find it difficult, if not impossible, to delight in an offended God. When conscious only of guilt, sinners cannot enjoy God; it is psychologically impossible.

Of course, not all sinful men and women are conscious of guilt. The truth is, not many people really think much about guilt before God at all. Consciousness of guilt before God is found only in those who believe and take seriously what the Bible teaches about God and man. They become aware of their essential sinfulness and all that sinfulness entails. If they respond with repentance toward God and faith in the Lord Jesus Christ, their guilt is removed. The separation between themselves and God is ended, and joy in God becomes more than a theoretical possibility; it becomes a wonderful and joyful reality.

If, on the other hand, they do not repent and believe the gospel, their natural hostility toward God deepens. Hostility may seem too strong a term. But in his letter to the Colossians Paul reminds them that "Once you were alienated from God and were enemies in your minds because of your evil behavior. But now he has reconciled you by Christ's physical body through death to present you holy in his sight, without blemish and free from accusation."[20]

Notice the combination of words: "alienated from God" and "enemies in your minds." Those twin themes—alienation and hostility—are struck more than once in Paul's writings.[21] They describe the human condition—alienated from God by sin and hostile toward him. God's answer is reconciliation and a renewed mind, which together make it possible for believers to enjoy God. We can enjoy him because the separation is ended and our minds have been cleansed of the old animosity, the old hostility, toward him. Says Paul, "We also rejoice in God through our Lord Jesus Christ, through whom we have now received reconciliation."[22]

Obviously, joy in God is possible only to the extent that we are conscious of the reconciliation achieved by Christ through his death and to the extent that we live as if we really believed it. On the other hand, to the extent that we consciously disobey God, or live carnally, we forfeit joy in God. Holy living and the enjoyment of God are inseparable.

Glorifying and Enjoying God Forever

Eternal life is not exclusively chronological. What we will be doing forever, we ought to be doing now, in this life. Sometimes, however, we think of eternal life only in chronological terms. You die, and if you know Christ you then begin to live eternally. But that view is incorrect. It ignores two truths: that eternal life is a present possession, and that its possession should affect profoundly the way its possessors now live.

The verb tenses used in the following passages are significant. "Whoever believes in the Son has eternal life, but whoever rejects the Son will not see life, for God's wrath remains on him."[23] "I tell you the truth, whoever hears my word and believes him who sent me has eternal life and will not be condemned; he has crossed over from death to life."[24] "My sheep listen to my voice; I know them, and they follow me. I give them eternal life, and they shall never perish; no one can snatch them out of my hand."[25] "Everyone who believes that Jesus is the Christ is born of God."[26] Those suffice to make the point, but I will give one more:

> And this is the testimony: God has given us eternal life, and this life is in his Son. He who has the Son has life; he who does not have the Son of God does not have life. I write these things to you who believe in the name of the Son of God so that you may know that you have eternal life.[27]

We could go on quoting Scripture to make the point that eternal life is not granted at the moment of death. It is conferred on every true believer the moment that person trusts Christ for forgiveness and salvation. It is important to understand that truth, because knowledge of it confers certain blessings on believers, including assurance of salvation and the wonderful comfort that comes with assurance. It also provides an incentive for holy living. If we already belong to God, if he has given us his Holy Spirit, and if salvation is assured, what kind of people ought we to be? The answer is clear: holy people. That is the point Peter makes so persuasively in his first letter.[28] Paul also speaks about living "a godly life in Christ Jesus."[29]

Eternal life begins now; but it is also true, of course, that it lasts forever. It is everlasting life. For most of us, the words *eternal* and *everlasting* may be used interchangeably as meaning the same thing. There are, however, important differences between them. *Everlasting* applies to duration alone, as in "everlasting punishment." *Eternal,* on the other hand, includes the idea of essential quality, as in "the eternal God," who has neither beginning nor end. We can therefore see why "eternal life" is a more suitable designation than "everlasting life." It is life with more than duration; it is a special quality of life, communicated to us the moment we trust Christ.

Yet eternal life is also everlasting life; it never ends. It lasts forever—not just for now or for a very long time, but forever and ever, for endless ages.

Where did the concept of eternity come from? It is not a cultural invention, an idea peculiar, for example, to the Hebrew writers through whom we received the Bible. It is a universal concept. Scratch the surface even of an atheist and you will find a man who, though denying the validity of the concept, is aware of it. His persistent denials attest to the pervasiveness of the idea. Ecclesiastes says that God has "set eternity in the hearts of men."[30] In other words, the concept is virtually instinctive.

Instinctive may not be the right word, but I cannot think of a better one. Neither could the translators of at least one Bible version, which records Paul as saying that "when Gentiles who do not have the Law do instinctively the things of the Law, . . . they show the work of the Law written in their hearts."[31] "Instinctively" is given as "by nature" in many translations. The idea is that some things are known because God built awareness of them into us.

The knowledge of God's existence is surely one of the things we know instinctively. The Bible says, "The fool says in his heart,

'There is no God.' "[32] It is not quite clear whether such a man says there is no God because he is a fool, or that he is a fool because he says it. In either case, he goes against nature; he denies what is instinctive and natural. Psalm 14 continues to say that such fools "all have turned aside,"[33] as if from that instinctive knowledge of the existence of God. Paul indicts the majority of mankind who, "although they knew God, they neither glorified him as God nor gave thanks to him, but their thinking became futile and their foolish hearts were darkened. Although they claimed to be wise, they became fools and exchanged the glory of the immortal God for images made to look like mortal man and birds and animals and reptiles."[34]

The concept of eternity and the nature of God, as known instinctively and revealed in Scripture, are closely related. In one of the loveliest passages in Scripture, God calls himself "the everlasting God, the Creator of the ends of the earth. He will not grow tired or weary, and his understanding no one can fathom."[35]

Through the ages God's people have been sustained by knowledge of his infinitude. He is eternal; he is everlasting. "Abraham planted a tamarisk tree in Beersheba, and there he called upon the name of the Lord, the Eternal God."[36] Moses wrote a prayer (which we call Psalm 90) in which he acknowledges the eternalness of God:

Lord, you have been our dwelling place
  throughout all generations.
Before the mountains were born
  or you brought forth the earth and
    the world,
  from everlasting to everlasting you
    are God.[37]

Psalm 102 has a similar affirmation of God's eternalness. The writer was conscious of his own perishability. He was getting old, but he knew that the God whom he worshiped was unchanging and imperishable.

Your years go on through all generations.
In the beginning you laid the foundations
    of the earth,
  and the heavens are the work of your hands.
They will perish, but you remain;
  they will all wear out like a garment.

Like clothing you will change them
  and they will be discarded.
But you remain the same,
  and your years will never end.[38]

That is the reason we are to enjoy God forever. He is the eternal and everlasting God. He never comes to an end. All those who know and enjoy him now will know and enjoy him *forever.*

2

The Bible and Its Authority

Our minds are at best finite and therefore limited in capacity. Consequently, God is unknowable except as he reveals himself. We have no way of finding out about God or of knowing his will on our own. We would have no way of glorifying God or of enjoying him if he did not show himself to us through his Word.

Our minds not only are finite but are damaged by sin, so that even the best mind that ever functioned may be described as spiritually darkened or blinded. Paul speaks of "the futility of their [unenlightened, pagan] thinking." He says that unconverted, Christless people are "darkened in their understanding and separated from the life of God because of the ignorance that is in them."[1]

That is strong language, but it is biblical language. In another place Paul says that God "has rescued us [Christians] from the dominion of darkness."[2] These and similar passages teach that our minds are flawed in at least one important respect: they are incapable of discovering basic truth about God.

The second, and closely related, reason why we need help to know how to glorify God and enjoy him is his unknowableness. Some of God's attributes, such as his creativity and power, may be deduced. Paul says that "since the creation of the world God's invisible qualities—his eternal power and divine nature—have been clearly seen, being understood from what has been made."[3] The universe reveals his power and brilliance. The immensity of outer space and the structure of the atom alike declare God's greatness. The problem, however, is that the divine attributes that may be deduced from his creative activity do not tend to draw us to him or teach us how to glorify and enjoy him. We may prostrate ourselves before the Almighty, but if all we know about him is his almightiness, we do not (in fact, as sinners we *cannot*) love or enjoy him. He is too great for us, too powerful, too good, too wise, too overwhelming.

God Is Speaking

Knowing God's power and greatness may be enough to make us worshipers in a formal sense. We may fall down before him in awe and reverence. In this limited sense, we glorify him. But we cannot really love and enjoy him unless, by pondering his creation, we conclude that he made the world *for us* and therefore *must* be personal and loving to some extent. The link between God's creative activity and his love is there, but we have to think about it to see it. Even then, it seems too theoretical for most of us. It is still only guesswork, and it does not satisfy our heart's longing to know God. Like Job, we sigh, "If only I knew where to find him; if only I could go to his dwelling!"[4]

Poor Job was born several thousand years too early, so to speak. Not that he was limited to knowledge of God that he attained through contemplating nature. He knew far more about God than his creative power and wisdom. He knew, for example, that God would judge the world and set right every wrong, and that he, Job, would see God in the resurrection.[5] In that regard Job knew more than most modern men and women. But he did not have the advantage of the Scriptures, even in the incomplete form enjoyed by David and his contemporaries. If, as is probable, Job lived about the time of Abraham, he knew only what God revealed to him directly or what had been passed down through oral tradition. He never saw a copy of any part of Scripture, because none of it had yet been written.

Did that matter? In Job's case, no. God provided him knowledge of everything he needed to know. But in our own day, not knowing what the Bible teaches is an appalling disadvantage. Why? Because the Bible is God's Word, his revelation of himself and of his will.

Other than that which still is apparent in nature, God no longer reveals truth as he did in ancient times. Yet he reveals vastly more about himself and his ways than in the past. It may seem surprising that God changes his methods of self-disclosure, but that fact is clearly stated in the Epistle to the Hebrews: "In the past God spoke to our forefathers through the prophets at many times and in various ways, but in these last days he has spoken to us by his Son."[6]

That statement does not discredit divine revelation in the past, as if somehow it was unreliable. The source of the earlier revelation was God, but the revelation was limited. Consequently, not even David, the eloquent psalm-writer, had access to as much information about God as is now available to anyone willing to spend a little time reading the Bible.

The Word of God

The Bible uses the phrase *Word of God* in two ways: first, as a designation of God the Son; second, as the divine written communication that we know as the Bible. The opening words of the Gospel of John are: "In the beginning was the Word, and the Word was with God, and the Word was God." Later, John says that "the Word became flesh and lived . . . among us."[7] The identification here is clear: the Word of God is God the Son, the Second Person of the Godhead, Jesus Christ.

But the Word of God is also used to refer to Scripture. "All Scripture is God-breathed," Paul tells us.[8] The word *Scripture* stands for the sacred writings. Immediately before the verse just quoted, Paul uses the plural form. Speaking to Timothy he says, "From infancy you have known the holy Scriptures, which are able to make you wise for salvation through faith in Christ Jesus."[9]

The Old and New Testaments

Originally a legal term (as it still is), the word *testament* entered English Scripture translations as an equivalent of the Greek word for covenant. Latin writers in the early church used it to designate the two collections of sacred writings belonging uniquely to the people of Israel and to the Church respectively. That is the way it is most commonly used today in regard to the Bible.

In its technical sense a testament is a legal document by which a person determines the disposition of his property after his death, as we see in "last will and testament." The word *testament* is used in this sense in the Authorized Version of the Book of Hebrews.[10] One writer suggests that the Holy Scriptures are called a "testament" because "they are the last will of the glorious Testator . . . concerning the spiritual legacies therein bequeathed to his spiritual seed."[11]

Knowing and glorifying God are achieved only by giving attention to the Bible. Certainly this is what the Bible itself teaches. As mentioned above, Paul congratulated Timothy on his childhood exposure to the Scriptures. It is through the Scriptures that a person acquires the wisdom that leads to salvation through faith in Christ Jesus. Not only that, but the Scriptures are profitable for all the requirements of spiritual growth and maturity. "All Scripture is God-breathed and is useful for teaching, rebuking, correcting and training in righteousness, so that the man of God may be thoroughly equipped for every good work."[12]

Scripture teaches us how to glorify God. It tells us what kinds of words and actions honor and please him and what kinds enhance his reputation. Christian men and women who study and obey his Word glorify God to the extent that this is humanly possible.

The Bible even tells us how to love and enjoy God. Nowhere is that truth more prominent than in Psalm 119, the first two verses of which strike a note that is sounded again and again:

> Blessed [i.e., happy] are they whose ways are blameless,
> who walk according to the law of the Lord.
> Blessed are they who keep his statutes
> and seek him with all their heart.

The man who composed that Psalm, the longest in the entire book, delighted in the Word of God. He enjoyed it, and in enjoying it, he enjoyed God.

Is the Bible the only revelation of God, or are there other revelations—such as tradition, intuition, or continued communications directly from the Holy Spirit himself? The teaching of the Bible, and therefore of orthodox Christianity throughout history, is that it is God's complete revelation. It is not a partial revelation which must or can be supplemented by oral or written traditions, by intuition, or by any other alleged source of information or authority. The Bible not only is complete; it is the *only* reliable source of knowledge in spiritual matters.

That is the Bible's own position. When God gave his commandments to ancient Israel, he said through his spokesman Moses, "Do not add to what I command you and do not subtract from it, but keep the commands of the Lord your God that I give you."[13] The warning clearly implies that additions or deletions would alter the commandment in such a way that the people would not keep it as they should.

Jesus rebuked Jewish religious leaders of his day because their scrupulous attention to oral and written traditions caused them and their followers to transgress the commandments of God.[14] He called them "blind guides."[15] They were blind because they could not tell the difference between the important matters of God's law and the picayune nonsense that characterized many of their human traditions. They were blind guides because they traveled about on land and sea to make one convert, and when they had him they made him "twice as much a son of hell as [they were]."[16] Had he come back to life in Jesus' time, Moses doubtlessly would have told them that their blindness was the result of their adding to or taking from the Word of God. How much safer to stick with Scripture than to rely on human traditions!

The prophet Isaiah would have agreed with Moses. When his contemporaries were turning restlessly to other sources of knowledge, he warned them to test those ideas by the Word of God. "To the law and to the testimony!" he said. "If they [i.e., mediums and spiritists] do not speak according to this word, they have no light of dawn."[17] Everything is to be tested by the unchanging Word of God.

The Primary Teaching of God's Word

If the Bible is God's Word, what are its primary teachings? On a certain occasion Jesus had a dialogue with some of his opponents. They were learned students of the Old Testament Scriptures, a fact that Jesus acknowledged. "You diligently study the Scriptures," he said, "because you think that by them you possess eternal life." They read the Bible constantly, but they completely missed its principal message. The Scriptures, Jesus told them, "testify about me, yet you refuse to come to me to have life."[18]

That is one of the most frightening passages in the Bible. It reveals the possibility of a lifetime of Bible study that is zealous and assiduous but unprofitable. Men and women who know how to dot every i and cross every t can miss the main message. What do the Scriptures *primarily* teach? What are the most important things they teach, the things we absolutely need to know? Those are the critical questions.

First, Scripture primarily teaches what man is to believe about God—not just that God exists eternally and is almighty and so forth, but that he is revealed in the divine person of Jesus Christ. "No one has ever seen God, but God the only Son, who is at the Father's side, has made him known."[19] As Jesus says, "the Scriptures . . . testify about me." How to find God through Christ is the principal thing by far.

Biblical truths are all equally true, but are not equally important. It is 100 percent true that chief Oholibamah descended from

Esau, as the Bible says, but chief Oholibamah's genealogy is not nearly as important as the truth that Christ died for the ungodly, as the Bible also says.[20]

Moreover, the Bible teaches many important things that are not the primary things. Old Testament narratives are important, but many of them are not primary, even in the Old Testament. They do not teach us what we must know about God and what he expects of us. This is not to imply that the narratives are without merit; if they were unimportant or had nothing to say to us, they would not be part of the Bible. But they are not given to us as primary teachings; they do not tell us what we need to believe about God or what God requires of us.

Belief in God The most important truth of Scripture is that man must believe in, have faith in, God. The dictionary compares similar words *(belief, faith, persuasion,* and *conviction)* and says they agree in the idea of assent. It also distinguishes between them: *belief* and *faith*, for example, differ chiefly in that belief, as a rule, suggests little more than intellectual assent, whereas faith also implies trust or confidence. A *persuasion* is an assured opinion, as: "It is my persuasion that he is bad." Persuasion sometimes implies that this assurance is induced by one's feelings or wishes, rather than by argument or evidence. *Conviction* stands for a fixed or settled belief, as: "His belief is likely to have been a persuasion rather than a conviction."[21]

Those who know the Bible fairly well will agree that it generally uses those words as they are defined in the dictionary. I say "generally" because there are exceptions. In Scripture, *belief* and *faith* usually mean the same thing. A true believer believes in God; that is, he has faith in God. In some biblical accounts, however, belief is seen to be little more than intellectual assent. When the crowds saw the miracles Jesus performed, they believed in his name; but the Bible says, "Jesus would not entrust himself to them, for he knew all men."[22] Under pressure of persecution or of great demands, such "believers" fall away. Paul was afraid that some of his converts in Galatia were superficial believers. Their belief was not a fixed conviction and, accordingly, it would not last.[23]

Belief, if it is worth anything at all, must be genuine—the fixed belief of one who, having seen "many convincing proofs," is persuaded that the gospel is true. Consequently, he *lives* as one who unwaveringly trusts God.[24]

Two legitimate questions must be answered. First, why should anyone believe the Scriptures? Second, do the Scriptures really require belief? A thorough answer to the first question would take a book, and many such books have been written.[25]

Evangelicals believe that all Scripture is given by inspiration of God. We believe that:

> The whole Bible is inspired in the sense that holy men of God "were moved by the Holy Spirit" to write the very words of Scripture. We believe that this divine inspiration extends equally and fully to all parts of the writings—historical, poetical, doctrinal, and prophetical—as appeared in the original manuscripts.[26]

If you accept that view of Scripture—its being divinely inspired in its entirety—you have the answer to both questions posed above. If the Bible is God's Word, it not only merits belief, but demands belief. Think about it! If the Bible is true, then it *should* be believed, as with everything else that is true. Only ignorant or arrogantly stubborn people refuse to believe the truth. If the Bible is God's truth, it *must* be believed.

The Bible demands belief. Near the end of his Gospel, John says that he was selective in the material he used. He omitted much that could have been recorded. But, he explains, "These are written that you may believe that Jesus is the Christ, the Son of God, and that by believing you may have life in his name."[27] Near the end of his first letter the same apostle tells why we should believe:

> We accept man's testimony, but God's testimony is greater because it is the testimony of God, which he has given about his Son. Anyone who believes in the Son of God has this testimony in his heart. Anyone who does not believe God has made him out to be a liar, because he has not believed the testimony God has given about his Son.[28]

John takes it for granted that the Bible is God's Word. He says, in effect, that believing what God says should be easy for at least three reasons. First, believing is as natural as breathing. People make mistakes and people tell lies, but if we did not generally take others at their word, we could not function as a society. If, then, we are naturally inclined to accept the testimony of men, the testimony of God should be even easier to accept. He neither makes mistakes nor tells lies. Second, when we believe the gospel, there is an inner assurance that we have believed the truth. Third, the alternative to belief is unbelief, which is tantamount to calling God a liar. If the Bible is true, refusal to believe it is the same as accusing God of deceit.

Responsibility to God Before God gave his ancient people Israel the Ten Commandments, he said something about himself: "I am the Lord your God."[29] That great statement laid the foundation for the call to duty. Nothing less would provide the required incentive to obey the commandments. So the order of teaching in Scripture is theology first, morals second. Faith comes first, then works.

In our zeal for the central biblical truth that salvation is granted in response to faith alone, evangelical Christians sometimes give the impression that works do not matter or are not terribly important. But that is not the case, as the Bible makes clear. Here is how Paul states the truth in Ephesians:

> For it is by grace you have been saved, through faith—
> and this not from yourselves, it is the gift of God—
> not by works, so that no one can boast. For we are God's workmanship, created in Christ Jesus to do good works,
> which God prepared in advance for us to do.[30]

In that biblical statement, the order of faith and works could not be clearer: first faith, then duty. Nor could it be more clearly stated that faith does not stand alone; true faith produces good works. Belief comes first, but if it is not manifested by good works, it is, as the Apostle James tells us, not true faith at all. "Faith . . . not accompanied by action, is dead."[31]

3

Knowing God

There are many fine books on systematic theology. All of them, without exception, devote a great deal of space to theology proper. Theology, the study of God, is to be distinguished from ecclesiology (the study of the Church) and all of the other "ologys" (anthropology, the study of man; hamartiology, the study of sin; soteriology, the study of salvation; etc.) which are associated with theology in its broadest sense. The space theologians give to theology proper is justified. If Scripture primarily teaches what man is to believe about God, then books attempting to systematize what the Bible teaches will inevitably deal at great length with the subject of God.

We are not going to plow through a textbook on theology. We will also avoid the speculations of philosophy—though it is tempting to quote Aristotle, Hegel, and other philosophers, just to contrast their conjectures with the assured word of the Bible. Other sources, however, will be cited occasionally to help interpret and explain what the Bible itself says.

The Bible takes for granted that God exists and that he is, in common terminology, "the Supreme Being." In that approach the Bible is not greatly different from philosophy, which, despite any claims to the contrary, always begins with certain assumptions. In *The Universe Next Door,* author James W. Sire shows how world views (that is, philosophies of life) are determined to a great extent by the concept of God with which they begin.[1]

But the Bible does not take the nature or purpose of God for granted. From beginning to end it is made clear that God's nature, purpose, and will can be known by us only because God has revealed them.

God Is Spirit

The most fundamental truth about God's nature is that he is spirit, and the source of that truth is Jesus himself. Jesus' definition of God is found in John's Gospel: "God is spirit, and his worshipers must worship in spirit and in truth."[2] God is not *a* spirit, as if one among many; he *is* spirit. The word *spirit* defines his essence, not his rank or personality.

Perhaps the simplest way to understand the term *spirit* is to contrast it with matter. Our bodies are matter. When from the cross Jesus cried, "Father, into your hands I commit my spirit," he meant that his life was leaving his body.[3] Later, when he was raised from the dead and showed himself to his friends, they were badly frightened. They thought they were seeing a ghost—which is Anglo-Saxon for spirit. He calmed their fears, telling them that he was in the body. A spirit, he said, "does not have flesh and bones, as you see I have."[4]

But if God is spirit, why does the Bible mention his eyes, ears, hands, and other bodily parts? Those references are not intended to be taken literally, but are used to illustrate some of God's spiritual characteristics. His eyes and ears suggest his knowing and awareness, his omniscience. His hand is a symbol of power, his face a symbol of his favor or disapproval, as in the Twenty-seventh Psalm: "Your face, Lord, I will seek. Do not hide your face from me."[5] If the Bible did not sometimes speak of God in physical terms, our finite minds could not begin to comprehend many of his attributes.

What significance is there in the spiritual, as contrasted with the material, nature of God? First, it is idolatrous to attempt any material representation of God. Carvings, castings—in short, all likenesses, whether effigy, image, or statue—are forbidden by the second of the Ten Commandments. Addressing the people of Israel after God gave the commandments, Moses said:

> Then the Lord spoke to you out of the fire. You heard the sound of words but saw no form; there was only a voice. . . . You saw no form of any kind the day the Lord spoke to you at Horeb out of the fire. Therefore watch yourselves very carefully, so that you do not become corrupt and make for yourselves an idol, an image of any shape, whether formed like a man or a woman, or like any animal on earth or any bird that flies in the air, or like any creature that moves along the ground or any fish in the water below. And when you look up to the sky and see

> the sun, the moon and the stars—all the heavenly array—do not be enticed into bowing down to them and worshiping [them].[6]

God's essence is spiritual, not material. He must therefore never be represented in any material form or likeness.

God is so much greater, so much higher than you and I, so transcendent that human minds cannot adequately conceptualize him. At this point philosophers must give up. But those who believe the Bible know that the invisible God made himself known in the person of Jesus Christ. As John says, "No one has ever seen God, but God the only Son, who is at the Father's side, has made him known."[7] Near the end of his earthly life, Jesus said, "Anyone who has seen me has seen the Father."[8] God is spirit, but he is knowable.

God Must Be Worshiped in Spirit

That God is spirit implies more than the fact that he is not physical. Jesus' definition of God was given in response to the Samaritan woman's confusion about the proper place in which to worship God. "Our fathers worshiped on this mountain," the sincere but theologically naive woman told Jesus, "but you Jews claim that the place where we must worship is in Jerusalem."[9] In reply, Jesus said that neither place was where men ought to worship God. He did not mean that worship could not be offered in either of the two places, but that they were not the *only* places of worship in the world. His point was that because God is spirit, he is incapable of being localized. He may be worshiped *anywhere.*

Jesus also said that those who worship God must worship in spirit and in truth. What did he mean? He meant that worship is a spiritual exercise, not physical. You can go through quite a few physical exercises—the kind often associated with worship, such as bowing down, standing up, raising your arms, etc.—without ever coming before God in worship. Because God is spirit, true worship must be spiritual. You worship with your heart and mind and soul, not your body.

That is the point Paul made in his appeal to the philosopher-theologians in ancient Athens. "The God who made the world and everything in it is the Lord of heaven and earth and does not live in temples built by hands," he told them. "And he is not served by human hands, as if he needed anything."[10]

We can worship God in church, but we do not have to go to church to find him. Physical activities or positions, such as kneeling and closing our eyes, may help us get mentally prepared for worship and help us focus on God, but they are not in themselves worship. All worship is from the inside, from the spirit and the mind and heart. It is possible to do everything properly according to a ritual or liturgy, or according to our own favorite pattern, and yet completely miss God. God is spirit, and those who worship him must worship in spirit.

God Must Be Worshiped in Truth

God's spiritual nature also requires, as Jesus told the Samaritan woman, that those who worship him must worship in truth.[11] Notice the emphasis on the word *truth*. We cannot just daydream about God, or worship him in whatever way suits our fancy or feelings. We have to worship him in truth.

How do we do that? The answer lies in a statement Christ made about eternal life. At the time, he was praying to his Heavenly Father. "Now this is eternal life," he said, "that they may know you, the only true God, and Jesus Christ, whom you have sent."[12] Having eternal life depends on knowing the only true God.

The importance of Christ's statement should be obvious. Knowing God brings eternal life; it also makes it possible for us to worship him in truth, meaning as he really is. Sincerity is not enough. We cannot worship God in truth if our concept of him is something we or some other human being has imagined or made up. If we want to worship the only true God, we must worship him as he really is.

How can we know him as he really is? Here is where we see how indispensable the Bible is. It tells us all we need to know about Jesus Christ. And who was Christ? He was God in human form, whom the Father sent to make himself known. The truth is breathtaking, but it is the essence of Christianity. In Christ, whose earthly name was Jesus, God is given visibility. He is revealed, so that we may better worship him as he really is. As John says, "No one has ever seen God, but God the only Son, who is at the Father's side, has made him known."[13] In his prediction of the Messiah (the Christ), the prophet Isaiah said that he would be called "Immanuel," which means, as Matthew explains, "God with us."[14]

It is hard to grasp the fact that we know what God is like by knowing Christ. The disciples found it hard to understand. Philip asked Jesus to show them the Father. He meant, "Tell us what God is like." Jesus rebuked him mildly for not having already understood what he then repeated for the disciples' benefit, and for ours: "Anyone who has seen me has seen the Father."[15]

If we really want to worship God in truth, all it takes is the knowledge of God as revealed in Jesus Christ. If we know Christ, we know God.

4

What God Is Like—His Attributes

God's nature is often spoken of in terms of his attributes. His attributes show us what he is like. An attribute is a characteristic or quality that is ascribed to, or inherent in, someone or something. A man may *become* merciful, so that it may be said of him that one of his best qualities is mercy. But mercy is not an attribute of that man, because it is not an inherent quality. God, by contrast, is inherently merciful. He does not become merciful; he *is* merciful. In him, mercy is an inherent, essential attribute.

Technically, what we call attributes are, in God, perfections of his nature. Divine perfections are called attributes because they are ascribed or attributed to him. For example, David ascribes certain perfections to God in one of his prayers: "Yours, O Lord, is the greatness and the power and the glory and the majesty and the splendor, for everything in heaven and earth is yours. Yours, O Lord, is the kingdom; you are exalted as head over all."[1] Greatness and power and majesty are really divine perfections; they are part of his nature. But because we ascribe, or attribute, them to him, whether in prayer or songs of praise, his perfections are called attributes.

Theologians commonly speak of God's attributes as incommunicable and communicable. Those are scholarly terms, but their meanings are simple. God's incommunicable attributes are divine qualities which cannot be found among his creatures; they belong only to God. For example, only God has infinity. The rest of us are quite finite.

God's communicable attributes, on the other hand, may also, to a certain extent, be found in his creatures. God is holy; hence holiness is a divine attribute. Believers also may be holy. Otherwise, God would not exhort us to be holy, as he repeatedly does in

Scripture. "Be holy, because I am holy," he says.[2] The difference between his holiness—or his righteousness, goodness, or any other communicable attribute—and ours is that in him those qualities are infinite, eternal, and unchangeable, whereas in us they are only partial and severely limited.

But it should be a source of comfort and encouragement to know that in our limited way we may display the attributes that make God adorable. By his power and help we, too, can be good! None of us is perfect, but we can be immeasurably better than we would be if we did not know God! We can also be true, honorable, right, pure, lovely; and to the extent that we display these qualities, we reflect the glory of our God and Savior.

God Is Infinite

The first incommunicable attribute of God is his infinity. It is the first of three incommunicable attributes that we will look at. The other two are his being eternal and unchangeable.

What does it mean to say that God is infinite? It means that he is without limits of any kind. in the Book of Job, Zophar asks: "Can you fathom the mysteries of God? Can you probe the limits of the Almighty? They are higher than the heavens—what can you do? They are deeper than the depths of the grave—what can you know? Their measure is longer than the earth and wider than the sea."[3]

You and I are limited, but God is not. He is immense, infinite, without any limits or boundaries. As Solomon said, "The heavens, even the highest heaven, cannot contain [him]."[4] He is immeasurably greater than any created thing.

Included in God's immensity, his infinitude, is the concept that he is omnipresent, present everywhere at once. For Christians that truth is a source of comfort. Among other things it teaches that no believer is ever forsaken. He who said, "Never will I leave you; never will I forsake you,"[5] obviously is omnipresent. He is every believer's constant companion on the way home to heaven.

The omnipresence of God also means that "where two or three come together in [Christ's] name," wherever they may be, in no matter how many groups, he himself is present with them.[6] He always is with his people when they come together in his name.

God's infinity means that nothing is too remote for him to handle. Even when we pass through deep water or walk through the fire, he will be with us.[7] For him, there are no limits.

God Is Eternal

We know the difference between time and eternity even if we have never looked up the words in the dictionary or made a study of them. The dictionary defines time in terms of periods, moments, epochs, and such things. Time is measurable. Eternity, on the other hand, cannot be measured. It is endless; it had no beginning, and it will have no end. It has always gone on, and it will always continue to go on and on.

The dictionary also distinguishes between eternal and everlasting. It says: "*Eternal,* as used of duration, strictly implies absence of either beginning or end, commonly as the result of inherent quality; *everlasting,* though often interchangeable with *eternal*, more often applies to future duration alone, and is less often thought of as implying inherent quality; as, the *eternal* God; *everlasting* punishment."[8]

Christian theologians and the compilers of that dictionary use the terms in identical ways. God is eternal, and his eternity is an inherent quality of his nature. Moses acknowledged God's eternity in the Ninetieth Psalm: "Lord, you have been our dwelling place throughout all generations. Before the mountains were born or you brought forth the earth and the world, from everlasting to everlasting you are God."[9] God had no beginning and he has no end. He is the eternal God.

We also will live forever, but the difference between God and us is the difference between an inherent and an acquired quality. His eternity is one of the perfections of his nature; ours is everlastingness. We all had a beginning (the moment we were conceived in the wombs of our mothers), and our everlastingness is derived from God and is dependent on his will.

For unbelievers, eternity is a reason for terror, because God will punish them with everlasting destruction. As Paul says, "He will punish those who do not know God and do not obey the gospel of our Lord Jesus. They will be punished with everlasting destruction and shut out from the presence of the Lord and from the majesty of his power."[10]

For believers, God's eternity is a source of great comfort. As Moses told the children of Israel, "The Lord your God goes with you; he will never leave you nor forsake you."[11] We may therefore say, "My flesh and my heart may fail, but God is the strength of my heart and my portion forever."[12]

God Is Unchangeable

One of the Church's best-loved hymns is "Abide with Me," the first stanza of which is:

> Abide with me, fast falls the eventide;
> The darkness deepens; Lord, with me abide;
> When other helpers fail, and comforts flee,
> Help of the helpless, O abide with me!

Nearly everyone has heard that stanza at some time in his life. Not as well known, however, is the third:

> Swift to its close ebbs out life's little day;
> Earth's joys grow dim, its glories pass away;
> Change and decay in all around I see;
> O Thou who changest not, abide with me!

This stanza draws attention to one of God's glorious attributes: his unchangeableness. Henry F. Lyte, author of the hymn, was conscious of change in himself and in others. He was getting old, and his friends were getting old, and he was saddened by the changes. In his distress he turned to the One who changes not—to the infinite, eternal, unchangeable God.

Where did he get the idea that God is unchangeable? From the Bible. Psalm 102 contrasts the unchanging God with the aging, changing universe:

> In the beginning you laid the foundations
> of the earth,
> and the heavens are the work of your hands.
> They will perish, but you remain;
> they will all wear out like a garment.
> Like clothing you will change them
> and they will be discarded.
> But you remain the same,
> and your years will never end.[13]

Malachi, author of the last book in the Old Testament, quotes the Lord as saying, "I the Lord do not change."[14]

God cannot change, because change is possible only in those

who can get better or worse. Because he is perfect, God cannot improve or deteriorate. Because he is a holy God, he cannot be less than perfect. Therefore he cannot change; he is the unchanging God. As James says, he is "the Father of the heavenly lights, who does not change like shifting shadows."[15]

What about passages in the Bible that speak of God's repenting or changing his mind? When the citizens of ancient Nineveh repented in sackcloth, "[God] had compassion and did not bring upon them the destruction he had threatened."[16] The explanation is simple: God did *not* change. He merely responded to Nineveh's repentance in harmony with eternal principles which he himself clearly states in his Word. For insights into those principles read Jeremiah 18 and Ezekiel 18.

How wonderful that God is unchanging. As Micah says, "He delights in unchanging love."[17] All the promises of God are sure. What he has promised to us, he will surely bring to pass, so that when we sing or pray, "O Thou who changest not, abide with me," we *know* that we are heard and that our prayer is answered. Who is our God? He is the Father of the heavenly lights, who does not change like shifting shadows.

5

What God Is Like—His Being

The attributes that we will be discussing in this and the following chapter are called communicable, because men can to some extent share in those attributes.

God's Being

What is *being*? The dictionary tells us that being is existence, and specifically conscious existence. Alexander Whyte says that being, as used of God, "expresses reality of existence as contrasted with non-existence."[1] Being means that God *is*; he is the great I Am, as contrasted with all of us *derived* creatures, who are created and dependent beings. God is the eternally self-existing One who brought us into existence. We derive *our* being from *God's* being.

In trying to understand God's being, we must keep three things in mind. First, as with all his attributes, his being is infinite, eternal, and unchangeable. Second, because all other beings are created and dependent, God alone is worthy of worship. To worship anyone or anything else is to be base and brutish.[2] Third, the God who gives being to his creatures can give substance to all his promises. He can even give us being that is infinitely better than our present being.

Here is how J. B. Phillips translates a paragraph from the first chapter of Ephesians:

> For God has allowed us to know the secret of His Plan, and it is this: He purposes in His sovereign will that all human history shall be consummated in Christ, that everything that exists in Heaven or earth shall find its perfection and fulfilment in Him. And here is the staggering thing—that in all which will one day belong to Him we have been promised a share (since we were long ago destined for this by the One Who achieves His purposes by His sovereign Will), so that we, as the first to put our confidence in Christ, may bring praise to His glory![3]

God, who is infinite, eternal, and unchangeable in his being, brought us into being, and he will perfect our being for eternity!

God's Wisdom

In thinking about God's wisdom we have to consider the difference between his knowledge and his wisdom.

Theologians often speak of God's omniscience, which means knowledge of everything. Hannah prayed, "The Lord is a God who knows."[4] The context suggests that she was thinking of God's ability to read her mind; he knew what she wanted even before she asked for it.

Sometimes we do not know what we ourselves think. Often, for instance, we do not know what we really want, or even whether we are innocent or guilty in regard to a given matter. Paul once said that he was not aware of sin in his life, but that the absence of a guilty conscience did not prove he was innocent. God alone knew the full truth, and he alone was qualified to judge Paul.[5] Only God's knowledge is perfect and total.

That truth is expressed beautifully in Psalm 139.

> O Lord, you have searched me and you know me.
> You know when I sit and when I rise;
>   you perceive my thoughts from afar.
> You discern my going out and my lying down;
>   you are familiar with all my ways.
> Before a word is on my tongue
>   you know it completely, O Lord.
> You hem me in—behind and before;
>   you have laid your hand upon me.
> Such knowledge is too wonderful for me,
>   too lofty for me to attain.[6]

It is not just that God is omniscient, that he knows everything, but that *everything* includes complete and intimate knowledge of each of us individually. He knows me and he knows you infinitely better than we know ourselves. Before a word can be formed on our lips, God knows the thought that shaped it. His knowledge is perfect, and it is total. There is nothing about any of us that he does not know.

That truth can both trouble and encourage us. On the one

hand, it can trouble us because sometimes we like to try to cover our tracks, so to speak. Having done something stupid or sinful, we like to think we can get away with it. But there is not a chance! Not a sparrow falls to the ground without God knowing it.[7]

But on the other hand, God's omniscience can also encourage us, because he knows the good intentions no one else can see. All they can see is our actual performance. How can they know that we wanted desperately to do it much better? Only God knows. He knows us immeasurably better than our friends or loved ones do. Even when our own hearts accuse us, he is greater than our hearts, because he knows all things.[8]

What, then, is the relationship between God's knowledge and God's wisdom, as revealed in the Bible? Earlier we saw that all of God's communicable attributes—such as his being, wisdom, power, and holiness—are all characterized by his incommunicable attributes of infinity, eternity, and unchangeableness. God not only knows the minds and hearts of all men, but can speak of future things, such as Christ's taking his throne, as if they were already done. He says, for example, "I have installed my King on Zion, my holy hill."[9] God has not done that yet, but anything he plans is as good as accomplished. He knows the future just as certainly as he knows the past.

This is where God's wisdom is especially important. As James Fisher says,

> His infinite knowledge comprehends all things in heaven and earth, by one intuitive glance of his infinite mind; but his infinite wisdom directs these things to the proper ends, for which he gave them their being.[10]

God's knowledge is aware of all things; his wisdom directs all things to their proper ends.

By his wisdom God is able to bring good out of evil. Take the evil that began when Adam sinned in Eden and then spread to all of his descendants. Speaking of that catastrophe, Paul says, "Where sin increased, grace increased all the more, so that, just as sin reigned in death, so also grace might reign through righteousness to bring eternal life through Jesus Christ our Lord."[11] In his wisdom, God is able to redeem lost mankind without compromising his holiness. His grace triumphs over sin.

God can turn every evil thing, including tragedies that sear and scar, to the ultimate advantage of his people. That is what is meant in the much-loved statement that "in all things God works for the good of those who love him, who have been called according to his purpose."[12] God does not cause all things—certainly not sinful things—to happen, but he does cause all things—including sinful things—to work together for the eventual good of his people. He can bring triumph out of tragedy.

No wonder Paul used a doxology to end his essay on the temporary unbelief of Israel: "Oh, the depth of the riches of the wisdom and knowledge of God! How unsearchable his judgments, and his paths beyond tracing out!" The last line of that doxology says, "For from him and through him and to him are all things. To him be the glory forever! Amen."[13] The apostle closes that letter with the words: ". . . to the only wise God be glory forever through Jesus Christ! Amen."[14]

To further distinguish between knowledge and wisdom, we can say that knowledge is acquaintance with facts, whereas wisdom is the ability to deal with facts that are known. A father and his six-year-old son may both witness an accident, and therefore both have knowledge of what happened. But all the son knows is what he saw; he is too young to know how to interpret what he has seen or what to do about it. The father, however, comprehends the significance of the accident and has some idea of what to do about it.

You cannot have wisdom without appropriate knowledge. A truly wise, man, however, need not be highly learned. He need not have gone to the best universities and taken dozens of courses. By today's standards, the ancients did not *know* much. Aristotle, for example, never heard of nuclear physics or computer science. Yet he probably was incomparably wiser than many people today who teach those subjects.

How is that possible if wisdom and knowledge are so closely related? It is possible because the relationship between wisdom and knowledge is not mathematical. Wisdom, like knowledge, is acquired, but it comes more slowly and painfully than knowledge. Given the opportunity, a smart young man may get much more education than his parents, having a doctorate by his twenty-fifth birthday. Yet he may be completely impractical, essentially helpless and unproductive outside the ivy-covered walls of the university.

According to the Bible, the best-educated man in the world is a fool if he is an atheist.[15] A student of God's Word, on the other hand, can say with the psalmist:

Your commands make me wiser than my enemies,
  for they are ever with me.
I have more insight than all my teachers,
  for I meditate on your statutes.
I have more understanding than the elders,
  for I obey your precepts.[16]

The secret of that man's wisdom—as contrasted with the mere knowledge of his unbelieving enemies, his teachers, and even the aged of the land—was his trust in God and his Word. He studied and believed the right things—God's commandments, God's statutes, and God's precepts. More than that, he observed them; he applied them to his life. Obeying God's will is of a higher order of wisdom even than acknowledging it.

The first few chapters of Proverbs have a great deal to say about wisdom, and about the human responsibility to *seek* wisdom "as for hidden treasure."[17] Knowledge is often relatively easy to acquire. We have only to take a few courses or read a few books. But wisdom comes more slowly and demands greater effort; it is the reward of time and meditation. And the wisdom that really counts is rarer still. It is God's gift, given to those who earnestly seek it from him.[18]

God's Power

We hear a lot about power these days, often with negative connotations. When Mount St. Helens erupted, geologists measured the power of the blast in megatons. Lumbermen surveyed the many square miles of flattened forests and calculated the loss in financial terms. Nations are frequently rated according to their respective military power. Politicians also are frequently rated according to their power.

Power includes the ability to act, which explains why some small-time politicians who may not have much prestige or recognition are more powerful than some mayors or high state officials. In their respective areas they can get things done. They have influence and the authority to act. They have power.

But the power of a volcano, a nation, or a politician are all temporary and limited. God's power, on the other hand, is unlimited power, eternal power, unchangeable power. It cannot be diminished or increased—which explains the Bible's frequent use of the descriptive title, Almighty God.

God manifests his power in various ways. Theologians usually speak of divine power in creation, in providence, and in redemption. When Mount St. Helens blew its top off, the world was awed by the great manifestation of energy. But what was that compared to the creation of the entire world! God asked Job:

> Where were you when I laid the earth's foundation?
> Tell me, if you understand.
> Who marked off its dimensions?
> Surely you know!
> Who stretched a measuring line across it?
> On what were its footings set,
> or who laid its cornerstone—
> while the morning stars sang together
> and all the angels shouted for joy?[19]

That is a poetic way of describing creation. Genesis says simply that God spoke, and creation was done. We do not know *how* God did it, but certainly the creation of the cosmos took an absolutely immeasurable amount of energy. Yet the whole of creative activity is described briefly in the Bible as the work of God's fingers.[20] For him it was child's play to make a universe, or a thousand universes. What was that to him! He is Almighty God, whose power is infinite, eternal, and unchangeable.

Early in the history of the human race, God decided to show us that he can do anything. He told a ninety-year-old woman that she would have a baby. The old woman laughed, and the Lord rebuked her with a question: "Is anything too hard for the Lord?" It was a rhetorical question, because the answer was obvious. Within months the old woman had a baby. She then understood that God can do anything; he is Almighty God.[21]

Centuries later a prophet named Jeremiah praised God for his power. "Ah, Sovereign Lord, you have made the heavens and the earth by your great power and outstretched arm. Nothing is too hard for you." The prophet linked God's creative power with his ways of dealing with his ancient people, Israel. The power that had been exerted to bring universes into existence was turned to providential uses; it brought Israel out of the land of bondage. The same powerful, outstretched arm that created the cosmos worked on Israel's behalf when she left Egypt.[22]

History repeats itself, we are told. Whether or not that is true, we know that God sometimes repeats himself. What he did for ninety-year-old Sarah, he did for Elizabeth, another childless old woman related to the girl who became the mother of our Lord. When the angel told Mary that Elizabeth was pregnant, he reminded her that "nothing is impossible with God."[23] Even a virgin birth was not beyond his power to perform.

History will yet repeat itself. Zechariah predicted an exodus much greater than the one from Egypt under Moses. The coming exodus will be out of the land of the east and the land of the west. God will regather scattered Israel to its historic land. When the Lord told the prophet he would do that, he said, "It may seem marvelous to the remnant of this people at that time, but will it seem marvelous to me?"[24] Again, a rhetorical question. The answer is obvious.

God's power is unlimited, and it acts on his people's behalf. He protected his ancient people, making plans for them which will be fulfilled, and he now protects his Church, for which also he has plans. Jesus said, "I will build my church, and the gates of Hades will not overcome it."[25] He is more powerful than anything or anyone who may oppose him or his people.

The infinite, eternal, unchangeable power of God is working on our behalf. No wonder Paul calls for a doxology—"To the King eternal, immortal, invisible, the only God, be honor and glory forever and ever. Amen."[26]

God's Holiness

God's holiness affects or is characteristic of all his other attributes. God's power is *holy* power. God's goodness is *holy* goodness. We might say that holiness is God's attribute of attributes.

The word *holy* is derived from an Old English word meaning "whole," suggesting inward health or wholeness. Is this what the Bible means when it speaks of God as being "majestic in holiness"?[27] Yes, if we take "inner, spiritual wholeness" to mean entire freedom from evil. In the Bible, as in much Christian literature, health or wholeness and freedom from evil are virtually synonymous. The General Confession in *The Book of Common Prayer* reads in part:

> Almighty and most merciful Father, we have erred, and strayed from thy ways like lost sheep. We have followed too much the devices and desires of our own hearts. We have offended

> against thy holy laws. We have left undone those things which we ought to have done; and we have done those things which we ought not to have done; and there is no health in us.[28]

"There is no health in us." We see, by contrast, the root meaning of holiness. Unholy people are spiritually unhealthy people. God, on the other hand, is "whole." He is holy because he is wholly right, wholly as he ought to be; he is entirely free from evil in any form or degree.

God is infinitely, eternally, and unchangeably wise, powerful, and holy. He is a holy God, and all his attributes are holy—his wisdom, power, justice, goodness, and truth.

In heaven, his holiness is acclaimed. John saw "four living creatures" which did not cease to say, "Holy, holy, holy is the Lord God Almighty, who was, and is, and is to come."[29]

God Hates Sin The fact that God is completely holy, entirely free from evil, means many things of profound importance. First, if God is holy, it follows that he hates sin. Second, if he hates sin, he will judge sin and, of necessity, everybody who loves it and clings to it. Third, he demands that those who submit to him be holy even as he is holy.

How do we know God hates sin? The Bible reveals God's hatred of sin, and it does so in two ways. First, it says in plain words that God hates sin. Second, it records divine actions which clearly reveal his hatred of evil.

Take these words from Psalm 5:

> You are not a God who takes pleasure in evil;
> with you the wicked cannot dwell.
> The arrogant cannot stand in your presence;
> you hate all who do wrong.
> You destroy those who tell lies;
> bloodthirsty and deceitful men the Lord abhors.[30]

Does that conflict with the biblical teaching that God loves people? No, it says merely that he hates sin in sinners. And when sinners cling to their sin, they become inseparable from it.

God abominates sin. Through Jeremiah, God condemned ancient Israel for having "filled my inheritance [the land] with their detestable idols."[31] God termed their idolatry "this detestable thing that I hate."[32]

The Book of Hebrews quotes a Psalm which, its author says, contains words that God the Father addressed to God the Son, whom we know as Jesus Christ. Listen to what they say about Christ's hatred of sin.

> But about the Son he says,
> "Your throne, O God, will last for ever and ever,
> and righteousness will be the scepter of your kingdom.
> You have loved righteousness and hated wickedness;
> therefore God, your God, has set you above your
> companions
> by anointing you with the oil of joy."[33]

God Judges Sin God's first judgment was his judgment of the angels who sinned; the second was his judgment of the ancient world by means of the Flood; and the third was his destruction of Sodom and Gomorrah. Peter cites all three in his second letter, and he asks us to consider the lessons implicit in those judgments. Here is what Peter says:

> If God did not spare angels when they sinned, but sent them to hell, putting them into gloomy dungeons to be held for judgment; if he did not spare the ancient world when he brought the flood on its ungodly people, but protected Noah, a preacher of righteousness, and seven others; if he condemned the cities of Sodom and Gomorrah by burning them to ashes, and made them an example of what is going to happen to the ungodly; and if he rescued Lot, a righteous man, who was distressed by the filthy lives of lawless men . . . then the Lord knows how to rescue godly men from trials and to hold the unrighteous for the day of judgment, while continuing their punishment.[34]

Here we see a series of facts and two conclusions based on those facts. God has judged evil. He judged angels who sinned; he judged an entire civilization, sparing only eight people; and he judged entire communities (Sodom and Gomorrah), leaving only Lot and his two daughters. Those are the facts. The conclusions are, first, that

God is consistent. If he expressed his wrath and indignation against sin in the past, he may be expected to do it again. That is what Peter meant when he said, "the Lord knows how to rescue godly men . . . and to hold the unrighteous for the day of judgment, while continuing their punishment."

Second, past judgments were designed to be warnings to all who may be inclined to live ungodly lives. Peter says that God "made them [Sodom and Gomorrah] an example of what is going to happen to the ungodly."[35] Third, the world is expected to weigh its actions in light of the past. Scoffers who claim that the world goes on as it always has "deliberately forget" the past, Peter says. But they will be held accountable, and they will learn to their eternal sorrow that "the present heavens and earth are reserved for fire, being kept for the day of judgment and destruction of ungodly men."[36]

A popular saying is, "Those who do not learn from history are condemned to repeat it." To apply that proverb to Peter's words about the history of divine judgments is sobering.

God Demands Holiness I would like to call attention to two aspects of holiness: first, the evidence of divine holiness, and second, the response expected of us.

The supreme evidence of divine holiness is Christ's cross. The subject can and should command our attention for the rest of our lives. But for our immediate purposes a glance at two texts of Scripture must suffice. In his account of the crucifixion Matthew tells us: "About the ninth hour Jesus cried out in a loud voice, 'Eloi, Eloi, lama sabachthani?'—which means, 'My God, my God, why have you forsaken me?' "[37] That is mysterious, but it tells us that God turned his back on the Sufferer.

The second text is in 2 Corinthians: "God made him who had no sin to be sin for us."[38] That may be Paul's comment on Jesus' cry of anguish just quoted above. At the very least, it suggests one profound aspect of the death of Christ—that God treated Jesus as if he were sin itself. That is why the Father turned away from the sin-bearing Sufferer. A holy God cannot endure sin.

What should be our response to God's hatred of sin? First, we thank him that divine judgment against sin fell on Christ, our substitute, rather than on us. Second, we accept the standard of conduct God sets for us, as indicated in Scripture. Says Peter: "As obedient children, do not conform to the evil desires you had when you lived in ignorance. But just as he who called you is holy, so be holy in all you do; for it is written: 'Be holy, because I am holy.' "[39]

Neither in nature nor in practice can any human being ever be as holy as God. But we are called to live holy lives to the extent that holiness can be practiced. Two texts in Hebrews 12 help us understand this truth. First, "God disciplines us for our good, that we may share in his holiness." And second, "Make every effort to live in peace with all men and to be holy; without holiness no one will see the Lord."[40]

No one can be sinless, but everyone can sin less; and that is the least God expects of us as Christians.

6

What God Is Like—Just, Good, and True

The last three of what are often called God's communicable attributes—those in which we can share to some extent—are his justice, his goodness, and his truth. As with the first four, these are all characterized by God's incommunicable, or divinely unique, attributes—his being infinite, eternal, and unchangeable.

God's Justice

What is justice? According to the dictionary, justice is "the maintenance or administration of that which is just . . . the strict and judicial rendering of what is due."[1] The word is Latin in origin. An Anglo-Saxon equivalent is "righteousness," which a Bible dictionary defines as "the divine holiness applied in moral government and the domain of law."[2] So we now have three related, but not quite identical, terms: justice, righteousness, and holiness.

Here is how an ordinary dictionary distinguishes between holiness and righteousness: "*Holiness* suggests inherent or intrinsic state or quality. *Righteousness* differs from *holiness* in connoting rather unswerving rectitude or conformity to the divine law than spiritual purity or freedom from sin."[3]

We are getting close to the biblical meaning of divine justice. It is not quite the same as holiness, which is God's inherent freedom from evil. It is more like holiness in action; it is his "unswerving rectitude or conformity to the divine law" in all his ways. Among other things, God's justice is his righteous administration of the cosmos. His holiness and his justice complement each other. Holiness refers primarily to God's nature, justice to his activity. Because he is holy, God is also just; *everything* he does is right.

The people of Israel were impressed by divine justice. In the Song of Moses, that facet of the divine nature is underlined:

I will proclaim the name of the Lord.
  Oh, praise the greatness of our God!
He is the Rock, his works are perfect,
  and all his ways are just.
A faithful God who does no wrong,
  upright and just is he.[4]

We see the significance of God's justice when we read that he is Judge.

The Bible teaches and history attests that human judges are often corrupt and unjust. They do not act with "unswerving rectitude or conformity to the divine [or even human] law."[5] But God is always a just Judge, and he will judge the world with perfect justice.[6] He will judge with the "integrity and uprightness of a true judge with whom is no respect of persons."[7]

Since we are sinful people, divine justice should be a terrifying prospect. We need mercy, not justice. The good news of the gospel is that God offers us mercy. God himself reassures us with these words:

And there is no God apart from me,
a righteous God and a Savior;
  there is none but me.
Turn to me and be saved,
  all you ends of the earth;
  for I am God, and there is no other.[8]

God is just, but he is also a Savior.

But how does God's justice relate to us? The first thing that may be said about divine justice is that it is exactly what the word says; it is *just*. It is true justice, or, as Paul says, "righteous judgment."[9] It is in marked contrast to much that passes for justice in the world in which we live!

His Legislative Justice Old-time theologians often distinguished between God's legislative and distributive justice. Legislative justice is God's gift or proclamation of just and good laws. A text in the prophecy of Micah illustrates this:

In the last days
the mountain of the Lord's temple
  will be established
as chief among the mountains; . . .

Many nations will come and say,
"Come, let us go up to the mountain of the Lord,
to the house of the God of Jacob.
He will teach us his ways,
so that we may walk in his paths."
The law will go out from Zion,
the word of the Lord from Jerusalem.
He will judge between many peoples
and will settle disputes for strong nations
far and wide.[10]

When God's laws are proclaimed the law of the land and administered justly, the world will be like the Garden of Eden—at least by comparison with the world of our day.

Most nations have laws that, intentionally or not, reflect divine law in that they call for justice. The rub is, fallen man is normally not inclined to take justice seriously, except when his own rights or privileges are violated. Then, of course, his concept of justice is flawed by self-interest. Consequently, even the loftiest legislative codes frequently have loopholes worked into the design. Those who know the codes best are usually able to make them work to their own advantage, often at the expense of others. But the day is coming when "a king will reign in righteousness and rulers will rule with justice," when "justice will dwell in the desert and righteousness live in the fertile field"[11]—which was Isaiah's way of saying that justice will prevail everywhere, whether in sophisticated or undeveloped societies. Only God can rule the world so that justice prevails everywhere.

His Distributive Justice Another type or aspect of God's justice is what may be called the distributive. If legislative justice is God's proclamation of just laws, distributive justice is his holding men and women accountable to those laws. It is his applying just laws justly, his rendering to everyone his rightful due. In Romans 2:5-11 Paul speaks of the righteous judgment of God, who will render to every man according to his deeds without partiality. That is a grim prospect. Who wants to be judged according to his just deserts? Certainly no thoughtful person, because he knows that he fails miserably to keep the laws of God or to live according to the dictates of his own conscience. No one does as many righteous deeds as his conscience tells him he should do. And no one refrains from everything evil that his conscience tells him is wrong.

We do not measure up even to our own standards, much less to God's. Therefore the thought of receiving from God our just due should be anything but pleasant. If he judges us according to our deeds, and if our deeds do not win his seal of approval, where does that leave us? In the same passage just referred to above, Paul says there will be tribulation and distress for everyone who does evil, to the Jew first and then the Gentile. In the next chapter (Rom. 3:5, 6), Paul says that God is the God who brings wrath and who will judge the world.

If that were all the Bible had to say, we would be doomed. But it says more. It says that God laid on Christ the penalty due us. Paul praises the Son of God, "who loved me and gave himself for me."[12] Peter says, "He himself bore our sins in his body on the tree [that is, on the cross]."[13] He also says, "Christ died for sins once for all, the righteous for the unrighteous, to bring you to God."[14] The God who brings wrath against sin did not shrink from his divine duty. But instead of bringing it on all of us sinners, he found a substitute, the beloved second person of the Godhead. Christ suffered on our behalf. That is the central fact of the gospel. That is why the holy God is able to show mercy to unholy people. In Christ—that is, in union with the Savior—we are safe. Justice is done, yet we escape the wrath which we so richly deserve.

His Satisfied Justice One more aspect of God's justice needs to be considered—his withholding wrath from some persons while inflicting it on others. Is it just that the God who declares that he is holy and impartial should spare some and punish others? The answer is yes. We have already touched on this briefly, in quoting passages such as Galatians 2:20, where Paul speaks of the Son of God "who loved me and gave himself for me." How did the Son of God give himself for Paul, and for us? The apostle explains: "Christ redeemed us from the curse of the law by becoming a curse for us, for it is written: 'Cursed is everyone who is hung on a tree.' "[15] Elsewhere Paul says, "God demonstrates his own love for us in this: While we were still sinners Christ died for us."[16] The punishment due us was transferred to Christ. He suffered it on our behalf. Consequently, in response to simple faith in Christ as personal Savior, God credits us with the death that Christ died. God views us as if we had actually suffered the penalty.

But is it right that an innocent person suffer for guilty people? Normally no. However, in this case the innocent person was himself the Judge; and he volunteered. It was his own will and plan. Hence, his death was a completely moral act that enables God to be just and the justifier of the one who has faith in Jesus.[17]

Christ died for all the ungodly, which includes everyone and excludes no one. John says that "the Father has sent his Son to be the Savior of the world"[18] and that "He is the atoning sacrifice for our sins, and not only for ours but also for the sins of the whole world."[19]

But if Christ died for everyone, why are some eternally lost? Does God exact the penalty twice? No. The answer is that some refuse God's offer. Nothing prevents them from being saved but their own refusal to accept God's offer. In their case, therefore, Christ's death is in vain. It accomplishes nothing for them except to increase their guilt. He died for them, but because they do not receive him, his death does not avail for them. They go to death unforgiven, having nothing to present to God. What remains for them, then? Let the writer of Hebrews tell us. First, he asks us rhetorically, "How shall we escape if we ignore such a great salvation?"[20] Second, he says, "Anyone who rejected the law of Moses died without mercy on the testimony of two or three witnesses. How much more severely do you think a man deserves to be punished who has trampled the Son of God under foot? . . . It is a dreadful thing to fall into the hands of the living God."[21] The passages are painfully clear. They need no comment, only tears.

God's Goodness

What is God's goodness? First we will look at the dictionary's definition of goodness, which is "excellence, virtue." It is also sometimes defined as kindliness. Andrew Bonar, a nineteenth-century Scottish minister and hymnist, defined God's goodness as the Old Testament version of God's love. Three Hebrew and two Greek words are often translated "goodness" in the Bible. While there are nuances in each word, the fundamental meaning is kindness. If you have access to a lexicon or concordance, you may want to look up the verses in which *goodness* and *kindness* appear.

These statements in the Psalms are particularly meaningful. "You are kind and forgiving, O Lord, abounding in love to all who call to you."[22] "Good and upright is the Lord; therefore he instructs sinners in his ways."[23] Finally, "You are good, and what you do is good."[24] What is God's goodness if not himself in action? Think about this great passage from Exodus: "The Lord, the Lord, the compassionate and gracious God, slow to anger, abounding in love and faithfulness, maintaining love to thousands, and forgiving wickedness, rebellion and sin" (34:6, 7). The word here translated "love" is "goodness" in some older versions and "lovingkindness," "unfailing love," or "constant love" in some modern translations. God's goodness is a special kind of kindness; it is lovingkindness. How good it is to know that the earth is full of the lovingkindness of the Lord.

No study of God would be complete without consideration of this great attribute. He is infinite, eternal, and unchangeable. He is filled with wisdom, power, and holiness. That causes me to fall down before him in awe. But when I read that he is good, that his lovingkindness is infinite and eternal and unchangeable, my heart is touched. He is good, and he does good to all men. He causes his sun to rise on the evil and the good, and he sends rain on the righteous and the unrighteous. He richly supplies us with all things to enjoy. Indeed, as the psalmist says, the earth is full of the goodness, the lovingkindness, of the Lord.

R. Alan Killan notes that in some passages God's goodness carries the idea of perfection. After each day of activity in the creation, for example, God saw that it was good. In being good it was perfect, like its Creator. In Psalm 16:2 David praises the Lord for his goodness: "You are my Lord; apart from you I have no good thing." Goodness in this sense is not quite the same as kindness or lovingkindness. It has been defined as that which is worthy of approbation because of its inherent moral value and because of its beneficial external effect. God's goodness is a moral perfection like his other divine attributes. It is distinct from them, however, in that it is active and its immediate external effect—that is, the effect of its action on others—is beneficial.

In the little chorus "God is so good," the refrain is repeated over and over again. That is not, I am sure, because the composer could not think of anything else to say, but because he wanted to emphasize the nature of God's work. Whatever he does is beneficial; it is good. In Paul's list of qualities produced in us by the Holy Spirit of God, goodness follows kindness.[25]

God expects us to be like him, kind and good. He wants us to be kindly disposed toward others and ready to put our feelings into action. He wants us to manifest his goodness to the extent that this is possible. Anything less than the attempt is not true Christianity.

God's Truth

In some respects truth is the most difficult of God's attributes to analyze. Pilate's remark suggests the reason. When Jesus said, "For this reason I was born, and for this I came into the world, to testify to the truth," Pilate said, "What is truth?"[26] I think his voice was heavy with cynicism. It was not an honest question; he was not really interested in truth. Perhaps having heard philosophers wrangle about it endlessly, he may have concluded that truth is whatever anyone wants to believe, as many people today think.

Every system of philosophy has its ideas about the nature of truth. There are, for example, the coherence theory of truth, the correspondence theory of truth, the performative theory of truth, and Pilate's kind, the pragmatic theory of truth.

In Scripture, truth refers to that aspect of God's nature that stands in contrast with, or in opposition to, everything that is false. In one of the great declarations of the Bible Jesus said, "I am the way and the truth and the life."[27] Jesus is divine truth personified.

The Truth That Saves A distinction must be made between facts and ideas that are true, and "the truth" as set forth in the Bible. It is true that 2 plus 2 equals 4. But that fact is not what Jesus had in mind when he said, "I am the truth." It is also true that I am a male citizen of the United States. That is true but entirely beside the point of what Jesus was talking about. Such facts are not the truth of which Christ is the embodiment. He was speaking of truth as it touches on the nature of God and man and the relationship of God to man and man to God. He was speaking of the truth that saves. That is indicated in the rest of Christ's statement: "I am the way and the truth and the life. No one comes to the Father except through me."

If we want to know the truth about God and the truth about ourselves, truth that teaches us how to go to God, we must come to Jesus. There is no other source of that kind of truth. How good and reassuring to realize that we can know how to come to God. We can know without speculating, without wondering whether our teachers are right, without fearing that in the future a new theory of truth may prove us wrong. On the Mount of Transfiguration the disciples heard God the Father say, "This is my Son, whom I love; with him I am well pleased. Listen to him!"[28] That advice is straight from heaven. God's Son speaks the truth that saves.

God's Truth Versus Satan's Lies Now I would like to concentrate on another aspect of truth. In calling himself the truth, Jesus draws attention to the contrast between himself and the devil. "I am . . . the truth," Jesus says. The devil, on the other hand, is deceit personified. As Jesus explains, "He [Satan] was a murderer from the beginning, not holding to the truth, for there is no truth in him. When he lies, he speaks his native language, for he is a liar and the father of lies."[29]

It is unlikely that Jesus was thinking of so-called "little white lies"—fibs people tell, sometimes to spare a friend an unpleasant truth. The devil no doubt encourages the telling of every kind of lie, including "white" ones, but the lies Jesus had in mind were theological or ideological. The notions that God does not exist, that he is not good, and that he withholds blessings from his children are among Satan's most common lies.[30]

Satan not only denies the truth about God; he invents lies about God. Paul says that certain religious ideas come from the devil and his agents. Says Paul, "The Spirit clearly says that in later times some will abandon the faith and follow deceiving spirits and things taught by demons."[31] Some satanic doctrines call for various kinds of asceticism, which appeals to many minds as the highest, most admirable form of religion. Paul, however, says that hair shirts, scourgings, starvation diets, enforced celibacy, and other such self-afflictions "have an appearance of wisdom . . . but they lack any value in restraining sensual indulgence."[32]

Every cult is founded on denial of the truth as it is in Christ, and on at least one doctrine of demons. Each cult in its own way brings its victims into bondage. The truth, on the other hand, is wonderfully liberating. As Jesus says, "If you hold to my teaching, you are really my disciples. Then you will know the truth, and the truth will set you free."[33]

Paul warned believers in Colosse not to allow anyone to take them "captive through hollow and deceptive philosophy."[34] Paul was anxious that the believers "know the mystery of God, namely, Christ, in whom are hidden all the treasures of wisdom and knowledge."[35] That is the important truth. It is *the* truth, both to know and to have. The believers at Colosse had received Christ by faith, and Paul did not want them to be misled by persuasive but false arguments.

Instead, they were to continue in faith, believing that their union with him who was (and is) the embodiment of truth was all they needed to know and to have the truth.

What is truth? Truth is whatever Christ says it is. Truth is "the whole revelation of God that has been at any time, or in any manner, made to man; all that it is God's glory to reveal, and man's blessedness to believe and enjoy. Truth, the highest and surest truth, is that God is true, and that Jesus Christ is his truth."[36]

Response to Truth The fact that Christ teaches truth and is himself the embodiment of truth demands response. The only acceptable response is twofold: belief and action. The alternative is unbelief, which dishonors God by calling his integrity into question. Says John, "Anyone who does not believe God has made him out to be a liar, because he has not believed the testimony God has given about his Son." He goes on to say that the witness is this, "God has given us eternal life, and this life is in his Son."[37]

In light of that, it should be obvious that the only acceptable response to the testimony God gives in the Bible is belief and appropriate action. We believe because God has spoken, and we believe what he has said. Sophisticates of a certain disposition deride the little chorus that says, "God says it, I believe it, and that settles it for me." They sneer that this is "simplistic." Some people, presented with an unpalatable spiritual truth, are prone to dismiss it by such responses. Simplicity, however, is not necessarily simplistic; simplicity is often profound. On the other hand, seemingly complex answers given in involved sentences are sometimes quite *un*profound, being merely turgid and wanting in substance—windy attempts to complicate an essentially simple proposition, or verbose smoke screens for ignorance.

Genuine belief in God's truth expresses itself in action. John says he had no greater joy than to hear that his children in the faith were "walking in the truth."[38] The truth has an effect on a genuine believer's manner of life. Among other things, believers testify to the truth. The writer of Hebrews gives this exhortation: "Let us hold unswervingly to the hope we profess, for he who promised is faithful. And let us consider how we may spur one another on toward love and good deeds."[39]

7

The Trinity

Only One God

The oneness of God is emphasized throughout the Old Testament and is stated in the earliest confession of ancient Israel, called the Shema: "Hear, O Israel: The Lord our God, the Lord is one."[1] Two things may be said about that great call to worship. First, it is a positive expression of the truth given negatively in the first two of the Ten Commandments. The first commandment says, "You shall have no other gods before me," and the second says, "You shall not make for yourself an idol in the form of anything in heaven above or on the earth beneath or in the waters below."[2] Those two commandments prohibit the acknowledgement or worship of any other than the true God, who is one.

Second, though the four Hebrew words which compose the Shema have been translated in slightly different ways, the meaning is clear: "Yahweh [Jehovah] was to be the sole object of Israel's worship, allegiance and affection."[3] Says Professor J. A. Thompson, "The word 'one' or 'alone' implies monotheism, even if it does not state it with all the subtleties of theological formulation. . . . the affirmation that Yahweh alone was Sovereign and the sole object of Israel's obedience sounded the death-knell to all views lesser than monotheism."[4] Israel was called by God himself to be a monotheistic people, a people of one God.

Israel's confession was more than a resolution to worship only one God; it expressed the great truth that there *is* only one God. The so-called gods who were worshiped by Israel's pagan neighbors—and tragically sometimes by Israel herself—were not gods at all. The true God is not one among many, or even the best among many; he is absolutely unique, the *only* God.

Among other things, that truth means that God alone is worthy to receive worship and homage. When John was given a vision of heaven, he saw heavenly beings worshiping him who, John says, "lives forever and ever." They were proclaiming, "You are worthy, our Lord and God, to receive glory and honor and power, for you created all things, and by your will they were created and have their being."[5]

The Living and True God

At first thought it might appear unnecessary to say that God is living and true. If he exists (and his existence is not in question), he is obviously living. But the word *living*, as it is used of God, does not mean mere existence. It means that God has life in himself and the ability to impart life to his creatures. He not only is alive, but he is the source of all life.

That truth is expressed in many passages in Scripture. Here is what Paul, while in Athens, told the city's philosophers: "The God who made the world and everything in it is the Lord of heaven and earth and does not live in temples built by hands. And he is not served by human hands, as if he needed anything, because he himself gives all men life and breath."[6] The living God does not merely exist. He is the Fountain of Life. As Paul went on to explain to the same crowd, "In him we live and move and have our being. As some of your own poets have said, 'We are his offspring' " (v. 28).

Another helpful passage is 1 John 1:2—"The life appeared; we have seen it and testify to it, and we proclaim to you the eternal life, which was with the Father and has appeared to us." John was, of course, speaking of Christ, the One who said, "I am the way and the truth and the life."[7] Christ was divine life manifested. John also tells us, "And this is what he promised us—even eternal life."[8] Our God is not merely living, as contrasted with lifeless wood or stone; he gives life, breath, and eternal life to as many as are willing to accept it.

In the religious systems of the world there are many false gods. None of them even has life, much less can impart life. Paul was familiar with some of them, and he said, "For even if there are so-called gods, . . . for us there is but one God, the Father, from whom all things came."[9] There is but one God, the living and true Lord. We exist for him.

One God in Three Persons

Studying God's triune nature is not easy. One writer observes that the doctrine of the Trinity is difficult but not more so than some others.

He goes on to note that neither paganism nor rationalism can rise to the idea of one God who governs the world. No one could or would have invented Trinitarianism.

Another writer, Stephen Neill, reminds us that to say that something is difficult is not the same as to say that it is not true. He points to analogies in nature (e.g., the three dimensions of a single object: length, breadth, height; the three modes of time: past, present, future; etc.) and says that while those things do not in themselves reveal much about God, they do help remove some of the mental difficulties of belief in the doctrine of the Trinity.[10]

Another analogy of the Trinity is man's own three-part nature—body, soul, and spirit (though some theologians argue for only two parts, considering soul and spirit to be the same). The cosmos is made up of the "trinity" of space, matter, and time; each is distinct in nature but they are integrally related. None of these analogies can begin to explain the Trinity, but they do help us realize that the basic principle of three-in-one is not unique to the divine Trinity.

Although the word *Trinity* is not used in Scripture, the truth of that doctrine is plainly taught. The concept of the Trinity is clearly seen in Paul's closing benediction in his second letter to Corinth: "May the grace of the Lord Jesus Christ, and the love of God, and the fellowship of the Holy Spirit be with you all."[11] There is no ancient Christian creed or catechism that does not agree with that Trinitarian statement. The Apostles' Creed, which is almost as old as Christianity itself, reads in part, "I believe in God the Father Almighty, Maker of Heaven and earth, and in Jesus Christ, His only Son, our Lord . . . and in the Holy Spirit." The Apostles' Creed is unmistakably Trinitarian, as are all other orthodox Christian statements about the nature of God.

The idea of the Trinity is somewhat overpowering. As J. H. Large says, "One cannot meditate on the awesome and insoluble mystery of Eternal and Infinite Being without being made to realize that any enquiry into the nature of God and the mode of His existence must be entered upon with reverent caution and utter dependence upon what God has been pleased to reveal."[12] We have no other source of information than God himself. All we can know of him is what he is willing to reveal.

The Heidelberg Confession makes this point in its twenty-fifth question. "Since there is but one divine essence," the question asks, "why speak of Father, Son, and Holy Ghost?" The answer is: "Because God has so revealed Himself in His word that these three distinct persons are the only true and eternal God."[13] In other words, the Church teaches that God is triune, a Trinity of persons, because this is what God himself reveals in the Bible. The Church did not invent the doctrine. As Canon Frank Colquhoun says,

> We must accept in faith the facts about God as he has revealed himself to us in his Son, the Lord Jesus Christ. That revelation is embodied . . . in the Holy Scriptures. From the study of the Scriptures we learn truths about God which we could never have discovered by our own conjectures or speculations.[14]

What Is a Divine Person? As Canon Colquhoun further comments, "Within the unity of the Godhead there is a distinction of 'persons,' so that he is at once God the Father, God the Son, and God the Holy Spirit."[15] The writer puts the word *persons* in quotes, thereby drawing attention to its inadequacy. God is a "person" (actually *three* in *one*), but not in the sense that you and I are persons. The English word comes from the Latin *persona,* a mask used by an actor through which his voice resonated. Alexander Whyte points out that it is a long step from the original sense of the word *person* to the use we are most familiar with when it is applied to an individual of the human race. But it is a still longer step from our ordinary use of the word up to the scriptural and theological use applied to the three Persons in the divine nature.[16]

Then why use the term? Because, as Whyte explains further, the Latin theologians could find no better word in their language; nor can modern languages supply one that is more adequate. If you test a few (such as *being, existence, essence*) you will see the difficulty. *Person* is probably the best word we can find, provided we remember that God is not like human persons or personalities we know or have known.

In his monumental work *The Creeds of Christendom,* Philip Schaff comments helpfully:

> In modern philosophical usage, the term *person* means a separate and distinct rational individual. But the Tri-personality of God is not a numerical or essential trinity of three beings, like Abraham, Isaac, or Jacob, for this would be Tritheism; nor is it only, on the other hand, merely a three-fold aspect and mode of manifestation in the Sabellian or Swedenborgian sense; but it is a real, objective, and eternal, though ineffable distinction in one Divine Being.[17]

Another term that perhaps needs to be clarified is *Godhead.* This unusual-sounding word is simply a modified form of Godhood. The "hood" is a suffix that means "state, condition, quality, or character," as in manhood or statehood. *Godhead,* therefore, refers to the divine nature, to God in his fullness, his complete Godliness.

It is not easy to think of God as triune in nature. But two important facts justify the effort. First, that is what God, in his own Word, reveals himself to be. Second, spiritually healthy churches have always given attention to this truth. I personally believe that right Christian worship and right Christian living require both spirituality and understanding. Paul says repeatedly to his readers, "I do not want you to be unaware [or "ignorant"] . . ."[18]

Trinitarianism, Not Tritheism As pointed out above in the quotation from Philip Schaff, it is of the utmost importance to distinguish between the terms *Trinitarianism* and *Tritheism.* Tritheism is the concept that the Father, Son, and Holy Spirit are three distinct Gods. Many Jews, Muslims, and other monotheists (those who believe in one God) falsely accuse Christians of being Tritheists, of worshiping "the triple God." Trinitarianism, on the other hand, is simply a term used to describe the biblical doctrine of the union of those three Persons in one Godhead. The three Persons of the Trinity are one as to substance, yet three as to individuality. Christians do not worship three Gods; we are not Tritheists. There is but one God only—the Father, the Son, and the Holy Spirit; and these three are one God, equal in substance, power, and glory.

Alexander Whyte defines "a person in the Godhead" as "the whole Godhead distinguished by 'personal properties.' " He goes on to say that the Godhead—that is, the divine nature or Godhood,

> neither is nor can be divided into parts; each of the Three Persons has in Himself the one whole indivisible Godhead. But . . . they are distinguished by their personal properties—that is to say, it is the personal property of the Father to beget the Son; and of the Son to be begotten of the Father; and of the Holy [Spirit] to proceed from the Father and the Son.[19]

There are differences but no inequalities among the Persons of the divine nature; each of the three is God. It may be helpful to think of the Trinity as expressed in the Church of England catechism: "First, I learn to believe in God the Father, who has made me, and all the world. Secondly, in God the Son, who has redeemed me, and all mankind. Thirdly, in God the Holy Spirit, who sanctifies me, and all the elect people of God."

The Persons of the Godhead are the same in substance, yet different in function. The Father made me, the Son saves me, and the Holy Spirit sanctifies me. That, of course, is an oversimplification, because all three Persons were involved in creation, and are involved in salvation and sanctification. But the division helps us somewhat to see the works that each Person does. As already mentioned, our human vocabularies and categories simply are not able to do God justice—particularly in an area as imponderable as the Trinity. We can only say that our great God, the God of Scripture, is the great Three-in-One and One-in Three.

Trinitarianism, Not Unitarianism Such passages as John 1:18 ("No one has ever seen God, but God the only Son, who is at the Father's side, has made him known") led Christian thinkers to state their belief in God in Trinitarian terms. Unitarianism, which denies the Trinity, appeals to minds that are either unfamiliar with the New Testament or are unwilling to believe it. In any case, the Unitarians' god is certainly not the God of the Bible, and they do not claim it to be. Their god is therefore defective. Stephen Neill makes this point in a series of contrasts. For example:

> The Christians' God loved the world so much that he entered into the world and was willing to live among men as Man. The Unitarians' God did not love the world enough to enter into it and live among men as Man.
>
> The Christians' God knows *by experience* what it is to be tired and hungry, sorrowful and lonely. The Unitarians' God may understand *by sympathy*, but he does not know *by experience* what it is to be tired and hungry and sorrowful and lonely.[20]

The list could be extended, of course, but the point is clear. Trinitarianism is not just dry theology; it describes the true and merciful God who, for our sakes, became man. Although the word *Trinity* does not appear in Scripture, the truth that it represents is exactly what the Bible teaches. It is a truth that Bible-believing Christians in all generations have acknowledged and cherished.

The Father Is God

God the Father does not stand alone, as if he were God Almighty and nothing else. He is the Father in heaven, and Christ is his Son. Paul refers to him as "the God and Father of our Lord Jesus Christ."[21] In another place Paul speaks of him as "the God of our Lord Jesus Christ, the glorious Father."[22] The idea of God's fatherhood of the Son is not generation, as when we speak of a human father and his son, but is a relationship.

The fatherhood of God has another dimension as well, an extremely important dimension as far as we are concerned. God is *our* Father, the Father of those who have put their trust in the Son. In the Lord's Prayer we say, "Our Father who art in heaven, hallowed be thy name."[23] God is also a type of Father of all human beings, though only in the sense of being their Creator. When Paul was in Athens, he told certain Greek philosophers, who knew nothing about Christ or Christianity, that all of us (that is, all mankind) are God's offspring.[24]

In regard to the Trinity, however, it is God's fatherhood of the Son, Jesus Christ, that is of supreme importance. God the Father and God the Son are the same God.

The Son Is God

The Son is often referred to as the second person of the Trinity, a term which is not meant to imply inferiority. He is second, but not secondary. The Son, of course, is Jesus Christ. Many passages in the New Testament identify Jesus as God's Son. In John's Gospel, for example, we read the beautiful and familiar words, "For God so loved the world that he gave his one and only Son, that whoever believes in him shall not perish but have eternal life."[25] In his first letter, John says that "if anyone acknowledges that Jesus is the Son of God, God lives in him and he in God," and that "he who believes that Jesus is the Son of God" is the overcomer.[26]

When a person first reads the Gospels he may decide that Jesus was just a man, despite the unusual and extraordinary things he was said to be and to have said and done. But repeated reading cannot help leaving the impression that if Jesus of Nazareth was anything like what the Gospel writers say he was like, then he was more than an ordinary man, in fact was more even than an extraordinary man. The evidence becomes overwhelming, and the honest reader will soon begin to feel its weight. Here was a man who though he ate, drank, slept, and became tired as do all other men, also multiplied wine and food, gave sight to the blind, healed incurable diseases, stilled storms, cast out demons, and even raised people from the dead! Either those writers were deluded, deceptive, or both, or they told of a man who was unlike any other man who has ever lived. His companions asked, as any thoughtful person asks, "Who is this?"[27]

The answer is, he is God. He said he was God, and his disciples came to believe him, and that conviction led to the preaching that built the Church. Every believer holds it. Otherwise he or she, no matter how religious, is not a Christian. As Paul says, "If you confess with your mouth, 'Jesus is Lord,' and believe in your heart that God raised him from the dead, you will be saved."[28]

The New Testament establishes the truth that Jesus is God in at least three ways: first, by direct statements; second, by statements that imply his deity; and third, by use of quotations that, in the Old Testament, refer to Jehovah or Yahweh.

Jesus said, "I and the Father are one." His enemies got the point immediately. They tried to kill him because, they explained, "we are not stoning you for [a good work] but for blasphemy, because you, a mere man, claim to be God."[29] They understood clearly the import of what he said about himself.[30]

Jesus repeatedly called himself by the name or designation reserved for Jehovah. This is very clear in the conversation with his enemies when he said, "before Abraham was born, I am!"[31] The Jewish leaders obviously took that to be a reference to Jehovah God. When, after the experience at the burning bush, Moses asked how he should identify the Lord to the people, he was told, "This is what you are to say to the Israelites: 'I AM has sent me to you.' "[32] In Isaiah, Jehovah is the First and the Last, a title that in the Book of Revelation is given to Christ.[33]

Jesus is God. That is who he said he was, and that is what the disciples who wrote the New Testament proclaimed him to be.

The Holy Spirit Is God

Jesus spoke of the Holy Spirit in terms that cannot be misunderstood. He said, "I will ask the Father, and he will give you another Counselor to be with you forever—the Spirit of truth. The world cannot accept him, because it neither sees him nor knows him. But you know him, for he lives with you and will be in you."[34] At the same time Jesus identified the Counselor as the Holy Spirit whom, he said, "the Father will send in my name, [and who] will teach you all things and will remind you of everything I have said to you."[35] The Greek word here translated "Counselor" is used of Christ himself in John's first epistle. Christ is described as our "Advocate" *(King James Version),* the "one who speaks to the Father in our defense."[36]

When Ananias and Sapphira tried to deceive the early church into thinking they were generous givers, Peter rebuked them in terms that underline the deity of the Holy Spirit. "How is it that Satan has so filled your heart that you have lied to the Holy Spirit?" Peter asked Ananias. Then he explained the seriousness of the attempted deceit: "You have not lied to men but to God."[37] You see the significance of the question and the statement. Ananias and Sapphira lied to the Holy Spirit, which meant that they lied to God.

The thirteenth chapter of the Book of Acts tells how missionary work among the non-Jews of the ancient world began. While Christians at Antioch were ministering to the Lord and fasting, "the Holy Spirit said, 'Set apart for me Barnabas and Saul for the work to which I have called them.' "[38] In the light of Paul's subsequent statements about his appointment to the ministry,[39] the significance of that verse in Acts is unavoidable: the Holy Spirit is God.

Among Jesus' last words to his disciples were these from what has come to be called the Great Commission: "Therefore go and make disciples of all nations, baptizing them in the name of the Father and of the Son and of the Holy Spirit."[40] Almost as familiar is Paul's beautiful benediction given to the church at Corinth: "May the grace of the Lord Jesus Christ, and the love of God, and the fellowship of the Holy Spirit be with you all."[41] Again the conclusion is unavoidable: the Holy Spirit, along with the Father and the Son, is God.

Scripture does not give us a full explanation of the Trinity, but it unmistakably teaches the reality of it. Martin Luther claimed that denial of the Trinity was a violation of the first commandment, which forbids having other Gods than the Lord. "When do men have other gods?" Luther asks. "When they believe in a god who is not the Triune God."[42]

The Same Substance

Theologians often speak of the Father, Son, and Holy Spirit as being "of the same substance." As already pointed out, no word or group of words, in any language, could do justice to any aspect of God's nature. But *substance,* rightly used and understood, is a helpful term.

One dictionary defines substance as "that which underlies all outward manifestations; real, unchanging essence or nature; that which constitutes anything; that which it is.[43] That definition is rather complete, and it squares with definitions found in standard works on philosophy.

But how can we understand the term with reference to God? It usually is associated with matter. The substance of chocolate cake, for example, is made up of flour, eggs, cocoa, and whatever other ingredients go into it. The substance of a knife blade is steel. But God is not matter, he is spirit. How can spirit have "substance"? Matter has qualities such as size, weight, shape, and chemical composition. Spirit also has qualities—such as wisdom, power, holiness, justice, goodness, and truth. All of those are qualities or characteristics of God—qualities that we have discussed in previous chapters.

To say that the three Persons of the Trinity are the same in substance, therefore, is to say that they are equally divine, equally God, in every way. As the Creed of St. Athanasius puts it, "Such is the Father, such is the Son, and such is the Holy Spirit." The truth is hard to grasp, but that is what the New Testament teaches about God. There are three Persons in the Godhead, and they are the same in substance, the same in nature.

After everything has been said, the Trinity remains a great and wonderful mystery. We cannot fathom its depths. But because Jesus Christ can bring us to God, we can know the Father, and we can know the Son, and we can know the Holy Spirit. When we accept what Christ has done on our behalf, they will come and make their home with us and eventually take us to be at home with them.[44]

8

The Eternal Purpose of God

Theologians who think about the purpose of God inevitably turn to the following passage in the Book of Ephesians:

> Praise be to the God and Father of our Lord Jesus Christ, who has blessed us in the heavenly realms with every spiritual blessing in Christ. For he chose us in him before the creation of the world to be holy and blameless in his sight. In love he predestined us to be adopted as his sons through Jesus Christ, in accordance with *his pleasure and will*—to the praise of his glorious grace, which he has freely given us in the One he loves. In him we have redemption through his blood, the forgiveness of sins, in accordance with the riches of God's grace that he lavished on us with all wisdom and understanding. And he made known to us *the mystery of his will* according to his good pleasure, which he purposed in Christ, to be put into effect when the times will have reached their fulfillment—to bring all things in heaven and on earth together under one head, even Christ. In him we were also chosen, having been predestined according to the plan of him who works out everything in conformity with *the purpose of his will,* in order that we, who were the first to hope in Christ, might be for the praise of his glory. And you also were included in Christ when you heard the word of truth, the gospel of your salvation. Having believed, you were marked in him with a seal, the promised Holy Spirit, who is a deposit guaranteeing our inheritance until the redemption of those who are God's possession—to the praise of his glory.[1]

In these verses the will of God is specifically mentioned three times. Paul speaks of "his pleasure and will," "the mystery of his will," and "the purpose of his will." The immediate impression we get is that God can do anything he wants to do—which is exactly Paul's basic point.

In light of God's nature, I am glad he is working according to the pleasure of his will. I am glad he is determined and able to achieve on earth and in heaven whatever is according to the pleasure of his will, or the mystery of his will, or the counsel of his will. Dora Greenwell says it for us in her hymn:

> I am not skilled to understand
>   What God hath willed, what God hath planned;
> I only know at His right hand
>   Stands One who is my Savior!
>
> That He should leave His place on high,
>   And come for sinful man to die,
> You count it strange?—so once did I,
>   Before I knew my Savior.[2]

The Decrees of God

God's purposes are often referred to by theologians as his decrees. A decree, as used in theology, signifies an eternal purpose of God that foreordains some event or condition. The expression is found in Psalm 2:7-9, which reads as follows:

> I will proclaim the decree of the Lord:
> He said to me, "You are my Son;
>   today I have become your Father.
> Ask of me,
>   and I will make the nations your inheritance,
>   the ends of the earth your possession.
> You will rule them with an iron scepter;
>   you will dash them to pieces like pottery."

As used by theologians, however, the term is more technical, adopted to express the idea that God has set before himself certain divine objectives to be attained. Many of those objectives are inferred; that is, they are not flatly stated as purposes. For example, though creation is included in a theologian's list of decrees, the Bible nowhere says that God purposed to create the world. It says simply that he did so. "In the beginning God created the heavens and the earth."[3]

The fall of man is often included in lists of God's decrees. But the Bible does not say that God decreed the fall of man; it simply describes the Fall. Speculation about divine purpose in creating the world and in permitting sin to spoil it may be interesting, but it is just speculation. Furthermore, much of the arguing about the proper sequence of the so-called elective decrees is no more helpful than the old debates about the number of angels who could dance on the head of a pin. We are on safer ground when we stick strictly to Scripture.

In the passage from Ephesians quoted above, Paul links the purpose of God with our eternal welfare. God chose us in Christ, Paul says, "before the creation of the world to be holy and blameless in his sight. In love he predestined us to be adopted as his sons through Jesus Christ." In Christ, we have been predestined to obtain an inheritance. In other words, though life itself is often hard, disappointing, and puzzling, God planned a magnificent future for his people, and that future will come. What that truth means for us while we wait is beautifully expressed in Joseph Parker's hymn:

> God holds the key of all unknown,
> And I am glad:
> If other hands should hold the key,
> Or if He trusted it to me,
> I might be sad.[4]

God holds the key, and in his own good time he will unlock the future. Then we shall see that everything he planned will be exactly as he planned it.

God Works All Things

When Paul said that God "works out everything in conformity with the purpose of his will," he obviously did not mean that *everything* that happens happens because God foreordained it. As theologian Charles Hodge explains, "The decretive and the preceptive will of God can never be in conflict. God never decrees to do, or to cause others to do, what He forbids. He permits men to sin, although sin is forbidden. But God cannot decree to make men sin."[5] Hodge is right. What God plans to make happen and what he allows to happen are often vastly different. In every generation, however, some Bible students have interpreted such texts as the one above from Ephesians with a type of literalness that results in giving God credit (or blame) for all the human tragedies that make life so wretched for many.

In Hebrews 2:17 we read that Christ "had to be made like his brothers in every way." Does the writer of that statement intend us to take "every way" literally, as including everything? That is impossible, of course, because it would mean, among other things, that Christ was born with a sinful nature, as all the rest of mankind has been. Yet the sinlessness of Jesus is a cardinal doctrine of the New Testament. Certain details of his birth—such as the fact that his mother was a virgin—no doubt were given in part to explain his sinlessness. He was like us, but not in every single way. He did not come into the world with a fallen nature, and he committed no sin of any sort to any degree.

This is so obvious that it would not have occurred to the writer of Hebrews that the words "every way" might be misapplied. Nor would it have occurred to Paul that readers might think that God "who works out everything in conformity with the purpose of his will" actually planned evil or causes any hurtful thing. Paul expected his readers to begin reading with certain assumptions. Commenting on words taken from Psalm 8:6 Paul says, "Now when it says that 'everything' has been put under him, it is clear that this does not include God himself, who put everything under Christ."[6]

Some things are so self-evident that it should not be necessary to point them out. It is clear, for instance, that God did not foreordain *everything* that comes to pass. He did not plan the fall of man, and he does not foreordain men's moral failures, the suffering caused by untimely death, or the affliction of children with incurable diseases. But he knew those things would happen, and before they happened he thought of ways to bring good out of evil. That is what is meant by the marvelous statement that God "works out everything in conformity with the purpose of his will."

God has planned a future world without sin, a world ruled by Christ. And "the staggering thing," as J. B. Phillips says, is that in all which will one day belong to Christ, we believers have a part.

God's Purpose in Creation and Providence

In our generation, according to popular perceptions, science now makes it impossible to believe in creation. Popular wisdom holds that everything just happened, possibly as a result of a big bang in outer space. If that is true, then no one need take the Bible seriously, or even God seriously. If God did not create the universe, why should it be thought that he has a purpose for it or is in any way involved in our lives?

If God did not create the world, why should he get involved with it? If he did not create the world, we would even have reason to doubt that he *could* get involved with it. If he could, he would be an intruder into a world that just happened and over which he would have no claim. The thought, of course, is absurd.

The divine purpose envisaged in Ephesians 1 clearly involves creation. The apostle there is saying: God purposed something, and the specifics of that something required creation of the earth and of mankind to populate it. Creation in turn calls for providence. In the words of the Phillips translation, God is the "one who achieves his purposes by his sovereign will."

9

The Work of Creation

Previously we saw the link between divine purpose and creation. If God planned our future, he obviously had to arrange for our existence. The initial step was the creation of the earth. The first truth to emphasize is that the Bible clearly teaches that God created the universe. That fact is the declaration of its opening words: "In the beginning God created the heavens and the earth."[1] Every subsequent biblical reference to origins states or assumes that God created the world.

For example, take these two passages from the prophet Isaiah: "This is what God the Lord says—he who created the heavens and stretched them out, who spread out the earth and all that comes out of it, who gives breath to its people, and life to those who walk on it."[2] And, "For this is what the Lord says—he who created the heavens, he is God; he who fashioned and made the earth, he founded it; he did not create it to be empty, but formed it to be inhabited."[3] Looking up the words *create* and *make* in a concordance will show that the uniform testimony of Scripture is that God created the world and everything in it.

But we wonder about some things in the world—poisonous plants, rattlesnakes, scorpions, rats, harmful bacteria, etc. The doctrine of creation does not hold God accountable for all the forms into which the various kinds of created things have changed. As we will see in more detail later, the world as it came from God's hands, and everything in it, was "good."[4]

If God created the world and everything in it, creation includes us. He is the Creator, and we are his creatures. What this means, among other things, is that we ought to worship him. This is the truth in Paul's mind when he rebuked certain idolaters who, he says, "worshiped and served created things rather than the Creator—who is forever praised."[5]

God Created out of Nothing

Aristotle, the great Greek philosopher who lived in the fourth century B.C. said, *"ex nihilo, nihil fir,"* which means "out of nothing, nothing comes." That seems to make good sense; nothing can come from nothing. Within man's power and experience the principle is true. But with God it is false. On the other side of Aristotle's principle was the parallel idea that matter is eternal. In other words, nothing comes into existence that does not already exist, and nothing that already exists will ever cease to exist. Thus, in his view the world was not made out of nothing; it was made from eternally existing materials.

If you investigate the cosmogonies of the ancient Greeks, you will find that Aristotle's view was typical. The Greeks believed that in the beginning chaos prevailed. All matter already existed, but it was formless. Out of Chaos came Erebus and Night, and from them "the various parts and forms of existence in the world, in successions that are differently given by different poets who have repeated the legends."[6] Ancient Assyrian and Babylonian legends held similar views; they all "assume a primeval chaos independent of any deity."[7] Differences in the Assyrian and Babylonian legends are like the differences in the Greek legends. Some trace origins to a spontaneous evolution of life from a watery abyss, others to the action of a deity of some kind. However, as James S. Candlish says, "Even those philosophers who . . . held that the order of nature could not be accounted for without a mind presiding over its changes, did not rise higher than the belief of a deity moulding and ordering an eternally pre-existent matter; as Plato, for example, represents the subject in the *Timmaeus*."[8]

But the Bible makes it clear that matter is *not* eternal. As Paul says, "for us [Christians] there is but one God, the Father, from whom all things came and for whom we live; and there is but one Lord, Jesus Christ, through whom all things came and through whom we live."[9] God created the universe (universes, plural, to be technically accurate) out of nothing. The Apostle John tells us that in heaven the twenty-four elders whom he saw laid their crowns before the throne and said, "You are worthy, our Lord and God, to receive glory and honor and power, for you created all things, and by your will they were created and have their being."[10]

Is it important that God created out of nothing? Canon T. C. Hammond lists four reasons why that truth matters to Christians. First, if there was uncreated matter, what assurance do we have that

God was able to control it? Second, if there was some form of matter over which God had no control, which spontaneously began to evolve, what assurance do we have that there are not *other* forms of matter which God cannot control? Third, if God used existing matter to make the world, what assurance do we have that it turned out the way he wanted it? Independently existing materials may not have responded to his will. Finally, if some other person or substance exists by as good a right as God himself, "how can we be certain that his ultimate purpose for the Church will not be frustrated by a catastrophe over which he will have no control?"[11]

God's creation out of nothing not only is biblical but is required by logical necessity. If the God whom the Bible sets forth as the only God actually exists, at some point in time (actually *before* time began) he was alone. He did not coexist with any person or thing or material of any kind. He was eternally alone, and creation was a free act. This is implied in the Genesis account, where it says repeatedly that "God said" and it was done. If we link creation with God's eternal purpose, we see that creation was a loving act. God created the world as a step toward the accomplishment of his eternal purpose. Paul speaks of that "eternal purpose which he accomplished in Christ Jesus our Lord." Included in that purpose is our present privilege of access to God. "In [Christ] and through faith in him we may approach God with freedom and confidence," says Paul.[12] Think of that! Freedom to approach God was made possible through—as the initial step—the creation of the universe! God created the world out of nothing, in order that we might approach him with freedom and confidence.

Denials of Creation

One is inclined simply to ignore the many denials of God's creation. But they are much too pervasive and influential to ignore. Most modern denials are based on supposed facts of evolution. Says Julian Huxley: "In the evolutionary pattern of thought there is no longer either need or room for the supernatural. The earth was not created; it evolved. So did all the animals and plants that inhabit it, including our human selves, mind and soul as well as body and brain."[13] Huxley maintained that the earth evolved, but he did not say from what, though he implies that something was there from which it could have evolved. Thus atheists like Huxley have just drawn up in modern garb the notion of the ancients that matter is eternal. In their search for origins, they get no farther back than did Aristotle, Plato, or the ancient Babylonians.

Hindus and other Eastern thinkers believe that the universe "was made out of the substance of the deity."[14] That explanation of origins is called the emanation theory, and it is taught in the Hindu Vedic hymns and the Upanishads.

Most of us are more familiar with pantheism, which is quite similar to the emanation theory of the universe. Says Professor James S. Candlish, "Spinoza and modern Pantheists of the Hegelian school have adopted views of the origin of the universe very like the emanation theories of the Brahmans."[15] What these views have in common is their identifying God with nature, the Creator with the things he created. A pantheist will see himself, and by extension see God, in the fluttering of a leaf. That is idolatry, of course.

God Created by His Powerful Word

In the Book of Hebrews we read that "By faith we understand that the universe was formed at God's command, so that what is seen was not made out of what was visible."[16] That verse echoes Psalm 148:1-5, which after calling on the heavens, the heights, God's angel hosts, the sun, the moon, and the stars to praise the Lord says, "he commanded and they were created." If God created the universe, we can hardly imagine his doing it any other way. He said, "Let it be," and it was so.

By faith we lay hold of that truth. Our eternal welfare depends on God's power. If God, who decreed eternal blessing for his people, were not powerful enough to create a world by his word, how could he then create a new heaven and a new earth? How could he provide an eternal home for his redeemed people? Scripture links God's power as Creator with his ability to bring everything to conclusion according to his will.[17] There is great comfort in knowing that the God to whom we look for present help is also the Creator. "I lift up my eyes to the hills—where does my help come from? My help comes from the Lord, the Maker of heaven and earth."[18]

The Six Days of Creation

When Genesis says God made the earth in six days, does the word *day* mean a twenty-four-hour day or a geological age? Scholars who take the Bible seriously—that is, devout men who believe the Bible is divinely inspired—disagree in the answer to that question. For the past hundred years or so, belief in creation—especially a six twenty-four-hour day creation—has not been considered intellectually respectable in many circles. Except for fundamentalists, few openly proclaimed creation in six days. Even some fundamentalists were uneasy. If they took science courses in a secular college or university, they likely were presented with seemingly overwhelming evidence that the earth is billions of years old, and that everything in it has evolved according to the principles of uniformitarianism—the theory that natural laws have always operated in exactly the same ways in which they do now.

For those among this group who wanted to believe the Bible, it seemed wonderfully reassuring to think that Genesis 1 could be made to harmonize with the findings of science by interpreting each creation "day" as being a geological age. In my judgment, however, modern so-called creationists or creationist scientists are right in insisting that the days of Genesis 1 are twenty-four-hour days. They cite biblical and scientific reasons. Henry Morris says that "there are more than twenty serious contradictions between the biblical order and events of the creative days and the standard geologic history of the earth and its development, even if it were permissible to interpret the 'days' as 'ages.' "[19]

Biblically there is no reason to interpret the days as ages, and very good reasons for taking them for what they seem to be—twenty-four-hour days. Among other reasons is the Lord's command to observe a six-day work week being based on the six days of creation. "Six days you shall labor and do all your work, but . . . on [the seventh day] you shall not do any work. . . . For in six days the Lord made the heavens and the earth."[20] Since Moses was the human author of both Genesis and Exodus, it is reasonable to conclude that he uses the word in the same way in both passages. In Exodus the word *must* be taken literally. A day is a day. Hence, in Genesis also a day is a day—twenty-four hours in length. Commenting on the various nonliteral interpretations of Genesis 1, Derek Kidner says, "The assumption common to these interpretations is that God would not have us picture the creation as compressed into a mere week. But this may be exactly what God does intend us to do."[21]

God Made Everything Good and Beautiful

After each day of creative activity, God saw what he had made and he "saw that it was good." When the work was finished, God saw "all that he had made" and the last verse in the chapter says, "it was very good."[22] In the beginning the world was orderly and beautiful. As a bumper sticker says, "God did not make junk." God saw what he had done, and in his eyes it was good, meaning well-done and lovely to look at.

It seems that in every generation some serious-minded people have been uneasy about beauty in any form, as if it were satanic or at least less than holy and pure. Perhaps they feel guilty about enjoying something that is physically beautiful. But God, not Satan, is the Creator of beauty—physical, moral, and spiritual. Satan cannot produce true beauty; the hideous and ugly is his special province. Appreciation of true beauty is part of our heritage as creatures made in the image of God.

There is much truth in the saying, "Beauty lies in the eyes of the beholder." A man in love may see beauty in a woman others view as quite ordinary. Is the man deluded, or is there in his beloved a beauty that only a loving heart can see? Something in her gives pleasure to *his* senses, if not to yours or mine. Furthermore, what he sees in her exalts his own mind and spirit. In other words, she brings out the best in him. That is the effect her beauty has on him.

Is beauty, then, an objective reality? Is it *there*, or is it just an invention of the viewer's mind, a purely subjective thing? Philosophers love to debate the question. I think its answer is found in the often repeated line in Genesis 1: "God saw that it was good." Goodness here represents rightness, perfection, and beauty. It turned out exactly as it should have turned out. Its goodness and beauty were not a figment of God's imagination. Those qualities were *there*, inherent in the universe he had created.

Thus, when we say that beauty lies in the eyes of the beholder, we are not entirely correct. The beauty is actually there, in the girl whom the beholder admires; and an inner faculty in him enables him to see it. Probably everyone has an inner eye; it is part of the image of God in us. God who created beauty gives us the ability to see it. But not all see as well as some. If our inner eye were trained, we would see beauty in nearly everyone. We would see the image of God in them, and we would see what Paul urges us to see in them—namely, "whatever" is lovely."[23]

Everyone sees some kinds or degrees of beauty. David was strikingly handsome; his was male beauty of an extraordinary kind. Abigail was beautiful, as was Bathsheba. Theirs, of course, was female beauty, and it was so intense that everyone could see it.[24]

Most people appreciate scenic beauty, especially in the spectacular beauty of high mountains and deep valleys. The most enduring beauty, however, is spiritual. In Psalm 90 Moses prays, "Let the beauty of the Lord our God be upon us."[25] Gypsy Smith may have been thinking of that prayer when he sang, "Let the beauty of Jesus be seen in me." There is no beauty like the beauty of character that the Lord Jesus Christ can produce in a person. When God sees that beauty, he says, "That's good!"

The statement "God made the world good and beautiful" may raise questions in our minds, because vast tracts of the earth obviously are *not* beautiful. We can always find *someone* who will say that the ugliest place in the world is beautiful. But not many are convinced; most of us think that certain areas of the Sahara and similar wastelands are far from beautiful. It is hard to believe that God made deserts or fields of lava or seemingly endless flat swamps of rotting vegetation. If God made the world beautiful, how do we account for the ugliness?

The answer is, sin came into the world and spoiled God's creation. Genesis 3:17-19 says that God cursed the ground because of Adam's sin.

> Cursed is the ground because of you;
>   through painful toil you will eat of it
>   all the days of your life.
> It will produce thorns and thistles for you,
>   and you will eat the plants of the field.
> By the sweat of your brow
>   you will eat your food
> until you return to the ground,
>   since from it you were taken;
> for dust you are
>   and to dust you will return.

Before the Fall (that is, before Adam's first sin), Adam worked the soil, and it was easy work.[26] After the Fall it was hard work; the conditions under which Adam (and, of course, all his descendants) worked were vastly different. The soil brought forth weeds and thorns, and Adam had to sweat to produce his food. Paul tells what happened to the earth: "For the creation was subjected to frustration, not by its own choice, but by the will of the one who subjected it, in hope that the creation itself will be liberated from its bondage to decay and brought into the glorious freedom of the children of

God."[27] The whole creation (the cosmos, the universes) has been groaning up to the present time.

That is the Bible's explanation of the ugliness that abounds. Nature now speaks in a minor key. God made the world good and beautiful, but when sin came the beauty was marred. The creation is now in bondage to decay; it is growing old, and there is no hiding the wrinkles.

Yet, just as moral and spiritual beauty are more wonderful than physical beauty, so is moral and spiritual ugliness more hideous and barren than a thousand Saharas. Christ can change our inner appearance; he can make us beautiful in him. Peter says that a gentle and quiet spirit has unfading beauty. That is the way "the holy women of the past who put their hope in God used to make themselves beautiful."[28] With God's help, all of us can have that inner beauty.

10

The Creation of Man

In a brief summary of the biblical teaching about the creation of man, the Westminster Shorter Catechism says, "God created man male and female, after his own image, in knowledge, righteousness, and holiness, with dominion over the creatures."

That is a good outline. God created man; he created man male and female; and he created man in his own image. That is the central truth: God made man, male and female, in his own image. The terms that follow—knowledge, righteousness, and holiness, with dominion over the creatures—help explain the concept of the image of God in man.

The first Scripture passage to consider is from Genesis 1:

> Then God said, "Let us make man in our image, in our likeness, and let them rule over the fish of the sea and the birds of the air, over the livestock, over all the earth, and over all the creatures that move along the ground." So God created man in his own image, in the image of God he created him; male and female he created them. God blessed them and said to them, "Be fruitful and increase in number; fill the earth and subdue it. Rule over the fish of the sea and the birds of the air and over every living creature that moves on the ground."[1]

Two brief passages from the New Testament are also especially significant. To the Christians at Colosse Paul wrote, "The new self . . . is being renewed in knowledge in the image of its Creator."[2] To the Ephesians he wrote, "Put on the new self, created to be like God in true righteousness and holiness."[3]

Creation, Not Evolution

I would like to underline the fact of creation as opposed to evolution. I say "fact of creation," but I am not going to attempt to *prove* that creation is a fact; I am going to do what the Bible itself does: assume it and state it.

Scripture clearly teaches that God created man in his own image, and if Scripture teaches it, the question is settled, at least for all who accept the Bible as inerrant and authoritative. If I seem to belabor creation as opposed to evolution, the explanation lies in the pervasiveness of evolutionary teaching in our society. I said *pervasiveness,* not *persuasiveness.* The acceptance of evolution pervades our school systems and much of the rest of our society, but at least for Christians who believe Scripture, it is not persuasive. We do not believe it.

Notice the change in language in Genesis 1 when the creation of man is introduced. For the first five days of creation the account begins with the words, "God said, 'Let there be . . .' " Then, whatever God wanted to happen, happened. On the first day God said, " 'Let there be light,' and there was light"; on the second day he said, "Let there be an expanse [or firmament] between the waters to separate water from water," and that is exactly what happened. And so on through the fifth day.

On the sixth day, however, he did not say, "Let man come into existence," or something like that. Instead God said, "Let us make man in our image, in our likeness." As Alexander Whyte explains,

> Instead of a creative command, as on the preceding days, there is heard the language rather of counsel, deliberation, and resolution. The Creator now speaks as if a work was about to be wrought altogether distinct from, and immeasurably superior to, all that had hitherto been made.[4]

In Genesis 2:7 the distinction between the creation of man and the rest of God's works is emphasized by the additional detail that is provided: "The Lord God formed man from the dust of the ground and breathed into his nostrils the breath of life, and man became a living being."[5]

What we see, then, are two basic truths: man (that is, the first man and woman from whom all the rest of us descended) was created, and man was (and, of course, still is) distinct from other created things. One immensely important implication of creation, therefore, is this: If God created us, he is over us and we are answerable to him. It is small wonder that many people prefer evolution to creation!

Male and Female

The books *The Naked Ape* and *Beyond Freedom and Dignity* were immensely popular for awhile. The view they set forth—that man is nothing much more than a talking animal—is still popular. It is, in fact, virtually the only alternative to the biblical view. Man is either a rational animal, and only a rational animal, as the authors of the books just cited think, or he is *more* than a rational animal; he is what the Bible says he is: a creature of an entirely different and higher order.

What does the Bible say about man? It begins with a purely biological characteristic: gender or sexual difference. God created man male and female. That is obvious, of course. But the fact has a significance sometimes overlooked by many people who habitually read the Bible. The significance is that the woman, Eve, was not an afterthought. God did not make a man slightly defective, then correct the error by adding a helper. As Genesis 1:26, 27 says, "God said, 'Let us make man in our image, in our likeness, and let *them* rule . . . over all the earth.' . . . So God created man in his own image, in the image of God he created him; male and female he created them" (emphasis added). From the beginning, God planned the creation of *two* forms of human beings, one male and the other female. Those two, the male and the female together, were the first members of mankind.

Why, some may ask, does Genesis 2:18 say that God said, "It is not good for the man to be alone. I will make a helper suitable for him"? That sounds as if the woman were an afterthought. The explanation is, God wanted to emphasize a fundamental distinction between man and the animals. Adam was created after the animals, and like them, he had biological characteristics. He was a living, breathing creature. Lest it be thought that Adam was just like other created things, only smarter, the Holy Spirit records the divine intention to create a suitable partner for the man. Eve, who was made in the image of God, was a suitable partner; none of the animals was.

What that means, among other things, is that whatever man is, woman is also. Men and women are alike made in the image of God. Together they comprise "mankind." That is why Peter urges men to treat their wives as "heirs with you of the gracious gift of life."[6]

In God's Image

What does "the image of God" mean? Let us begin by defining the word *image* as it is commonly used. Then we will look at the creation of man and ask which of the two processes in that act refers to the image of God.

An image is defined in the dictionary as "a reproduction or imitation of the form of a person or thing." The word has other meanings, of course, but that is fairly close to what is intended in Scripture by "the image of God." It means that man resembles God. How? Certainly not in the first of the two processes of creation. Genesis 2:7 says that "the Lord God formed man from the dust of the ground." He took the clay of Eden and fashioned a man of flesh and blood and bones and tissue and everything else that a body has. Up to that point, the creature did not resemble God. How do we know that? Because, as we saw earlier, God is not a physical being; he is spirit. He has no bones or blood to resemble. Remember the statement of Jesus to the woman beside the well? "God is spirit, and his worshipers must worship in spirit and in truth."[7] No one *looks* like God, because God has no body. Whatever "the image of God" means, it does not refer to physical appearance.

The second stage, or process, in the creation of a man is indicated in the words that complete Genesis 2:7—"[The Lord God] breathed into his nostrils the breath of life, and man became a living being." That process turned mere clay into the image of God. How? By infusing into it its immaterial part, the soul. Here the term "being" stands for man's inner nature or personality. It includes that aspect of the immaterial part of man termed "spirit." We will not here try to distinguish between soul and spirit, or try to settle the question as to whether man is bipartite or tripartite. In Genesis 2:7, "being" sums up everything that can be said about the immaterial part of man. It is his soul that bears the image of God.

What then *is* the image of God in man? The place to begin is with God himself. What is God like? The least that can be known from the first two chapters in Genesis is that God is a person. He thinks, he wills, he feels, and he acts. In other words, he has intellect, will, emotion, and the ability to act in accordance with those things. Since we also have those qualities (they are part of our personhood), we conclude that those aspects of human nature are at least part of the image of God in us. There is more to the image of God than those things because, to a lesser extent, animals have the same qualities. But animals do not have self-consciousness or what may be termed a moral nature—a sense of right and wrong. Those qualities are uniquely human and, in addition to intellect, will, and emotion, constitute the image of God in man.

Image and *likeness* are virtually synonymous terms. God created man in his own image so that man could be like him. Since the image of God cannot be physical likeness, it must refer to moral and spiritual likeness. Theologian Gordon R. Lewis accentuates the following human properties which he believes constitute the image of God in man: self-consciousness and self-transcendence, self-determination, moral judgment, and communion with God.[8]

Self-consciousness is obvious. I am aware of myself, and I can analyze myself. As Paul says, "Who could really understand a man's inmost thoughts except the spirit of the man himself?"[9] Because I can analyze myself, even rebuke myself, I also have what theologians term "self-transcendence." I can rise above my knowledge of myself and of other persons and other things.

Self-determination is the ability to exercise self-control. I do not *have* to do what my nature or inclinations suggest. Paul said he beat his body and made it his slave, and he constantly exhorted his Christian friends to do the same thing. "Do not let sin reign in your mortal body so that you obey its evil desires."[10] To a considerable extent we can determine what kind of persons we will be, and we are responsible before God for the choices we make. "Each of us will give an account of himself to God."[11]

Finally, the image of God in man enables man to have fellowship with his Creator. Paul hints at this aspect of the image of God in a passage partially quoted earlier:

> For who could really understand a man's inmost thoughts except the spirit of the man himself? How much less could anyone understand the thoughts of God except the very Spirit of God? And the marvelous thing is this, that we now receive not the spirit of the world but the Spirit of God himself, so that we can actually understand something of God's generosity toward us.[12]

Admittedly that passage deals specifically with man as brought back to God through Christ. But fellowship with God was part of man's original state. Adam talked with God in the Garden of Eden, a privilege denied the animals.

Theologian T. C. Hammond lists the following elements of the image of God in man: first, human personality is in contrast to that of animals. Man is self-conscious, possesses the power of abstract thought, and has a spiritual nature. (Those properties were discussed above under self-consciousness, self-transcendence, self-determination, moral judgment, and communion with God.) Second, man has a moral resemblance to God, "in the laws which govern human relationships and human government at their best." Third, man has dominion over creation. And finally, he has "characteristics which argue in favor of his hope of immortality."[13]

The image of God in man consists in man's nature as moral and spiritual. As Erich Sauer says, man "gives expression in a creaturely manner to the *inward* characteristics of God."[14] Sauer notes that man's resemblance to God is presented in Scripture in two aspects: as something that can be lost (and was, in fact, lost at the fall of man) and as something that cannot be lost. Hence, man is still viewed in Scripture as having the image of God.[15]

In relation to the image of God that remains in man, Sauer draws attention to three attributes: will, intellect, and feeling. Three passages in the New Testament link those attributes with the image of God. In Ephesians 4:24 Paul says, "Put on the new self, created to be like God in true righteousness and holiness." That is a reference to the will. According to Colossians 3:10, we have "put on the new self, which is being renewed in knowledge in the image of its Creator." That is a reference to the intellect. Finally we need to consider what Sauer terms "the joyful experience of the glory of God," including "the joy of the *feeling*."[16] "We, who with unveiled faces all reflect the Lord's glory," Paul says, "are being transformed into his likeness with ever-increasing glory, which comes from the Lord, who is the Spirit."[17]

We can understand to some extent the concept of the image of God in man, but its implications overwhelm us. Man is not just a thinking animal; he is a creature made to express the inward characteristics of God. No wonder ancient Israel's King David cried out, "What is man?"[18] He was overwhelmed by the wonder of creation in the image of God.

Let us look at three words: knowledge, righteousness, and holiness. The link between the image of God and man's knowledge, righteousness, and holiness seems obvious. To the extent that it is possible in a mere creature, man's knowledge, righteousness, and holiness mirror the knowledge, righteousness, and holiness of his Maker.

Knowledge Adam was created with a certain fund of knowledge. We do not know how much he knew. It is easier to say what he did not know. He obviously did not know the English language, because English did not exist. Because there were no cars in the Garden of Eden, he did not understand automobile mechanics. Neither did Aristotle, Plato, or other brilliant men who lived many centuries after Adam. What, then, did Adam know? We do not know the full range of his knowledge. It is clear, however, that he knew how to talk; he understood something of agriculture; he knew the animal kingdom well enough to give the animals their names; and (surely the most important item in his fund of knowledge) he knew God and he knew that God is holy. That is evident from his shame and fear after the incident of eating the forbidden fruit.[19]

Adam probably taught his sons and daughters everything from agriculture to zoology. He was created knowing those things, or at least was sufficient in knowledge to function while he was learning. But Adam's children were *born,* not created directly as were their parents; and like all babies since that time, they had to learn slowly and sometimes painfully.

Still, in every human being there may be some kind of innate knowledge, some things which people in every culture would know if they were not brainwashed, so to speak. Two passages of Scripture come to mind in support of this idea. The first is John 1:9—"The true light that gives light to every man was coming into the world." The alternate reading is, "This was the true light that gives light to every man who comes into the world." The second passage is Romans 2:14—"When Gentiles, who do not have the law, do by nature things required by the law, they are a law for themselves, even though they do not have the law." It is as if those who have never heard of the Ten Commandments nevertheless know the substance of those commandments. It is as if some knowledge (specifically moral knowledge) is innate and instinctive.

We cannot, of course, resolve all the questions that come to mind. But one thing is certain: Adam was created knowing some things, and what he knew was true knowledge, not false knowledge. When God saw the man he had made, he said, "very good." What a pity mankind has lost its way! What a pity so many of our smartest people are, as Paul says, "always learning but never able to acknowledge the truth."[20]

Righteousness and Holiness Righteousness and holiness are qualities, along with knowledge, that were part of Adam's God-like nature as he came from the hand of his Maker. Holiness may be distinguished from righteousness as being its root or source. A truly holy person does what is right. His holy nature affects his will and his behavior. He behaves righteously. Adam's righteousness was inherent. As Solomon says in Ecclesiastes 7:29, "God made mankind upright." If Paul could describe fallen men as having by nature an instinct for what is right and good, how much more did Adam as he came from God.[21]

Alas, when Adam sinned he became unrighteous and unholy, as are all his descendants—meaning you, me, and everyone else who has ever lived. But there is good news! Paul says that an *imputed* righteousness is available. It is imputed as contrasted with inherent. Paul says in Romans 3:22 that "this righteousness from God comes through faith in Jesus Christ to all who believe." In 1 Corinthians 1:30 Paul says that Christ Jesus "has become for us wisdom from God—that is, our righteousness, holiness and redemption." What he is saying is that, through union with Christ Jesus, we recover the righteousness and holiness Adam lost. In us it is not inherent; but it can be imputed. We were born sinful, but when we trust Christ to save us, God credits us with righteousness and holiness. Practical sanctification means growing in righteousness, the process whereby a believer struggles to bring his everyday life into harmony with his new stature as righteous and holy in God's sight.

Dominion In the Eighth Psalm David expresses amazement at man's place at the pinnacle of creation:

> You made him ruler over the works of your hands;
>   you put everything under his feet:
> all flocks and herds
>   and the beasts of the field,
> the birds of the air,
>   and the fish of the sea,
>   all that swim the paths of the seas.[22]

I recall thinking of that Psalm when, while we were on the mission field, one of my sons was gravely ill and, the doctors said, dying. He had encephalitis, which according to lab tests had been caused by water contaminated by lice carried in the fur of rats. All things under man's feet; yet here was my son, being killed by a louse!

Dominion, like moral qualities such as righteousness and holiness, was real but was forfeited when Adam sinned. Yet it was not entirely lost. Man is not safe from predators on land or sea, but he is still clearly dominant over the creatures. The lost dominion was recovered for us by the man Christ Jesus.

Adam began life in a perfect world. The animals originally were all herbivorous; they all ate plants. None of the animals hunted and killed for its food.[23] In that state God brought them to Adam, and whatever Adam called a creature, that was its name. He named them all, from aardvarks to zebras, though not in English, of course. Every animal was as harmless and friendly as any in a Walt Disney movie.[24]

When Christ returns, the original dominion will be completely restored. That is a major theme of the prophets. The lovely eleventh chapter of Isaiah paints a Millennial picture. It says that then "the wolf will live with the lamb, the leopard will lie down with the goat, the calf and the lion and the yearling together; and a little child will lead them."[25] At that time man will again be in complete charge of a renewed and renovated creation.

How will that be accomplished? By and through Christ. That is the lesson of Hebrews 2, where Psalm 8 is quoted. The writer says we do not yet see all things subjected to man, though that was God's original plan. But, he says, we do see Jesus. We see him who "was made a little lower than the angels, now crowned with glory and honor because he suffered death."[26] When Christ returns, he will perfectly and permanently repair the damage done to his world.

A new world is coming. And in the world to come neither lion nor tiger nor shark nor killer whale, nor even a louse, will be able to kill a man. The world will once again be as God intended.

11

God's Providence

The subject of God's providence is more involved than it may first appear to be. It is also controversial.

I have two objectives as we look at this doctrine. First, I hope to develop a clear explanation of what the doctrine means, and second I hope to show that the explanation is biblical. It is possible to push a truth to such an extreme that an otherwise sound position becomes untenable. The doctrine of providence lends itself to abuse, which we hope to avoid.

The word *providence* is made up of two parts, which taken together literally mean "seeing before." It refers to the act of providing for or exercising foresight. The word has long been used to represent divine guidance or care, or an act or instance of such guidance or care. When capitalized, Providence stands for God.

God's Preserving

Divine providence primarily embraces two ideas: preserving and governing. We will take these one at a time and will turn to the Bible to see what it says about each.

What does God preserve? He preserves his creation. He made everything, including man. "Everything," of course, does not necessarily include a million and one different kinds of microbes, bacteria, etc. Surely some species and forms of life developed after the Fall. But everything God has made, whether in original or developed form, is the object of his preserving care. Otherwise, in a world condemned to change and decay, nothing would survive.

Is that what the Bible teaches? Yes, as witnessed by the following passages. First is Hebrews 1:3—"The Son is the radiance of God's glory and the exact representation of his being, sustaining all things by his powerful word." Second is Colossians 1:17—"He is before all things, and in him all things hold together." Third (and last, though many other passages could be cited) is 2 Peter 3:5-7—"Long ago by God's word the heavens existed and the earth was formed out of water and with water. By water also the world of that time was deluged and destroyed. By the same word the present heavens and earth are reserved for fire, being kept for the day of judgment and destruction of ungodly men."

God's creation includes the entire universe. We just quoted several passages of Scripture that teach that God himself keeps the universe from falling apart. Here is where the significance of entropy becomes apparent. In the nineteenth century scientists discovered (or formulated) the law of entropy. The term *entropy* is used in several ways, but as used here it stands for "the degradation of the matter and energy in the universe to an ultimate state of inert uniformity."[1] It may be helpful to elaborate. The law of entropy (also called the second law of thermodynamics) says that energy flows from the orderly to the disorderly, from the usable to the unusable. If order is created, it is done by causing greater disorder in the surrounding environment.

What is the connection between the law of entropy and providence? The connection is made clear by lining up three passages of Scripture. First consider Romans 8:20, 21.

> For the creation was subjected to frustration, not by its own choice, but by the will of the one who subjected it, in hope that the creation itself will be liberated from its bondage to decay and brought into the glorious freedom of the children of God.

That is the Bible's way of stating in nonscientific language the entropy law, or the second law of thermodynamics. The universe is running down; everything tends to proceed from order to disorder. The creation is in bondage to decay.

Now consider Hebrews 1:3—"The Son is the radiance of God's glory and the exact representation of his being, sustaining all things by his powerful word." Next look at 2 Peter 3:5, 7—"By God's word the heavens existed and the earth was formed. . . . By the same word the present heavens and earth are reserved for fire, being kept for the day of judgment and destruction of ungodly men."

The verbs "sustaining," "reserved," and "being kept" refer to God's providence, "his most holy, wise, and powerful preserving" of the universe, as someone has put it. When sin entered the world, God condemned the world to decay; it was he who set the law of entropy in motion. Yet it is also he who controls entropy in the universe, keeping the universe intact until the day of judgment. Peter continues to explain: "The heavens will disappear with a roar; the elements will be destroyed by fire, and the earth and everything in it will be laid bare."[2] Until that time God will continue to hold all things together. He is the holy, wise, and powerful Creator and Preserver of the universe.

Now we are going to consider a few biblical evidences of God's providence in the so-called vegetable and animal kingdoms. We will not be thinking about evidences of *design* in creation. That is a fascinating subject, but not ours to discuss at this time. We will be thinking of evidences of his preserving.

When we say that God preserves his creatures, we mean, among other things, that he provides for them. That is not to say that he keeps them from dying, or that he unfailingly meets every need of his creatures. In times of drought and famine or other natural disaster, many of God's creatures starve to death or are killed. Nevertheless, the norm is an unending cycle of seasons, each contributing to meet the needs of man and beast. In Genesis 8:22, after the great Flood, God said,

> As long as the earth endures,
> seedtime and harvest,
> cold and heat,
> summer and winter,
> day and night
> will never cease.

God made the seasons and the natural phenomena peculiar to each—cold winds in winter, warm winds in summer, etc. Many Bible passages speak as if God were personally and directly responsible for every wind that blows, every drop of rain that falls, every bolt of lightning that flashes. That does not mean that the writers of the Bible were unaware of "secondary causes" or "laws of nature." Careful study of passages in some of the Psalms and in Job reveal a remarkably intimate knowledge of nature and the way it works. But men of those days thought of creation as God's handiwork; hence, it was he who made the winds blow, the rain fall, and the lightning flash. Perhaps the closest they came to acknowledging secondary causes may be seen in passages such as Revelation 7:1, where four angels are seen "holding back the four winds of the earth to prevent any wind from blowing on the land or on the sea or on any tree." The angels held back the wind, which, if they had not been specially held in check, would have blown according to the laws that govern the wind.

In my judgment, the biblical way of ascribing natural phenomena to God is a fine corrective to the secular way of thinking and talking as if the universe were a closed, self-sufficient system, operating according to inexorable "laws of nature." This is God's world, and he can and does do what he wishes in it.

Psalm 104 is a powerful exposition of the truth that this is God's world and that he determines the laws that operate within it. Following are a few verses of that Psalm translated from a French version of the Bible:

> You set springs gushing in ravines,
>   running down between the mountains,
> supplying water for wild animals,
>   attracting the thirsty wild donkeys;
> near there the birds of the air make their nests
>   and sing among the branches.
>
> You made the moon to tell the seasons,
>   the sun knows when to set:
> you bring darkness on; night falls,
>   all the forest animals come out:
> savage lions roaring for their prey,
>   claiming their food from God.
>
> All creatures depend on you
>   to feed them throughout the year;
> you provide the food they eat,
>   with generous hand you satisfy their hunger.
>
> You turn your face away, they suffer,
>   you stop their breath, they die
>   and revert to dust.
> You give breath, fresh life begins,
> you keep renewing the world.

That is a lovely setting forth of the truth that God preserves his creatures.

God's Governing

The second aspect of God's providence is his governing all his creatures and all their actions.

The two ideas are often closely related, as in the experiences of Elijah reported in 1 Kings 17:1-16. You may recall the prophet's flight from the wicked King Ahab. God told the prophet to "hide in the Kerith Ravine," and then said to him, "I have ordered the ravens to feed you there." The ravens brought him bread and meat every morning and every evening until the brook dried up. Then God sent Elijah to Zarephath, to the home of a widow. "I have commanded a widow in that place to supply you with food," God said. The widow knew nothing of this, and when the prophet arrived and made a request for food she was dismayed. Why? Because she had barely enough for herself and her son for one more meal. When it was gone, they would starve. Nevertheless, she believed the prophet when he told her that feeding him would not hasten her death, but would ensure her life. "The jar of flour will not be used up and the jug of oil will not run dry until the day the Lord gives rain on the land," Elijah assured her. And that is the way it was; the flour jar and the jug of oil for cooking were never empty. By a daily miracle God met the needs of the widow, her son, and the prophet Elijah.

That is a lovely story, and many of God's people in desperate straits have been encouraged by it. For our purposes, the following lessons from it are helpful. First, creatures of instinct, the ravens, acted in obedience to higher orders than mere instinct; they acted in response to God, who governs all his creatures and all their actions. It would be silly to say that the ravens consciously chose to feed Elijah, or that they knew what they were doing. Like the lion that killed the disobedient prophet,[3] the ravens responded to a signal more powerful than instinct.

Second, God's use of ravens did not interrupt their normal activities. What do ravens normally do but fly around looking for food, then delivering it somewhere? God acted unusually in his world, but not bizarrely. Furthermore, his actions did not throw nature out of whack or introduce spectacular things. The brook dried up, as was to be expected in time of prolonged drought. Then God told the prophet to do what was natural under the circumstances—leave the drought-stricken land. In Zarephath a widow would take him in. It was perfectly normal, yet also miraculous in that God *caused* the widow to do it. She did not hear words or see visions; she just responded to the prophet's assurances. It may never have occurred to her that God specifically directed her to do what she did.

The ravens and widow alike prove that God both preserves and governs his creatures. Ravens, like the wind and sea, obey him mindlessly. The widow probably thought about her action, but she, no less than the ravens, was responding to him who governs his creatures.

Neither aspect of God's providence, his preserving or his governing, must be pressed to extremes. God preserves his creatures, but his creatures are nonetheless subject to laws that operate in a fallen world, including the law of decay and death. Similarly, God governs his creatures and all their actions, but he does not persuade or force them to commit sin.

Two or three years after the story just mentioned, when the famine was over and Elijah was home again, Queen Jezebel threatened the prophet, and, without waiting for a word from the Lord, he ran for his life. His flight was prompted by fear. The next day, in a despondent mood, Elijah prayed for death. God sent an angel to encourage him and forty days later, at Horeb, the word of the Lord came to him. "What are you doing here, Elijah?" God asked the prophet. The Lord asked him the same question twice, then sent him elsewhere.[4] Elijah was not a puppet on a string. As a man of God, he usually did what God wanted him to do, when God wanted him to do it. But he was also capable of lapses in faith, at which times he was inclined to erratic behavior.

The point is that at times the prophet acted independently of the Lord. He did what God did not want him to do. God's control over his creatures and their actions must not be interpreted in terms of ironclad, irresistible determinism. God permits the exercise of human will. Otherwise, how can we explain actions such as Elijah's flight or, say, Abraham's misconduct in Egypt?[5] We cannot blame God for those failures. As James says, "God cannot be tempted by evil, nor does he tempt anyone."[6]

We will return to that subject later, but for now we will focus on two ideas suggested by those incidents in the life of Elijah. First, God wants to govern the actions of his people; second, he refuses to neutralize or override our wills. He permits the exercise of human will, thereby running the risk, so to speak, that we will fail to do what he wants. God preserves his creatures, but only for special purposes does he prevent the normal operation of laws at work in a creation subject to bondage and decay. He governs the actions of his creatures, but he does not exercise absolute control. He could do so if he desired, of course; but he does not. We are free to rebel, if we choose. But happy is the person who makes it his ambition to be well pleasing to God! It is only a question of time before others come to grief.

God Uses Evil When we say that God governs all his creatures and all their actions, we do not mean that God is responsible for sin. No one really knows how to explain the origin of evil, or why God permits its continued existence. We do know, as we just saw from the quotation from James, that God does not tempt people to sin. He does not entice us to do things for which he then judges us.

What do we mean then when we say that God governs his creatures and their actions? We mean that he is *in total control* and, to the extent that evil serves his purposes, he exercises his control even over that which is against his will. If we so choose, we may rebel against him and commit terrible sins. But he is able to make our evil contribute toward the eventual fulfillment of his ultimate objectives.

Many passages in Scripture teach this truth. An example among many is Isaiah 10:5-7.

> Woe to the Assyrian, the rod of my anger,
> in whose hand is the club of my wrath!
> I send him against a godless nation,
> I dispatch him against a people who anger me,
> to seize loot and snatch plunder,
> and to trample them down like mud in the streets.
> But this is not what he intends,
> this is not what he has in mind;
> his purpose is to destroy,
> to put an end to many nations.

God took a violent, pagan nation bent on conquest and sent it against Israel in order to punish Israel. Thus, without prompting evil, God used an evil nation engaged in doing evil to discipline and purge his people Israel. Assyria was a rod, but the Lord was the one who used it.

A more familiar passage is Acts 3:11-26, which records Peter's second message to the people of Jerusalem. He accuses them of having disowned the Holy and Righteous One. They sent Christ to death! Peter says, however, that Christ's death was according to the Word of God, "foretold through all the prophets." Thus, their sinful act accomplished the will of God. Man's worst sin provided a righteous basis for divine forgiveness!

It would probably be wrong to infer, on the basis of activities positively identified in the Bible as divinely controlled, that *every* action of *every* man or woman contributes to the purposes of God. To take such a position ignores the parallel truth that "the whole world is under the control of the evil one."[7] Most people follow "the ways of this world and of the ruler of the kingdom of the air, the spirit who is now at work in those who are disobedient."[8] Much of human wickedness seems irredeemably destructive; in the lifetimes of its perpetrators and victims no apparent benefit results. It is a slander on the character of God to charge him with habitually achieving his purposes through the evil that men commit.

Nevertheless, God is in control. Satan is on a leash and under restraint. And he is working according to a timetable imposed upon him by God, who is Satan's Creator, Judge, and Conqueror. When Satan's time is up, his power will be broken forever. Then, when God assumes complete control, the world will see that even evil itself was *always* under divine control. Though God was not its author nor approver, he *managed* it for the ultimate good of redeemed mankind.

The Edenic Covenant Upon pain of death, God forbade Adam and Eve to eat of the tree of the knowledge of good and evil. That truth is seen in the first three chapters of Genesis, with special reference to 2:16, 17—"And the Lord God commanded the man, 'You are free to eat from any tree in the garden; but you must not eat from the tree of the knowledge of good and evil, for when you eat of it you will surely die.' "

Some theologians speak of a covenant between God and Adam. The word *covenant* is not used in the first three chapters of Genesis, nor is there any hint of an agreement between God and Adam. God did not promise Adam anything; he merely defined the conditions of existence, *and* he warned Adam that disobedience would cost him his life. As far as we can tell from Scripture, Adam did not violate a covenant when he sinned; he disobeyed a command.

But I do not strenuously object to the term *covenant* being applied here. God obviously gave Adam life, and possession of it was conditioned on obedience. God pointed to one solitary tree and told Adam not to eat from it or he would die. That was the only test of obedience; if there were others, Genesis 1—3 does not mention them; nor does any other part of Scripture. In any case, one test was sufficient.

If we accept the word *covenant* as appropriate to the terms of Adam's life in Eden, we call it the Edenic covenant. That covenant, which determined the conditions under which Adam and Eve lived, had seven elements. Adam was told, first, to be fruitful and multiply; second, to subdue the earth; third, to rule over the animal kingdom; fourth, to be a vegetarian; fifth, to cultivate the Garden; sixth to abstain from eating from the tree of the knowledge of good and evil; and finally he was warned that the penalty for disobedience would be death.[9]

But Adam disobeyed God; he violated the terms of his tenancy in the Garden. Nobody dickers with God. It is legitimate to talk about covenants; Scripture itself speaks of them. But, as used in Scripture of God's dealings with men, a covenant is a divine promise (or set of promises) that God pledges himself to keep. He gives and we get, provided we meet his terms. The terms are always the same: the obedience of faith. Accordingly, God offers salvation free of charge, and he pledges his honor to make good on the offer. No one gets salvation by earning it, but neither does anyone get salvation without taking it by faith. By believing the gospel and receiving Christ into our heart and life, we receive all that God offers.

The Tree of the Knowledge of Good and Evil Though Romans 5:12 says that "sin entered the world through one man, and death through sin," it is not certain that Adam was immortal before the Fall. According to 1 Timothy 6:16 God "alone is immortal." The presence in the Garden of the tree of life suggests that if Adam were to continue living, his life had to be renewed. After his sin, he was denied access to the tree of life.

But why did God forbid access to the tree of the knowledge of good and evil? The only satisfactory answer is that it was a symbol of all that was forbidden. Derek Kidner suggests that it "presented the alternative to discipleship: to be self-made, wresting one's knowledge, satisfactions and values from the created world in defiance of the Creator. . . . The tree plays its part in the opportunities it offers; like a door whose name announces only what lies beyond it."[10]

Were the tree of life and the tree of the knowledge of good and evil literal trees? I believe so. Kidner observes that "the fruit, not in its own right, but as appointed to a function and carrying a word from God, confronts man with God's will, particular and explicit, and gives man a decisive Yes or No to say with his whole being."[11]

That Adam and Eve said no to God is the real significance of their act. It was an act of rebellious self-will. They wanted their own way, or were tricked into thinking they wanted their own way, not God's way; and therein lies the tragedy of the Fall.

On the nature of the Fall and its effect, Alexander Whyte notes that "death here is something far deeper and more awful than the dissolution of the body. Death in the Bible sense is sinfulness; guilt and inward corruption, with all the unspeakable miseries that flow from them."[12] As Calvin said, "The miseries and evils both of body and soul, with which man is beset so long as he is on earth, are a kind of entrance into death, til death itself entirely absorbs him."[13]

Revelation 22 gives a picture of Eden restored and greatly improved. An angel showed John "the river of the water of life, as clear as crystal, flowing from the throne of God and of the Lamb down the middle of the great street of the city. On each side of the river stood the tree of life, bearing twelve crops of fruit, yielding its fruit every month. And the leaves of the tree are for the healing of the nations."[14] How tragic that Adam and Eve did not choose the tree of life rather than the tree they chose.

12

What Caused the Fall?

Some years ago, when I was teaching doctrine to African Christians, I soon discovered that most of them were more interested in the identity of our first parents than the theological implications of what our first parents did in disobeying God. In colonial times Africans chafed under the common charge that they were inferior beings. Naturally it fascinated them to learn in Scripture that all of us have a common parentage in Adam and Eve. That truth is of immense importance. Every human being who has ever lived descended from Adam and Eve.

But the significance of Adam's and Eve's disobedience of God is also of immense importance. Because they used their free wills to decide against God, they did not continue—and could not have continued—living in the innocent and sinless condition they were in when they came from the hand of God. They did not continue in the state in which they were created.

Freedom of the Human Will

Adam's and Eve's disobedience of God involved three basic things: human freedom, the sin itself, and the effect of that sin—the fall from the original pure state in which they were created. Our first parents were left to the freedom of their wills. That truth in itself is, of course, profound beyond our comprehension. Books and dissertations have been written on human freedom from both the secular and religious points of view. It is an important subject to philosophers and theologians alike. In our discussion here, however, we will look briefly at three aspects of man's free will. First, we will consider a definition of freedom; second, we will look at the distinction between freedom before the Fall and freedom after it; and, third, we will think about God's willingness to grant freedom to his creatures.

Here is how Thomas Boston defines freedom of the will: "Freedom of will is a power in the will, whereby it does, of its own accord, without force upon it, choose or refuse what is proposed to it by the understanding."[1] James Fisher defines freedom of will as a mutability, meaning the power to make choices that result in change.[2] He goes on to discuss changes that took place when Adam made the wrong choice. One of the effects of Adam's wrong choice was reduced freedom. Before the Fall, Adam had no inward urging to sin; he was truly free. After the Fall, he became less free; he was like us, having a strong tendency to do evil. For us, it is easier to yield to than resist temptation. Nearly all theologians agree that a distinction must be made between the freedom of human will before and after the Fall.

Scripture does not tell us why God bestowed upon our first parents what someone has described as the "perilous and in the event a fatal gift" of freedom. The answer may lie in man's nature as made in the image and likeness of God. James Fisher contends that God made man mutable, or changeable, because immutability, or unchangeableness of nature, is the essential property of God alone.[3] Whatever the reason, John Milton's words express the truth of man's being left with freedom of human will:

> God made thee perfect, not immutable;
> And good He made thee; but to persevere
> He left it in thy power; ordained thy will
> By nature free.[4]

The Effect of Adam's Sin

Sin is transgression of God's laws. In his great penitential Psalm, David says, "Against you, you only, have I sinned and done what is evil in your sight."[5] The act for which David repented was sinful because God had forbidden it. It was a transgression of God's law; it was a sin because it was against God's will.

The effect of Adam's sin was the Fall. The Fall is the subject of great works such as Dante's *The Divine Comedy* and Milton's *Paradise Lost*. The term stands for more than one specific sin; it stands for the entire human condition that resulted from that one sin, including human depravity and death.

Though it is not used as such in Scripture, the term *fall* is appropriate, because it echoes the language and teaching of Scripture. Satan is condemned because he does not hold to the truth.[6]

The New Testament consistently treats sin as a fall, a descent. Paul warns those who think they stand to take heed lest they fall.[7] The writer of Hebrews warns his readers not to "fall by following their [Israel's] example of disobedience."[8] Apostates are said to "fall away" from the faith.[9]

The Fall took place in Eden. But limited reenactments of the Fall—little falls spelled with a small f—occur every time a believer sins. Peter warns us against this. "Therefore, dear friends, since you already know this, be on your guard so that you may not be carried away by the error of lawless men and fall from your secure position."[10] There is nothing Satan likes better than to reenact, insofar as it is possible, the fall of our original parents. As Peter warns, we should constantly be on guard against his efforts to make us fall.

What Is Sin?

As has already been stated, sin is any transgression of or lack of conformity to God's will and law. Sin includes both omission and commission. Sins of omission are neglected duties. James tells us, "Anyone, then, who knows the good he ought to do and doesn't do it, sins."[11] Not doing something that God requires of us is sin. I find that standard very troubling, because it is so demanding. But James did not invent it; he echoed a statement of Jesus himself. Jesus accused religious leaders of neglect of important duties. They did some good things, such as tithing their possessions. But, Jesus said, "you have neglected the more important matters of the law—justice, mercy, and faithfulness. You should have practiced the latter, without neglecting the former."[12] Jesus was then speaking of sins of omission, the failure to conform to all the laws of God.

Sins of commission are the evil things we do, the transgressions we commit. In his first letter John tells us, "Everyone who sins breaks the law; in fact, sin is lawlessness."[13] In the same letter, the apostle says that "all wrongdoing is sin."[14] So we see that more than one definition is necessary. Sin is lawlessness, but not just lawlessness; it is any kind of wrongdoing. The Thirty-second Psalm uses five or six Hebrew words, all different and all required, to express the full extent of sin:

> Blessed is he
> whose transgressions are forgiven,
> whose sins are covered.

Blessed is the man whose sin the Lord does not count
against him
and in whose spirit is no deceit.
Then I acknowledged my sin to you
and did not cover up my iniquity.
I said, "I will confess my transgressions to the Lord"—
and you forgave
the guilt of my sin.[15]

Perhaps none of us in our effete times expresses himself as forcefully as the old Puritans, one of whom said:

> Shall I speak the last evil I can say of sin? It is an evil which in the nature and essence of it, virtually and eminently contains all evils of all kinds that are in the world, insomuch as in the Scriptures you shall find that all the evils of the world serve but to answer for it and to give names to it. Hence sin, it is called poison, and sinners serpents; sin is called vomit, and sinners, dogs; it is the stench of graves, and the rotten sepulchres: it is mire, sinners, sows; and sin, darkness, blindness, shame, nakedness, folly, madness, death, whatever is filthy, defective, infective, painful. . . . It is so evil that it cannot have a worse epithet given to it than itself; and therefore the apostle, when he would speak his worst of it, and wind up his expression highest, *usque ad hyperbolem,* calls it by its own name, sinful sin (Romans 7:13). It is sinning sin; you cannot call it by a worse name than its own.[16]

That is strong language, but every image in it is taken directly from the Bible.

The New Testament word for sin (Greek *hamartia*) originally meant "to miss the mark." The Greek poet Homer (ca. 900 B.C.) used the term to refer to a warrior's missing his enemy with a spear. The word was also used when a traveler missed the right road and went astray. About the time of Aristotle (ca. 350 B.C.), the term started to be used in a spiritual or moral sense.

The biblical meaning of sin is especially clear in passages such as Romans 3:23—"For all have sinned and fall short of the glory of God." We are like arrows that swerve aside, or spent arrows that fall to the ground before reaching their target. The explanation for our missing God's mark lies in man's nature as a fallen creature. The

Bible describes sinners as being "darkened in their understanding . . . because of the ignorance that is in them due to the hardening of their hearts."[17] No wonder we miss the mark!

Sin is also transgression, which is another word for disobedience. Paul says that "through the disobedience of one man the many were made sinners."[18] In the larger passage (Rom. 5:12-21) from which those words are taken, Paul uses three terms synonymously: sin, trespass, and disobedience. *Sin* is the generic term; the other words help describe its full nature. A transgression is the violation of a command. In violating a command, we disobey God who gave it. Thus, sin is disobedience. When David had Uriah killed, he not only sinned against Uriah but sinned against God, because it is God who forbids murder. David's sin ultimately was disobedience to God, as he himself later confessed.[19]

Sin is also rebellion, which is to say that it is not an isolated case of disobedience, an occasional lapse. The testimony of Scripture—which human history, both individual and collective, confirms—is that transgression of the law of God is chronic. In fact, the nature of man is such that awareness of the prohibition to sin usually inflames the desire to commit the very sin that is forbidden! That truth is the gist of Paul's comments in portions of Romans 7. He writes, "For I would not have known what it was to covet if the law had not said, 'Do not covet.' But sin, seizing the opportunity afforded by the commandment, produced in me every kind of covetous desire."[20]

Sin is failure to conform to the law of God. Sin is missing the mark. Sin is disobedience. Sin is transgression. Sin is rebellion. The more you think about it, the more frightening the subject becomes. How encouraging it is to know that the Bible deals with sin in terms of its forgiveness as well as its judgment and condemnation. Otherwise, we could only despair.

Forbidden Fruit

The specific sin whereby our first parents fell from their original sinless and innocent state was their eating the forbidden fruit. It was not a sin of omission, the failure to do something they knew they ought to do. It was a sin of commission; they did something they knew they should not have done. As we have already discussed, they ate forbidden fruit from the tree of the knowledge of good and evil.

At this point many discussions of sin become frivolous. Instead of taking the account of the first sin literally, some regard the tree and its fruit as mythical symbols. Accordingly, they suggest that the first sin was intemperance of some sort, possibly sexual. But Paul says plainly that Adam's sin was disobedience.[21] John says that sin is transgression of the law.[22] There is therefore no justification in viewing the tree and its fruit in terms of myth or symbol. It was a real tree bearing real fruit. But it stood there as a test of man's obedience. Would he accept a seemingly unnecessary restriction on his activity, thereby rendering obedience to God, or would he disobey his Creator?

The answer, of course, is history: he ate the forbidden fruit; he disobeyed God. Perhaps a better order would be: He disobeyed God; he ate the forbidden fruit. Whether he disobeyed God when he decided to take the forbidden fruit or when he actually took it is the kind of question theologians love to toss around. It is possible that the decision to disobey and the act of taking and eating were simultaneous.

But that issue is of little consequence. The important truth is that the sin was disobedience, which expressed itself in eating what God told them not to eat. Adam and Eve ate literal fruit from a literal tree, but the evil was in them, not in the tree or its fruit. They disobeyed God, and that is what made them fall from the beautiful and wonderful state in which they were created.

I am glad Christ never fell. We cannot conceive of him as capable of falling. Paul speaks of Christ as One whose life was a continuous act of obedience, culminating in the supreme act of obedience in going to the cross on behalf of fallen mankind. Consequently, says Paul, "just as through the disobedience of the one man the many were made sinners, so also through the obedience of the one man the many will be made righteous."[23] If it were not for this truth, the subject of sin would lead to despair!

Sin and Grace

The Bible says a great deal about sin, though sin is not its primary message. The world does not need a Bible to tell it that it is sinful, or to depict the varieties and shapes in which sin comes. Philosophers and novelists write eloquently about sin's many manifestations. The Bible's chief contribution in the field is threefold: it tells us how sin began in the world; it defines the nature of sin as transgression of God's laws; and it tells us that God will bring men to judgment for their sins.

Nevertheless, sin is not the Bible's main message. Its main message is redemption or salvation—God's provision for the reversal of the effects of man's sin. Yet sin clearly is a major topic in the Bible, a topic apart from which salvation, or redemption, would be meaningless. It is sin that makes salvation necessary. It is therefore against the backdrop of sin that the biblical teaching about redemption is presented. Paul tells us that "where sin increased, [God's] grace increased all the more."[24]

That brings us to the third reason for discussing sin: apart from a sense of sin which only God's Word can create, we could not appreciate the Bible's presentation of salvation. Not until we cry out, "Wretched man that I am!" do we, like the poor, lost wretch in *Pilgrim's Progress,* set out for the Heavenly City, by the way of the cross.

Adam's Fall—Our Fall

Adam was the world's first sinner, and in sinning he fell. Did his sin affect him alone, except for Eve, with whom he joined in the sin? At the time Adam and Eve were the only people on earth. But Scripture teaches that the rest of us were involved in that first sin. Paul tells us, "Therefore, just as sin entered the world through one man, and death through sin, . . . in this way death came to all men, because all sinned."[25] Paul leaves the sentence incomplete, but its meaning is plain, especially in light of statements that follow with reference to death in the world. Universal death presupposes universal sin. Even babies die, without having sinned in their brief lives. In another passage Paul tells us, "For as in Adam all die, so in Christ all will be made alive."[26]

In that one verse we have the central truths of sin and redemption. Adam's sin brought sin to all men; Christ's sacrifice offers salvation to all men. Solidarity with Adam in sin is more than compensated for by solidarity with Christ in his act of obedience. In Adam we lost everything—without personally having done anything. In Christ we gain infinitely more than we lost—again without personally having done anything. Through faith alone we are linked with Christ, so that all he is and has done is credited to our account.

The theologians who put together the Westminster Confession described Adam and Eve as "the root of all mankind," and they assert that Adam's sin "was imputed, and the same death in sin and corrupted nature conveyed to all their posterity."[27]

I like the phrase "the root of all mankind." It is well suited to expressing the truth that Adam was the moral head and representative of mankind, as well as its biological beginner. In the same chapter of 1 Corinthians quoted from above, Paul says, "So it is written: 'The first man Adam became a living being'; the last Adam, a life-giving spirit."[28]

In the context of those verses we see that Paul views Adam as the head and therefore the representative of *fallen* mankind—which includes every person. Christ is head and representative of *redeemed* mankind—which includes only those who through faith become part of his family.

It may not be easy to see how we could be implicated in Adam's sin before we were even born. Perhaps an analogy from biology will help. What I am physically—my size, color, hair texture, build, etc.—was in the loins of my forebears, as the ancient writers expressed the idea.[29] Today we would explain the phenomenon in terms of genetic codes. Either way, the truth is the same. The determination and pattern of what I am *physically* existed long before I was born. In the same way, what I am *morally and spiritually*—a fallen creature with a tendency to do evil—existed in Adam. It may be said, therefore (with a little exercise of imagination), that I was there when Adam sinned; I was "in Adam," as was all of mankind.

To some, that idea may sound silly. But Paul's reasoning about Adam and his posterity explains the basis for our hope of salvation. We were implicated in Adam's sin. And in the same way we may be implicated in Christ's great act of redemption! Adam, by his sin, ruined us. But Christ, by his righteousness, offers to save us. Hence Paul is able to say, "Just as we have borne the likeness of the earthly man, so shall we bear the likeness of the man from heaven."[30]

Christ was the one exception who did not descend from Adam by ordinary biological and spiritual descent. One of the fundamentals of the Christian faith is that Jesus was born of a virgin, and in such a way that Adam's sin was not passed on to him. As Alexander Whyte observes,

> God, in ways we cannot fathom, but at the same time in ways that show us that a singular exception was here made to the otherwise universal traduction of original sin, sent His Eternal Son in our nature, and yet did not send Him through Adam. The birth of Christ was rather a creation of a new humanity than a propagation and sanctification of the old. His flesh was

> the flesh of Adam's race, sanctified and united to the personality of the Son of God. Adam was the type of Christ, but he was not His father.[31]

Christ's generation was not ordinary; it was extraordinary. His human nature was not tainted by the sin passed on from Adam to his posterity. If we think about that aspect of Christ's virgin birth, we can see the importance of the doctrine. It is not stated incidentally in Scripture; it is required as the biblical explanation of the sinlessness of Christ. Accordingly, preachers and teachers who either minimize or deny the truth of Christ's extraordinary birth not only set aside the plain teaching of the Word of God, they also undermine the very basis of salvation—the sinless perfection of Christ which made him a worthy substitute for sinners.

You and I and every other human being who ever lived or will live descended from Adam by ordinary generation. Like him, we are sinful. Thank God for that one exception to the rest of us! Through his voluntary death, sinful people may be redeemed and fitted for heaven.

Adam's sin was imputed to all mankind before anyone else was born. Many people object to that idea. In their minds it is unjust of God to charge all mankind with Adam's guilt. But such people misunderstand the nature of guilt. As Canon T. C. Hammond comments,

> A careful distinction must be preserved between the guilt of an individual act and guilt resulting from corporate responsibility. It often happens in our ordinary life that one man becomes involved in responsibility for another's wrongdoing. No man today is condemned by God for the guilt of Adam's individual act, but if Adam is the fountainhead of the race, then it is reasonable to assume a corporate responsibility for the first act of sin. It lies in the very principle of the perpetuation of the race, that man coming into the inheritance tainted by early rebellion is himself not only involved in the guilt but adopts an attitude of revolt from the beginning of his conscious existence.[32]

Canon Hammond makes two more important points. First, "Man is not eternally condemned for sin other than his own. Actual sin and guilt are joined by God. Men themselves deliberately choose to sin. Those who have heard the Gospel message are left wholly without excuse, since they have deliberately rejected the pardon offered." Second, the imputation of original sin is met by the imputation of our Lord's obedience and righteousness, and, as discussed previously, "original guilt" is met by remission of sin by virtue of the atonement. "As from Adam men derive sin and guilt, so from Christ, the new Federal Head of the race (i.e., mankind), we derive forgiveness and righteousness."[33]

Those who have trusted in Christ as their Savior can rejoice with Peter: "He himself bore our sins in his body on the tree [i.e., the cross]."[34] Solidarity with Christ in his atoning death cancels out the effects of solidarity with Adam.

13

The Consequences of the Fall— Corruption and Depravity

In Romans 5, especially verses 10-21, we see that in Adam's sin we all lost something (original righteousness) and we all gained something—though "gained" is a poor word, since what we gained was guilt, the guilt of Adam's first sin.

Righteousness Lost

Evolutionary theory holds that man evolved and in fact is still in the process of evolving. In theory, he is evolving *upward*—getting smarter and better all the time. Man's anger and warlike tendencies are explained as vestiges of his animal past.

The Bible, on the other hand, teaches that man was created in the image of God, in knowledge, righteousness, and holiness, with dominion over the creatures. Before the Fall man was perfect. The anger and warlike tendencies, and every other ugly feature seen in human nature, are traced to Adam's sin and its immediate and pervasive consequence—the fall from the condition in which man was created.

Why was the consequence not confined to Adam and Eve alone? Because, as we have seen, they stood as representatives of as yet unborn mankind. God could have chosen to create people like angels, each a separate entity with no mutual relationship. Instead—for reasons which he alone understands—he made man in such a way that the solidarity of mankind is apparent to all. After creating Adam, God made Eve from Adam's rib, so that even Eve was linked to Adam. The rest of us proceed from that first couple; they are the human source of all that we are genetically. They are also the source of all that we are morally and spiritually—fallen, sinful people.

Guilt Gained

In Scripture, explains William Dyrness, "Guilt is the condition of liability to punishment at God's hands. This is not an automatic curselike retribution as in pagan religions, but a state of deserving God's wrath. It is an objective condition before it is a subjective awareness."[1] A guilty sinner is liable to punishment, whether he feels guilty or not.

Alexander Whyte notes that our English word *guilt* comes from a Teutonic base which meant "to pay."[2] A guilty offender had done something requiring atonement; he had committed a punishable offense. Whyte adds that the word as used in Scripture conveys the additional idea of "representation, suretyship, and solidarity." The guilt of Adam's first sin brought all of mankind's exposure to punishment on account of Adam's sin. His sin was imputed to the rest of us. The ground of that imputation is that we stood with him, so to speak, since he was our head and representative.

The idea is not as difficult as may first appear, and it is echoed in much literature. We see it clearly in John Donne's poem "For Whom the Bell Tolls." "No man is an island," he wrote. Every man is part of humanity. Hence, when the bell tolls—no matter whose body lies in a coffin at the moment—it "tolls for thee."

The truths of man's lost righteousness and his acquired guilt complement each other, and both are foundational to understanding the consequences of the Fall.

Corruption Resulted

Corruption may be defined as decay or depravity. *Depraved* in turn refers to someone in a state of serious deterioration. Thus, to say that man is corrupt in his whole nature is to say that human nature is depraved; it is in a state of deterioration.

Those are powerful words, which many people find objectionable. "We aren't that bad!" they protest. "Corrupt? Depraved?" Well, I understand the resistance. We tend to restrict usage of these terms to really bad guys. A politician who takes bribes is corrupt. A sexual pervert is depraved.

But Scripture clearly teaches that the finest person among us is by nature corrupt. That is, he is no longer pure, as was Adam at first, and he no longer possesses Adam's original righteousness. Instead, he possesses a nature that *tends* to think evil and do evil. It is true, as the Bible acknowledges, that men and women (probably everyone who has ever lived, including thoroughly wicked people) are capable of noble thoughts and deeds. But human nature has been spoiled. It is no longer perfect; it is corrupt, having been corrupted by sin.

Think about a comment on human nature found in Job. The speaker is Eliphaz.

> Can a mortal be more righteous than God?
>   Can a man be more pure than his Maker?
> If God places no trust in his servants,
>   if he charges his angels with error,
> how much more those who live in houses of clay,
>   whose foundations are in the dust,
>   who are crushed more readily than a moth![3]

Proofs of Corruption There are two proofs that mankind is corrupted. First is the testimony of the Word of God—that is, the Bible; and second is the testimony of experience. We will look at those proofs in reverse order.

For the testimony of experience all we need do is read a little history or, if history is too heavy, the daily newspaper, to see that human nature is corrupted from its original innocence. In 1883 a British commentator said,

> If a naturalist could come from Jupiter or Saturn to describe the inhabitants of this earth, he would say that man alone had instincts and tendencies which were constantly leading him to courses of action injurious to himself and to the race to which he belonged.[4]

A century has passed, and nothing has happened to alter the truth of that comment. On the contrary, much has happened to confirm it.

We do not have to think only of great social upheavals. We need only review our own lives during the past week for evidence of moral corruption. I am not implying that we are all corrupt by most human standards. Most of us maintain a basic integrity and decency by those standards. But measured against the standard of perfection, we see a different picture. Only one bad thought or only one failure to do something we know to be good proves the case. Our nature is corrupt.

A second test is this: Instead of thinking about what we did or failed to do, we can think about what we *wanted* to do, what we would like to have done but were reluctant or afraid to do. If we look within our hearts and do not see evil tendencies, the explanation is not that no evil tendencies are present, but that our concept of sin and evil is terribly deficient.

Here is where the first proof of universal corruption is important. The Word of God states the fact in various ways. It combines statements of truth with illustrations of it in the lives of men and women featured in its pages. One such statement of truth is: "For all have sinned and fall short of the glory of God."[5] Another is: "But God demonstrates his own love for us in this: While we were still sinners, Christ died for us."[6] following is a passage that combines doctrine with biography. Paul was writing to former pagans in Ephesus who had become Christians. To them he says:

> And you were dead in your trespasses and sins, in which you formerly walked according to the course of this world, according to the prince of the power of the air, of the spirit that is now working in the sons of disobedience. Among them we too all formerly lived in the lusts of our flesh, indulging the desires of the flesh and of the mind, and were by nature children of wrath, even as the rest.[7]

Even in the secular literature of the world, there is nothing that could be called great that does not testify in some way to the corruption of human nature.

That is the bad news. The good news is: "For by grace you have been saved through faith; and that not of yourselves, it is the gift of God; not as a result of works, that no one should boast. For we are his workmanship, created in Christ Jesus for good works."[8] When God saves us, he reverses the effects of corrupt human nature. He re-creates us and sets us on a new course.

Total Depravity A common, and controversial, phrase used to describe man's fallen state is total depravity. It is often objected to because of misunderstanding. If by "totally depraved" we mean that every human being is as bad as he possibly could be, then that view is erroneous and unscriptural. All of us could be worse than we are. We admit to corruption; we confess that we have an inclination to evil. We are sinful by nature. But none of us is as bad as we could be, and we often have generous, even noble, impulses.

Depravity, as it is used by theologians, does not mean that one is utterly, vilely depraved. The word primarily refers to loss of innocence, loss of the knowledge, righteousness, and holiness that came with man's original creation in the image of God. *Total* depravity means that the loss of original righteousness affects us in every part of our being—body, soul, and spirit. We are completely, though not to the *nth* degree, depraved.

Following is a quotation that helps us understand the theological use of the term *total depravity:*

> It is a term of *extensity* rather than *intensity*. It is opposed to *partial* depravity, to the idea that man is sinful in one moment and innocent or sinless in another; or sinful in some acts and pure in others. It affirms that he is all wrong, in all things, and all the time. It does not mean that man is as bad as the devil, or that every man is as bad as every other, or that any man is as bad as he may possibly be, or may become. But there is no limit to the universality or *extent* of evil in his soul. So say the Scriptures, and so says every awakened conscience.[9]

If we think about ourselves objectively—to the extent that that is possible—we will have to admit that even our finest impulses are tainted. Take love. Surely loving is man's noblest activity. Yet whose love is truly Godlike—completely pure, selfless, and eternal? Even our love for our children is, to a certain extent, self-seeking.

Are we totally depraved? Yes, we are. There is no limit to the extent of potential evil in every human soul. How glad we should be that we who have trusted Christ as Savior "are being transformed into his likeness with ever-increasing glory, which comes from the Lord, who is the Spirit."[10]

Original Sin *Original sin* is another term commonly used in relation to man's condition because of the Fall. As generally used by Christian interpreters and theologians, the term stands for one thing—hereditary sinfulness. It indicates a radical defect in human nature, which is inherited by every human being at birth. As J. P. Lilley explains,

> The doctrine concerning the state of man as fallen which prevailed in the early Latin Church was that of Augustine. He

> taught that man was created by God in His likeness, and therefore with inherent moral integrity. When he sinned, he not only lost this original righteousness, but thereby also corrupted his whole moral nature, and so became subject to physical death and all the other miseries that accompany it. The consequences that he thus brought upon himself, he, as the representative of the whole race, also entailed on his posterity. Every human being is at once born without original integrity and with a disordered moral nature. This native corruption is itself sinful; it has the nature of sin in itself, even before it be manifested in conscious voluntary sinful deeds.[11]

The two concluding sentences succinctly give the meaning of original sin.

A right and clear understanding of original sin goes a long way toward explaining the not-so-original sins that so commonly and noticeably trouble us—especially the sins we consciously commit. Only one human being—the Lord Jesus Christ—was not born in sin, and he was sinless all his life. The irony of the ages (I think it is legitimate to call it that) is that our sins were laid on him. God made him (who was neither born in sin, nor committed sin as a child or adult) to be sin for us. God treated him as if he were sin itself. Why? In order that he might be able to treat *us* as if we were *not* sinners. That is altogether amazing!

God did not create mankind sinful. Then how do we explain man's sinfulness? The Heidelberg Confession gives the answer this way: "From the fall and disobedience of our first parents, Adam and Eve, in Paradise; hence our nature is become so corrupt that we are all conceived and born in sin."[12]

Another statement of faith, the Confession of Augsburg, also gives helpful insights on the doctrine of original sin. That confession, written by Philipp Melanchthon and published in 1530, sets forth the views of Luther and his associates, as indicated in the words "They teach."

> They teach that after the fall of Adam all men, born according to nature, are born with sin, that is, without the fear of God, without confidence towards God and with concupiscence, and that this original disease or flaw is truly a sin, bringing condemnation and also eternal death to those who are not reborn.[13]

Roman Catholic teaching, as presented in the famed Council of Trent, strongly affirms the doctrine of original sin. In Session V, which convened on June 17, 1546, the Council of Trent presented the following three articles:

> 1. If anyone does not confess that the first man Adam, when he had transgressed the commandment of God in Paradise, straightway lost that holiness and righteousness in which he had been established, and through the offense of this disobedience incurred the wrath and indignation of God, and therefore incurred death, which God had before threatened to him, and, with death, captivity under the power of him who thereafter had the power of death, namely the devil, and that the whole of Adam, through the offense of that disobedience, was changed for the worse in respect of body and soul: let him be anathema.
>
> 2. If anyone asserts that the disobedience of Adam injured only himself and not his offspring . . . or that . . . only death and the pains of the body were transferred to the whole human race, and not the sin also, which is the death of the soul: let him be anathema.
>
> 3. If anyone asserts that the sin of Adam—which in origin is one and which has been transmitted to all mankind by propagation, not through imitation, and is in every man and belongs to him—can be removed either by man's natural powers or by any other remedy than the merit of the one mediator our Lord Jesus Christ . . . let him be anathema.

The doctrine of original sin is scriptural, and has been taught by the Church since the beginning. By *Church* I mean the mainstreams of historic Christian teaching. I do not mean the bizarre sects or cults, such as those spawned in the nineteenth and twentieth centuries. Those groups have nothing to say to Christians who want to know what Scripture teaches. For clear water you go to the source of the stream, not to muddied creeks miles downstream.

The doctrine of original sin is still being taught, but never was there a more critical time than now for affirming the truth that we were born in sin. Not until men and women turn from the shallow and unbiblical theories of human nature set forth by modern psychology and humanism, and grasp the painful truth that we were born in sin and are therefore in ourselves incurably sinful, will they seriously consider turning to Christ and, in turning to him, find him who is able to transform their very nature.

Opposition to the Idea of Original Sin

Throughout the history of the Church, however, there has never been a lack of teaching against the idea of original sin. First there was Pelagius, a British monk and theologian who lived between A.D. 360 and 420. Following is a brief description of his teaching about original sin.

> Pelagius completely rejects the doctrine of original sin, holding that man is inherently good and that the sin of Adam was not transmitted to posterity. That sin appears to be universal among men is due more to Adam's bad example than to the taint of original sin. The further implications are drawn that it is false that mankind suffered spiritual death through the sin of Adam and that the redemption of man is not due to the grace given by Christ but to the value of Christ's moral teachings.[14]

Pelagianism has at least two major flaws. First, it does not face up to the rather obvious fact of universal sin. With the possible exception of Pelagius himself, whom Augustine, his opponent, called "a saintly man," men and women who are more saintly than the rest of us are correspondingly more keenly aware of their inner defects of character. They are, in fact, the most intensely aware of their sinfulness. It would be nice if, as Pelagius thought, men were truly free to choose to be sinless, but the evidence of history is that no one has ever succeeded in living sinlessly.

The second, and more important, flaw in Pelagianism is that it does not square with Scripture. No doubt Pelagius thought it did; to the end, even after having been condemned for heresy, he continued to say that he was a Christian. The consensus of the Church, however, was then, and is now, that Pelgianism is a denial of the truth clearly stated in such passages as Romans 5:12—"Therefore, just as sin entered the world through one man, and death through sin, and in this way death came to all men, because all sinned . . ." Elsewhere in the same epistle Paul refers to "the law of sin and death," and "our sinful nature." The testimony of Scripture is clear that everyone is *born* sinful; we inherit a sinful nature from our parents, who inherited their sinful natures from their parents, who inherited theirs, and so on, all the way back to Adam.

We commit sins because we were born sinful. The sins we commit are committed because of the sin nature we inherited. Jesus said, "What comes out of a man is what makes him 'unclean.' For from within, out of men's hearts, come evil thoughts, sexual immorality, theft, murder, adultery, greed, malice, deceit, lewdness, envy, slander, arrogance and folly. All these evils come from inside and make a man 'unclean.' "[15]

Our Lord's analysis of human behavior echoes the prophets and is echoed by the apostles. Jeremiah said, "The heart is deceitful above all things and beyond cure. Who can understand it?"[16] The heart (that is, man's corrupt nature) is the source of his evil actions. Jesus' list of evil deeds in the above passage was not meant to be complete, but merely representative of all the sins man commits. In his letter to the church at Galatia, Paul adds to the list, and ends it with these words: "and the like," as if to suggest that he did not have enough time or space to mention every evil deed that men and women do.[17]

All the wicked, sinful things people do proceed from within. They are the natural expressions of sinful human nature. The following remark from Jonathan Edwards is archaic in language but clear in meaning.

> If we, as we come into this world, are truly sinful, he acts but a *friendly* part to us, who endeavors fully to discover to us our disease. Whereas, on the contrary, he acts an *unfriendly* part who . . . hides it from us; and so, in effect, does what in him lies to prevent our seeking a remedy for that which, if not remedied in time, must bring us finally to shame and everlasting contempt, and end in perfect and remediless destruction hereafter.[18]

14

The Consequences of the Fall—Cursed in Death

In addition to the consequences discussed in the previous chapter, several others resulted from man's fall through the disobedience of Adam and Eve.

Lost Fellowship with God

One of the most immediate and tragic consequences of the Fall was the lost fellowship of man with his Creator. In the New Testament the Greek word *koinõnia* is translated variously as "participation," "communion," "partnership," and "fellowship."[1] E. M. Blaiklock prefers "partnership," and in a comment on 1 John 1:3, where *koinõnia* is often translated "fellowship," he observes that "the word 'communion' is specialized in ecclesiastical speech. 'Fellowship' has become diluted in modern usage. 'Partnership' suggests business. But partnership is what the word means."[2]

The thought is stupendous! Were Adam and Eve partners with God? If so, they had to be able to communicate with God, for how can there be partnership, with all that entails, without communication? We know that God talked to Adam and Eve. Before the Fall, he told them to be fruitful and multiply and to rule over his creatures.[3] It is perfectly legitimate to assume that they replied. We know from Genesis 3 that after the Fall Adam and Eve answered when God called. It is therefore reasonable to conclude that before the Fall God and the couple conversed freely.

Doubtlessly they talked about their partnership. God created everything, and he assigned Adam and Eve the work of caring for it, to the extent of their human abilities. After the Fall God called them and they answered. But the relationship was now radically changed. Communication with God as they previously had experienced it was ended. Not that God no longer spoke to them or their descendants.

Even the murderous Cain heard God speaking to him, and he replied.[4] But it was mere communication, not communion. It was not communication based on the fellowship of minds. God has never stopped communicating truth to his creatures. But getting through to us whose minds are darkened is not easy, even for the Creator. Paul alludes to the difficulty in a passage describing Gentiles living in his time and, by extension, to pagans of all times, including pagans in twentieth-century America. Says the apostle:

> So I tell you this . . . that you must no longer live as the Gentiles do, in the futility of their thinking. They are darkened in their understanding and separated from the life of God because of the ignorance that is in them due to the hardening of their hearts. Having lost all sensitivity, they have given themselves over to sensuality so as to indulge in every kind of impurity, with a continual lust for more.[5]

Subjection to God's Wrath and Curse

The second additional consequence of the Fall was man's subjection to God's wrath and curse.

God's Wrath Wrath is intense anger, denoting the feelings of one provoked almost beyond measure. The Bible teaches that God is love and, accordingly, loving; but it also teaches that he is capable of great anger. How could it be otherwise? Would not a truly loving parent be angry at something or someone who menaced his beloved children? Well, God is the Father in heaven. He is angry at evil. Consider the link between God's anger and divine hatred. God loves righteousness and hates wickedness. He hates those who by their actions make themselves virtually identifiable with wickedness. Sin and sinners are sometimes indistinguishable. The wrath of God is directed toward all such. No doubt that is a shocking concept to some people, even to some Christians. Yet that is the import of passages such as Hosea 9:15.

> Because of all their wickedness in Gilgal,
> I hated them there.
> Because of their sinful deeds,
> I will drive them out of my house.
> I will no longer love them;
> all their leaders are rebellious.

In at least two of the Psalms, God is said to hate "all who do wrong" and "those who love violence."[6] In citing those passages I am aware of the risk that sensitive persons may misinterpret them. Let me reassure you. If you are troubled about your sins you need not fear God's displeasure; it is directed against callous sinners such as those who inspired Paul's comment in Romans: "Although they know God's righteous decree that those who do such things deserve death, they not only continue to do these very things but also approve of those who practice them."[7] Such persons love evil, and they love evildoers. These are not conscientious people who weep over their sins. These are people who, like Satan in Milton's poem, say, "Evil be thou my good."

The Bible says God's wrath comes upon the sons of disobedience. All of us, before conversion, were "children of wrath," that is, subject to the wrath of God. The unconverted continue to be subject to his wrath, which, Paul says, "comes on those who are disobedient."[8] In another place Paul warns us that, on account of immorality, impurity, passion, evil desire, and greed, "the wrath of God is coming."[9]

God's Curse We may have sung the hymn that includes these lines:

> Behold! a spotless victim dies,
>   My surety on the tree;
> The Lamb of God, the Sacrifice,
>   He gave Himself for me.
> Whatever curse was mine, He bore:
>   The wormwood and the gall,
> There, in that lone, mysterious hour,
>   My cup—He drained it all![10]

God's wrath is more easily explained than his cursing. God is angry at sin, and he is going to express his wrath. But what about his cursing? Did God in a fit of anger pronounce a curse against mankind? No and yes. God never does anything in a fit of anger. He has, however, pronounced curses. After the Fall he cursed the snake and he cursed the ground. He also cursed Cain for killing his brother Abel.[11] Paul tells us that "All who rely on observing the law are under a curse, for it is written: 'Cursed is everyone who does not continue to do everything written in the Book of the Law.' " The curse is the evil that God has determined will come upon lawbreakers. How glad we are that Paul goes on to say that "Christ redeemed us from the curse of the law by becoming a curse for us."[12]

Now we see what the hymn-writers meant. They were praising God for having transferred the curse (that is, death under the judgment of God) from us to Christ. It fell on him. He suffered and died. Thus he redeemed us, Paul says, "so that by faith we might receive the promise of the Spirit."[13]

Subjection to Trouble in This Life Loss of fellowship with God and subjection to his wrath and curse bring certain other consequences. The first is subjection to the difficulties and troubles of this present earthly life. These troubles affect both the soul and the body. They are internal and external. In the words of the Westminster Larger Catechism, the inward troubles are "blindness of mind, a reprobate sense, strong delusions, hardness of heart, horror of conscience, and vile affections."

A willful sinner becomes increasingly perverse and perverted. In some cases a fierce addiction to sin is sin's reward. In Romans Paul speaks of certain gross offenders whom God gave up to do what they wanted to do.[14] External sufferings are afflictions which may be either public or private. Under the first heading come such things as wars, famines, epidemics, and other calamities on a mass scale. Private miseries are sickness, accidents, poverty, and any of a thousand kinds of personal troubles people experience.

Obviously believer and unbeliever alike suffer both public and personal afflictions. In time of war, believers as well as unbelievers suffer the effects of a bombardment. Their houses are blown to pieces; their children are killed by flying shrapnel. They suffer because they are part of mankind, and all of mankind is under the wrath and curse of God.

Does that mean that God personally sends every calamity that comes our way? No, not at all! We live in a fallen world, and in a fallen world things fall apart. God cannot be accused of having driven a berserk killer mad. He cannot be accused of having told an arsonist to set fire to a house in which a family burns to death. God does not do that sort of thing, though he is able to bring good out of the evil men do in response to the inner urges of their own sin.

We cannot here attempt to explain all the misery in the world. But the following comments may be helpful. First, as John explains, "the whole world is under the control of the evil one."[15] Any explanation of misery that ignores the activity of Satan is terribly inadequate. He is directly responsible for much of the misery inflicted on mankind. It was he, not God, who killed Job's sons and daughters.[16] Second, God is able to make all things work together for the good of those who love him. An otherwise unmitigated disaster can be made to serve the purposes of God. Though not causing everything, God is in final control. It is he, not Satan, who determines the ultimate outcome of events.[17]

The basic truth is that if man had not sinned, there would be no misery or suffering at all in the world. Because Adam sinned, and we sin in Adam, we are subject to the sufferings and hardships of this life.

Subjection to Death The Bible makes it clear that there is a direct link between sin and death. All mankind, by their fall, were made subject to death. "Sin entered the world through one man, and death through sin, and in this way death came to all men, because all sinned."[18] In another place we are told that "the wages of sin is death."[19] Sin is clearly the cause of death, and, as Paul says, it is also death's "sting."[20] Death is doubly dreadful because of its link with sin.

It should be obvious that the death described in the passages just quoted is physical death. Our bodies die. Man "is destined to die once, and after that to face judgment."[21] The only exceptions of which we are told were Enoch and Elijah, who experienced the equivalent of the sudden transformation believers living at the end-time will undergo when Christ returns for his Church.[22]

Is physical death the same for believer and unbeliever alike? Superficially, yes. The immaterial soul leaves the material body, and death ensues. The experience may be easy or painful. But for believers and unbelievers, the immediate effect of death is vastly different. Death comes to believers in the hands of Christ, who says to us, in effect, "Death is yours. Come and share your Master's happiness."

To unbelievers, death comes from Satan who, as God's executioner, has the power of death. Says James Fisher, "To the one (that is, to unbelievers) death comes as an everlasting and irreparable loss; to the other as eternal and unspeakable gain; to the one as a conqueror, dragging the prisoner to the prison of hell; to the other as a vanquished enemy, paving the way to heaven and glory."[23]

Believers may die in agony or in a coma. The dying person often does not seem to know what is happening. But when death has done its work, when the believer has passed through its gates, he shouts in triumph with Paul, "Where, O death, is your victory? Where, O death, is your sting?"[24]

Unbelievers may also die in agony or have an easy death, slipping away as if sleeping. Yet, for them death's arrival is as the king of terrors.

The prospect of death should make every person, believer and unbeliever, think about the shortness of life. For the unbeliever it should also raise the question, What then?

Subjection to Hell Forever We do not know much about hell, because the Bible does not describe it in great detail. And if it were not such an extremely important subject, most of us would not care to know much about it. But hell is an immensely important and serious subject, the most serious subject in all the world.

What is hell? We could launch into a treatment of the words used for it in the Bible—*sheol, hades, Gehenna,* and *Tartarus.* All of them are sometimes translated "hell." Or we could give a treatise on conditional immortality, or philosophize about the morality of eternal punishment. Instead, we will stick to a few passages of Scripture, the meanings of which seem painfully clear and difficult to evade.

The first is in the Gospel of Matthew. Our Lord is speaking, and he predicts an event in the future when he himself will say to some of the people before him, "Depart from me, you who are cursed, into the eternal fire prepared for the devil and his angels." When the judgment is over, he continues to explain, "they will go away to eternal punishment, but the righteous to eternal life."[25]

Who will go to hell, and how long will they stay there? The answer to those questions may be found in careful study of the passage just cited, as well as from numerous others. John the Baptist said, "Whoever believes in the Son has eternal life, but whoever rejects the Son will not see life, for God's wrath remains on him."[26] Paul tells us:

> This will happen when the Lord Jesus is revealed from heaven in blazing fire with His powerful angels. He will punish those who do not know God and do not obey the gospel of our Lord Jesus. They will be punished with everlasting destruction and shut out from the presence of the Lord and from the majesty of his power on the day he comes to be glorified in his holy people and to be marveled at among all those who have believed.[27]

The last three chapters of the Book of Revelation confirm what we have seen already—that unbelievers, by virtue of their unbelief, are regarded as disobedient and wicked, and are sent to hell. For how long? Forever. "Those who do not know God and do not obey the gospel of our Lord Jesus . . . will be punished with everlasting destruction and shut out from the presence of the Lord."[28] The fate of the lost is to "suffer the punishment of eternal fire."[29] Unbelievers will suffer banishment forever and ever.

We are inclined to wish it were not so. It would be infinitely less tragic if the lost were only annihilated. But Scripture gives that notion no support. In the Fall, mankind became subject not only to death, but to eternal death, to the pains of hell forever.

But those who are subject to the pains of hell do not have to go there. "Come to Me," Jesus says.

> For God so loved the world that he gave his one and only Son, that whoever believes in him shall not perish but have eternal life. For God did not send his Son into the world to condemn the world, but to save the world through him. Whoever believes in him is not condemned.[30]

15

God's Gracious Provision

God did not leave mankind to its doom when sin entered the world. The loving and gracious Heavenly Father provided a way of escape from the terrible consequences of the Fall. "This is love," the Apostle John tells us, "not that we loved God, but that he loved us and sent His Son as an atoning sacrifice for our sins. . . . And we have seen and testify that the Father has sent his Son to be the Savior of the world."[1]

God does not offer salvation reluctantly, but cheerfully. Jesus tells us that it was the Father's "good pleasure" to reveal the way of salvation to those who simply and humbly trust in him.[2] In Paul's Epistle to the Ephesians he assures us that "He [that is, God] predestined us to be adopted as his sons through Jesus Christ, in accordance with his pleasure and will."[3] That verse, and several others in the same paragraph, makes two points about God's provision of salvation. The first is that God wills to save us; salvation is his will for lost mankind. The second point is that God takes joy in what he is doing; he does not save us grudgingly, as if it were his duty. The thought of redeeming mankind makes God divinely happy.

Another truth is evident in these and other Bible passages dealing with God's plan of salvation. It was entirely his idea, not man's. God did not offer a way of salvation because mankind was seeking one from him. Left to ourselves, we would never have thought about salvation. Salvation is solely the plan and work of the God and Father of our Lord Jesus Christ.

From All Eternity

In Ephesians 1:4 we read that God "chose us in him [that is, Christ] before the creation of the world." Says Dr. James S. Candlish in a comment on this verse:

> God's act in blessing us is performed in accordance with a choice that preceded our existence and that of the whole world. The idea is in harmony with the whole strain of Bible teaching, which represents God as knowing the end from the beginning, and having a purpose which He carries out by means of all things that take place.[4]

Salvation was not an afterthought, as if God was surprised by the Fall, then, after turning it over in his mind, decided to save rather than to destroy mankind. God chose us in Christ before the creation of the world, prior to the existence of any human being. Why did he make us, knowing we would sin? That is another question, which we will skip for two reasons. First, it is not germane to our subject. Second, and more significantly, there is no biblical answer, and therefore no reliable answer.

Before we think about the beautiful truth of election, a word of caution seems in order. We are not going to attempt to settle ancient and modern disputes about the doctrine. We will try to state the truth as clearly as possible and leave it at that.

Dr. Candlish gives further help.

> This choice (that is, the "choice" set forth in Ephesians 1:4ff.) is said to be 'in Christ,' and these words refer, as in verse 3, not to God, but to us. Not, God in Christ chose us; but, God chose us in Christ. As the actual blessings are bestowed on us in Christ, i.e. on Christ first and on us as united to Christ; so the choice, before the world was, is of Christ as the head, and of us as members of His body. Christ the God-man is primarily God's elect or chosen One (Isaiah 42:1-7; Matthew 12:18-21); but as the Servant of the Lord in the prophecy is sometimes the people, and sometimes He who is 'the covenant of the people,' so the election of Christ involves that of those who are to be holy and believing in Him.[5]

If we have believed the gospel, we are part of God's elect. As Paul says in the same passage quoted above, "You also were included in Christ when you heard the word of truth, the gospel of your salvation. Having believed, you were marked in him with a seal, the promised Holy Spirit."[6] The order is listening, believing, and being sealed in Christ with the Holy Spirit. That is how anyone can become one of God's elect.

Some of the questions about election that trouble people are not legitimate and come from unwarranted assumptions or conclusions. Questions about the conflict between the sovereignty of God and man's free will are among those illegitimate questions, because the conflict is contrived. It stems from presumed contradictions and inconsistencies in Scripture. I say "presumed" because real contradictions and inconsistencies do not exist. We think we perceive them because our understanding of God's exercise of his sovereignty and of man's responses is defective. Paul, as other writers of Scripture, teaches both God's eternal purpose and his election before the creation of the world, *and* man's obligation to respond. Francis Foulkes makes this point in a note on Ephesians 1:4.

> Paul emphasizes both the sovereign purpose of God and man's free will. He took the gospel of grace and offered it to all. Then to those who had accepted the gospel he set forward the doctrine of election for two reasons, both of which we find linked similarly together in John 15:16, Romans 8:29, 2 Thessalonians 2:13, 2 Timothy 1:9 and 1 Peter 1:2. First, the Christian needs to realize that his faith rests completely on the work of God and not on the unsteady foundation of anything in himself. It is all the Lord's work, and in accordance with His plan, a plan that reaches back *before the foundation of the world.* Second, God has chosen us that we should be *holy and without blame before him* (cf. v. 27 and Col. 1:22). Election is not simply to salvation, but to holiness of life. . . . We were "foreordained to be conformed to the image of his Son" (Romans 8:29 RSV).[7]

That is the thrust of the doctrine of election. Election and assurance of salvation are inseparably linked. It probably did not occur to Paul that theologians in later times would work his statements into rigid systems that raise questions about inconsistencies and paradoxes, or attempt to deny the possibility of salvation to hordes of allegedly nonelect people. In Paul's teaching, assurance of salvation rests on God's eternal purpose of love to choose a people out of this world for everlasting life. If we are among God's elect we are *eternally* saved. And if we are among God's elect, he chose us in order that we should be holy and blameless before him.

How can we know if we are among God's elect? If we have believed the gospel, we are included in God's elect. Because they responded to his preaching, Paul assured his friends in Thessalonica that they were chosen. They had turned from idols to serve the living and true God, and were waiting for his Son from heaven. Seeing the changes in their lives, the apostle was certain that God had chosen them.[8] We may test our own election by the same criteria.

In my judgment there would be far fewer problems troubling people if, in the past, theologians had simply let Scripture speak for itself. Instead, some of them developed rigid systems based on positions Scripture does not state, but which they (the theologians) thought were required for logical consistency. For example, some have held that the concept of the election of some to everlasting life also demands the opposite—the election of others to everlasting condemnation. It postulates the utter hopelessness of the nonelect. Because they were not chosen, they cannot be saved. But Scripture does not teach that. The Bible teaches that *anyone* who sincerely seeks the Lord will find him. Says Paul,

> The God who made the world and everything in it is the Lord of heaven and earth and does not live in temples built by hands. . . . From one man he made every nation of men, that they should inhabit the whole earth; and he determined the times set for them and the exact places where they should live. God did this so that men would seek him and perhaps reach out for him and find him, though he is not far from each one of us.[9]

At the first church council, held in Jerusalem about A.D. 48 or 49, James quoted the prophet Amos in support of Paul's and Barnabas's contention that God was saving Gentiles. Here is what the prophet said, as quoted in Acts:

> "After this I will return
>   and rebuild David's fallen tent.
> Its ruins I will rebuild,
>   and I will restore it,
> that the remnant of men may seek the Lord,
>   and all the Gentiles who bear my name,"
> says the Lord, who does these things
>   that have been known for ages.[10]

No one who believes in the authority and trustworthiness of Scripture seriously denies the import of those verses. Some interpreters, however, believe that man's fallen nature is such that he cannot seek God unless God himself helps him. The argument has merit. Fallen man's will is not truly free. His perception of issues, and therefore his understanding of those issues, is determined to a certain extent by factors over which he has no control—as many psychologists recognize.

But two other considerations have bearing on the subject. First, if God commands all men everywhere to repent, it may be assumed that men *can* repent. Otherwise, his command would be a mockery and could not be taken seriously. Furthermore, God is active in the world, leading men to repentance. He gives the necessary help, or at least offers it. Who is to say that God restricts his persuading to those who eventually turn to him? Who is to say, based on Scripture, that the unbelieving remain unbelievers because God ignores them or trifles with them? As Paul plainly tells us, the gospel "is the power of God for the salvation of everyone who believes."[11] In another letter he says, "God was pleased through the foolishness of what was preached to save those who believe."[12] The only ground for exclusion is unbelief. It does not make sense to say that God saves as many as believe, but that only his elect can believe. The truth is that those who believe are his elect. If a person listens to the gospel and believes it, he will become one of God's elect. As such, his eternal salvation is guaranteed.

Election and Predestination

We have used the terms *election* and *predestination.* Is there any difference or distinction between them? As theologian E. A. Litton explains,

> The terms 'predestination,' 'saints,' 'effectual calling,' represent the same fact under different aspects. Predestination signifies the general intention of God to provide a plan of salvation, and has no direct reference to the individuals comprised in the plan. . . . Election is predestination carried into effect in time, and . . . presupposes individuals as in existence.[13]

J. Edgar Beet makes the difference even plainer. He says, "Election determines the objects of salvation; predestination the goal to which God will lead them. Each is a divine purpose."[14]

What is that goal? Listen to Paul: "For those God foreknew he also predestined to be conformed to the likeness of his Son, that he might be the firstborn among many brothers. And those he predestined, he also called; those he called, he also justified; those he justified, he also glorified." The full passage, too long to quote entirely, ends with a powerful affirmation: "For I am convinced that . . . [nothing] will be able to separate us from the love of God that is in Christ Jesus our Lord."[15]

The New Covenant and God's Work of Grace

Some theologians speak of God's provision to save mankind through the sacrifice of his Son as a covenant of grace. A covenant is an agreement between two parties, though biblical covenants are essentially one-sided, since it is always God who initiates and determines the provisions of the covenants.

The covenant with Adam, if indeed it was a covenant, is often referred to as the covenant of works. If Adam had behaved himself, he would have been rewarded with life. Life is also the reward offered in the covenant of grace, but there is a great difference. As one theologian expresses it, "The Holy Ghost calls that blessedness of the old covenant of works *life,* but never *salvation,* for you are saved by grace."[16]

Before proceeding further, we should define grace. I am going to let Alexander Whyte do it. Here is what he says:

> Grace means favour, mercy, pardon. Grace and love are essentially the same, only grace is love manifesting itself and operating under certain conditions, and adapting itself to certain circumstances. As, for instance, love has no limit or law such as grace has. Love may exist between equals, or it may rise to those above us, or flow down to those in any way beneath us. But grace, from its nature, has only one direction it can take. *Grace always flows down.* Grace is love indeed, but it is love humbling itself. A king's love to his equals, or to his own royal house, is love; but his love to his subjects is called grace. And thus it is that God's love to sinners is always called grace in the Scriptures. It is love indeed, but it is love to creatures, and to creatures who do not deserve His love. And therefore all He does for us in Christ, and all that is disclosed to us of His goodwill in the gospel, is called *grace.*[17]

Let me emphasize the truth that grace is love or favor extended to *the undeserving*—like you and me. Let me also quote one of the

Bible's loveliest statements, taken from Paul's Epistle to the Ephesians: "For it is by grace you have been saved, through faith—and this not from yourselves, it is the gift of God—not by works, so that no one can boast."[18] That is the meaning of grace—undeserved salvation!

If God's grace is undeserved salvation, then a covenant of grace is a pledge of favor toward mankind which, apart from this act of God's love, would be forever unattainable by mankind. At least two questions remain unanswered. First, with whom did God make the covenant of grace, and second, where is it specifically taught in Scripture? Says Thomas Boston, "The covenant of grace was made with Jesus Christ, as the Second Adam, party-contractor. And Christ, in this covenant, represented all the elect, as the spiritual race, the parties contracted for."[19]

In a volume titled *The Doctrine of the Atonement as Taught by Christ Himself*, George Smeaton sets forth the same view. He presents a section headed "Sayings of Christ Which Assume That He is the Second Adam, and Acting According to a Covenant with the Father in This Atoning Work."[20] The author quotes mainly from John's Gospel to make his case. He uses such passages as John 6:39—"And this is the will of him who sent me, that I shall lose none of all that he has given me, but raise them up at the last day"; John 7:16—"My teaching is not my own. It comes from him who sent me"; and John 10:17—"The reason my Father loves me is that I lay down my life—only to take it up again."

It is debatable, however, whether there was a covenant among the Persons of the Trinity. As Lewis Sperry Chafer points out, the notion assumes "that separate Persons of the Godhead sustained individual interests."[21] That is not to say that all the concepts set forth in what are called the covenant of works and the covenant of grace are unscriptural. Many of the ideas are there, but as Charles Ryrie points out, the ideas are not "systematized and formalized by Scripture into covenants."[22]

But there is no debate among theologians about divine intention. As John says, "God so loved the world, that he gave his one and only Son, that whoever believes in him shall not perish but have eternal life."[23] Or, as the same apostle also says, "The Father has sent his Son to be the Savior of the world."[24] That, of course, is only part of the story, but it makes the point that, whether or not a special covenant of grace existed, God planned our salvation in grace. He was not willing that any should perish, but that all should come to repentance, and in coming be saved.[25] As Paul reminds us in his letter to Titus, "The grace of God that brings salvation has appeared to all men. It teaches us to say 'No' to ungodliness and worldly passions, and to live self-controlled, upright and godly lives in this present age, while we look for the blessed hope—the glorious appearing of our great God and Savior, Jesus Christ."[26]

16

The Person of Jesus Christ

Christology is the theological interpretation of the person and work of Jesus Christ. In this chapter we will be looking primarily at the person of Christ. We will look at his name, Jesus, and at his being Lord, Messiah (Christ), and God's eternal and only true Son.

Jesus

Jesus is not basically a title but a name. It is the Greek form of the Hebrew Joshua, which in turn is an abbreviated form of Jehoshua. In the King James Version of the New Testament, "Jesus" appears several times where "Joshua" ordinarily would have been used—and *is* used in most modern versions.[1] The name may have been more common in New Testament times than is generally thought. The Old Testament lists four different Joshuas, and in the New Testament there is reference to a friend of Paul's called Jesus.[2] The name was not restricted to Jesus of Nazareth, whom we know as our Lord Jesus Christ.

Joshua, or Jehoshua, is a compound word meaning "Jehovah [or Yahweh] saves." It suited the Old Testament Joshua, because he was an instrument in God's hands for the conquest of Canaan. In some respects he was a type of our Lord. But neither he (Joshua) or the "Jesus, who is called Justus" whom Paul mentions in Colossians really merited the name.

When Joseph discovered that his fianceé Mary was pregnant, he was upset. Before he could do anything, an angel of the Lord appeared to him in a dream and told him that she had conceived miraculously by the Holy Spirit. He told Joseph that Mary would bear a Son and that Joseph, as the legal human father, was to name him Jesus. Why Jesus? Because, the angel explained, "he will save his people from their sins."[3] Jesus, *our* Jesus, the Lord Jesus Christ, truly deserved the name!

As the angel announced to Joseph, the Jesus born to Mary became the Savior; he redeems his people out of all their bondage to sin. As used by him, Jesus is more than a name; it is also a title. Jesus is the Savior. Whether title or name, to believers it is lovely.

How sweet the name of Jesus sounds
In a believer's ear!
It soothes his sorrows, heals his wounds,
And drives away his fear.

It makes the wounded spirit whole,
And calms the troubled breast;
'Tis manna to the hungry soul,
And to the weary rest.

Dear name! the Rock on which we build;
Our shield and hiding place;
Our never-failing treasury, filled
With boundless stores of grace.

There are three more stanzas. The last is particularly beautiful. Building on the preceding stanza which refers to Christ's return, it says:

Till then we would Thy love proclaim
With every fleeting breath;
And triumph in that blessed name
Which quells the power of death.[4]

The Christ

Christ is the Greek form of the Hebrew *Messiah* and is primarily a title meaning, "the Anointed One." But as applied to Jesus it soon came to be used also as a name, as seen in our speaking about Christ without the definite article "the." Yet strictly speaking, Christ is a title. This is quite clear in Peter's great confession: "You are the Christ,"[5] by which he meant the Messiah, whom Jews had long expected. He is not simply Christ, but *the* Christ. When the Jewish high priest put Jesus on oath, he said, "I charge you under oath by the living God: Tell us if you are the Christ, the Son of God."[6] What did the high priest want to know? First, we have to remember that he was not speaking Greek but Aramaic. He did not say the Greek *Christos,* from which we get the English word *Christ,* but the Aramaic equivalent of Messiah.

The word *Messiah* is not found often in most English Bibles, because the Hebrew term is usually translated "anointed." For example, in Psalm 2 we read, "The kings of the earth take their stand, and the rulers gather together against the Lord and against his Anointed One."[7] On "Anointed One" some Bible editions have a marginal note explaining, "Or, Messiah." The Messiah is God's Anointed One. Instead of being translated, the Hebrew word could have been transliterated—that is, rendered "Messiah," which sounds close to the Hebrew original.

The King James translators did that in two verses in the Old Testament (Dan. 9:25, 26), in which the prophet predicts the death of the Messiah. The word could have been translated "the Anointed One," but "Messiah the Prince" seems to convey the sense better than, "the Anointed One, the Prince" or "the Anointed Prince." And by Daniel's time the hope of the coming of a powerful deliverer of the royal line of David was so strong that the term which had long been merely descriptive had become a title. The hope eventually became so strong, in fact, that even a Samaritan woman could say to Jesus, "I know that Messiah is coming." We can imagine her astonishment when he replied, "I who speak to you am he."[8] She then did what Andrew had done earlier. He went looking for his brother Peter, and when he found him he said, "We have found the Messiah."[9] The woman ran to town and said to the men whom she found there, "Come, see a man who told me everything I ever did. Could this be the Christ?" What she meant was, "This man *is* the Messiah, the Christ, isn't he?" He was indeed the Christ and, as the men later acknowledged themselves, he was "the Savior of the world."[10] That is who Jesus Christ is—God's Anointed Savior.

The Lord Jesus Christ

Nearly everyone knows who Jesus was, although from time to time we read about surveys that reveal abysmal religious ignorance. Many people, including educated people, have no idea who Jesus was (much less, who he *is*), though they may have heard the name all their lives. But no one could understand who he was by that name alone. He is not just Jesus; he is the Lord Jesus Christ. As used by believers, His name Jesus is most often preceded or followed by titles.

Among other things, Jesus is the Lord and he is the Christ. The biblical basis for those statements is clear. Several familiar texts are the following ones: "If you confess with your mouth, 'Jesus is Lord,' and believe in your heart that God raised him from the dead, you will be saved."[11] Peter, in his famous confession of faith, declared, "You are the Christ, the Son of the living God."[12] James, our Lord's half-brother, who might have been expected simply to use the familiar name Jesus, called him "our glorious Lord Jesus Christ."[13] James, with the others, was obviously reluctant to use the name without a title. What that says to us should be clear: when speaking to unbelievers about Christ, it may be permissible to identify him as Jesus. Among ourselves, however, he is the Lord and the Christ. He is our Lord Jesus Christ.

Webster's defines *lord* this way: "One who has power and authority, as from headship or leadership; a master; ruler."[14] Bible students may consult a dictionary, but for a truly authoritatve definition they look to the Bible. In this case, the biblical use of "lord" means exactly what the dictionary says—"One who has power and authority . . . a master; ruler." Therefore, when we say "Jesus is Lord," we mean that he has power and authority over us; he is our Master, our Ruler.

Why does Jesus deserve the title Lord? He does for two reasons. First, he is divine by nature; as such, he has authority over us. Second, he earned lordship by what he did as man. As Alexander Whyte says, "He holds a lordship over us as the recompense and result of all He did and does for us as our Redeemer."[15] Following is a translation of Philippians 2:6-11, in which both those grounds of lordship are set forth.

> His state was divine, yet he did not cling to his equality with God but emptied himself to assume the condition of a slave, and became as men are; and being as all men are, he was humbler yet, even to accepting death, death on a cross. But God raised him high and gave him the name which is above all other names so that all beings in the heavens, on earth and in the underworld, should bend the knee at the name of Jesus and that every tongue should acclaim Jesus Christ as Lord, to the glory of God the Father.[16]

The Eternal Son

Failure to recognize that Jesus Christ is not only God's Son, but his eternal Son, undermines the biblical teaching about his very nature. In the past heretics have misused biblical statements such as "You are my son; today I have become your Father" to assert that Jesus was not the Son of God until after he was born in Bethlehem. According to such teachers, who have their modern counterparts, God conferred deity on the man Jesus. That teaching is heretical because it is unscriptural. Among other things, it ignores Paul's use of the above quotation from Acts as an anticipation of the resurrection, not the Incarnation. Paul's full statement was, "What God promised our fathers he has fulfilled for us, their children, by raising up Jesus. As it is written in the second Psalm: 'You are my Son; today I have become your Father.' "[17]

To apply that verse to the birth at Bethlehem also ignores many other passages that either imply or assert the eternal sonship of Christ. Paul told the Galatians, "When the time had fully come, God sent his Son, born of a woman, born under law, to redeem those under law, that we might receive the full rights of sons."[18] That passage makes clear that the One whom God sent was the Son. He did not become the Son at birth; he was eternally the Son—otherwise he could not have been "sent." That this is what is intended is made clear from the sixth verse in the same chapter: "God sent the Spirit of his Son into our hearts, the Spirit who calls out, 'Abba, Father.' " The Holy Spirit did not become the Spirit when God sent him into the world; he was always the Spirit. In the same way, the Son did not become the Son when Jesus was born. He was always the Son—God the Son, eternally one with the Father.

The man known in his life on earth as Jesus of Nazareth was the eternal Son of God. He was always divine; he did not become divine at birth. As he himself said, "I came from the Father and entered the world; now I am leaving the world and going back to the Father."[19] Unlike you and me, who began to exist in our mother's womb, he existed eternally; and when he was born, he came on a mission from the Father.

The Apostle John was present when Jesus said the words just quoted. Years later, after a lifetime of reflection, John wrote about that extraordinary life. It was manifested, John said, and, therefore, we (the apostles who knew him) "proclaim to you the eternal life, which was with the Father and has appeared to us."[20] John did not say that the life before Jesus' birth was with *God;* he said the life was with *the Father.* W. E. Vine explains the significance of John's choice of words.

> The term "Father" implies the existence of a son. The terms "father" and "son" are correlative. . . . There is no hint in the Scriptures of any time at which God began to be a Father; yet the above Scriptures make clear that His Fatherhood in relation to Christ was pre-existent to the Incarnation. The Fatherhood of the One being eternal, the Sonship of the Other must likewise have been eternal. In the light of this introductory statement in the Epistle, we are to understand the subsequent statement in chapter 4:14: "The Father hath sent the Son to be the Savior of the world." It was a Father who sent and a Son who came.[21]

That is not dry theology. The very nature of the One we call Lord is the issue. Is he the eternal Son or merely an exalted creature, as ancient heretics alleged and modern heretics agree? The answer, as given in the Bible, is that he was the eternal Son. He was always one with the Father. It is immeasurably important that Jesus be eternally divine, that in him is all the fullness of deity.[22]

Does it really matter? Of course it matters! Why? Because the value of Jesus' death is determined by his nature. No mere mortal, no matter how highly exalted, could atone for the sins of mankind. For that, a better sacrifice was required—the sacrifice offered by the eternal Son, who, the Bible says, through the eternal Spirit offered himself without blemish to God.[23] We can have confidence in such a sacrifice. We can believe that with such a sacrifice the Father was pleased.

Consider this statement by a twentieth-century theologian:

> If Christ be a creature, however great, there is no redemption, because there is no real point of contact between the sinner and the Holy God . . . salvation is only possible by Divine grace, and grace can only come through a Divinely human Savior. It will be seen from this that the very nature of Christianity is at stake, and all that Christianity means in regard to salvation from sin.[24]

Before the Incarnation, Jesus Christ was the eternal Son of God. On that truth rests the entire value for us of his life and his death.

17

The Incarnation—God and Man

At the Incarnation the eternal Son of God became man. After identifying the Word as God, John says: "the Word became flesh, and lived for a while among us. We have seen his glory, the glory of the one and only Son, who came from the Father, full of grace and truth."[1]

Here is how Paul records the same truth:

> Beyond all question, the mystery of godliness is great:
>
> He appeared in a body,
>   was vindicated by the Spirit,
> was seen by angels,
>   was preached among the nations,
> was believed on in the world,
>   was taken up in glory.[2]

God Became Man

The incarnation, as an ordinary dictionary says, is "the union of divinity with humanity in Christ."[3] The word is used to indicate the birth of Christ in a manger. But instead of saying "birth," we often say "Incarnation," because Incarnation means more than the birth of a baby. It means what the dictionary says it means, "the union of divinity with humanity in Christ."

Of the birth of Jesus Christ, Paul tells us, "But when the time had fully come, God sent his Son, born of a woman, born under law."[4]

The eternal Son of God became like us. He became man; not "a man," but "man." As one theologian has put it,

> We must ever remember, that though He was in nature perfect man, He was not man in exactly the same sense in which any

> one of us is a man. Though man, He was not, strictly speaking, in the English sense of the word, *a* man; He was not such as one of us, and one out of a number. His person was not human like ours, but divine. He who was from eternity, continued one and the same, but with an addition. His Incarnation was a 'taking of the manhood into God' . . . He was not a man made God, but God made man.[5]

Two Natures in One Person

When the eternal Son became man, he was not a mere man. He was a perfect man, but he was also, as we have already discussed, something else—the eternal Son of God. Any view of Christ's nature which ignores or denies his deity is heresy and is to be rejected.

The Incarnation as set forth in Scripture is not like approximations of it which are proclaimed in some oriental religions. In those, human beings may be elevated to deity; at the Incarnation of the eternal Son, deity became man.

When God became man, he received a genuinely human body and a genuinely human soul. Physically and "soulishly" he was like Adam had been in his unfallen state. He was *not* like you and me with respect to sin; we are truly human, but imperfectly so in virtue of inherited sin. Jesus not only was *truly* human but *perfectly* human.

Jesus was also not like you and me with respect to earthly parentage. He was born of a virgin. Mary had never known a man intimately. She conceived miraculously, and the agent of the conception was the Holy Spirit of God. That is very important; it is required as an explanation of Jesus' sinlessness. As explained previously, Jesus was immaculately conceived; a sinful nature was not passed on to him, as would have been the case had he been the product of normal human conception.

Such a conception was also required in order that Jesus be one person rather than two. If he had "come upon" an existing human being, taking possession of that person, there would have been two persons—one divine and one human. The testimony of Scripture, however, is that he was one person, or personality, with two natures—divine and human.

The Incarnation was done with a view to our redemption. Unlike the gods of the Greeks, who left Mount Olympus to make mischief or play around, the eternal Son of God became man in order to be in a position to save lost mankind. Had he not become man, with a truly human body, he could not have represented us in death.

As man, he was qualified by experience to be our High Priest. As God, he was qualified to become the propitiation for our sins, and to be a merciful and faithful High Priest.[6] As our great High Priest he gives us mercy and help when we need it, with the heart of a fellow-sufferer.

The concept of Jesus' being both human and divine is theological, not psychological. We are not talking about a split personality. He was one Person, not two. The subject is difficult, and because our minds are limited, we cannot expect to understand it thoroughly. Yet we can try. A statement in the Westminster Confession of Faith, though somewhat archaic in language, is helpful.

> The Son of God, the second person of the Trinity, being very and eternal God, of one substance, and equal with the Father, did, when the fulness of time was come, take upon him man's nature, with all the essential properties and common infirmities thereof, yet without sin; being conceived by the power of the Holy Ghost, in the womb of the Virgin Mary, of her substance. So that two whole, perfect, and distinct natures, the Godhead and the manhood, were inseparably joined together in one person, without conversion, composition, or confusion, which person is very God and very man, yet one Christ, the only Mediator between God and man.[7]

That is a clear statement of the biblical doctrine of the distinctness of two natures and the unity of the person of our Lord Jesus Christ. Not every believer agrees with that confession's Calvinistic views. But in regard to questions about the Person of Christ, it sets forth clear scriptural truths that have been held by the Church from the very beginning.

The Thirty-nine Articles of the Church of England, drawn up in 1563, express the same truths in this way:

> The Son, which is the Word of the Father, begotten from everlasting of the Father, the very and eternal God, and of one substance with the Father, took man's nature in the womb of the Blessed Virgin, of her substance; so that two whole and perfect natures, that is to say, the Godhead and Manhood, were joined together in one Person, never to be divided.

A document much older than any denominational confession is a statement from the Council of Chalcedon (A.D. 451), which sets forth the belief of the ancient church about the nature of Christ. It reads in part:

> We acknowledge one and the same Christ to be perfect God and perfect man; of the same substance with the Father as regards His Godhead, and of the same substance with us as regards His manhood—in all things like unto us, sin only excepted; begotten of the Father from everlasting, but in the last days born of the Virgin; subsisting in two natures, without confusion, conversion, division, or separation; the distinction between the natures not being destroyed by the union, but each preserving its own properties and both culminating in one Person and Hypostasis: one and the same Christ, not divided into two Persons.[8]

From the earliest times the Church has had to contend for the faith delivered to it by the apostles. Paul warned that from within would arise false teachers, who would "distort the truth in order to draw away disciples after them."[9] Peter echoed Paul's warning: "There will be false teachers among you. They will secretly introduce destructive heresies, even denying the sovereign Lord who bought them."[10]

Sure enough, such false teachers appeared in the churches, teaching heretical views about various things, including the person of Christ. Historians draw attention to several especially influential errors. Two widespread errors in the early church were Arianism, which denied the deity of Christ, and Apollinarianism, which denied the perfect manhood of Christ. The scriptural truths those heresies deny have been discussed in previous chapters. Two other heresies were Nestorianism and Eutychianism. Those cumbersome terms are derived from the names of the two men, Nestorius and Eutyches, who propagated views which denied, respectively, the unity of the person of Christ and the distinction of the natures of Christ.

How could one person have two distinct natures? It is not an easy question. In an attempt to shed some light on it, let me quote at length from W. H. Griffith Thomas:

> The union of the two natures in one Person is sometimes called the Hypostatic Union; that is, two natures in one. . . . In the

> New Testament there is a clear unity of consciousness throughout, and it is often quite impossible to distinguish between the human and Divine elements. It is, of course, a great mystery how two natures can be joined together in one Person, never to be divided, and the distinction between nature and Person must not be unduly pressed. Our knowledge of personality, as of psychology in general, is only small, and it is impossible to fathom the mystery of the union of two natures in one personality. We must emphasize the Divine Nature, the Human Nature, and the Divine Personality, without expecting to solve the problem of their correlation.[11]

Thomas continues by pointing out the dangers of emphasis on either the divine or the human elements in Christ's character at the expense of the other:

> The consideration of our Lord's life on earth tends to make some people lose sight of the Divine in the human, and the result is often a merely humanitarian Christ. On the other hand, a consideration of the glorified Lord tends to make some lose sight of the human in the Divine, and the outcome is often a craving for some Mediator between the Divine Lord and ourselves. . . . Our safety will be found in emphasizing and balancing both aspects, the Divine and the human."[12]

The four heresies mentioned in this chapter were exposed in four famous general councils of the Church. The Council of Nicea (325) opposed Arius's denial of the deity of Christ; the Council of Constantinople (360) corrected Apollinarius's denial of Christ's true humanity; at Ephesus, in 431, Nestorius's notion that Christ was two persons was condemned; and, finally, at Chalcedon (451), the notion that the two natures of Christ so intermingled that one was impaired by the other—the heresy of Eutyches—was condemned.

The Council at Chalcedon used four words to summarize the findings of the various councils, or, as Thomas Hooker says, to set forth "whatever antiquity has at large handled either in declaration of Christian belief, or in refutation of the foresaid heresies."[13] As translated from Greek by Hooker, a famous English theologian of the early seventeenth century, those words are *truly, perfectly, indivisibly,* and *distinctly.* Christ was declared to be "truly" God, "perfectly" man, "indivisibly" One, and as having two natures which are "distinctly" separate.[14]

Church councils may sound dull to us, but they were terribly important. In their way they were as important as Paul's confrontation with Peter, or as Paul's correction of the Judaizers, who tried to pervert the gospel by making it a mere extension of Judaism. Paul contended with fierce tenacity; he refused to yield a doctrinal point for even a moment, in order that "the truth of the gospel might remain with you."[15] Like Paul, other thoughtful men of the first four hundred years of church history refused to yield to teachers of error. They studied the Scriptures and, helped by the Holy Spirit, issued statements setting forth the true teaching of Scripture.

Now, some fifteen hundred years later, we may safely cite the ancient creeds and confessions, knowing that to the extent that we agree with them, we stand on the biblical and historic faith. Like those tenacious men of the first few centuries of Christian testimony, we also must contend for the faith that God has once for all entrusted to the saints.[16] Like them, we maintain that Jesus Christ is truly God, perfectly man, in two natures, and one person. "Jesus Christ is the same yesterday and today and forever."[17]

At Bethlehem the eternal Son of God, without ceasing to be what he can never cease to be—the Second Person of the Godhead—became what he had not been but which, having become, he will never cease to be—man. How many truths are implied by that great fact! Among them are those mentioned in Hebrews: "Because Jesus lives forever, he has a permanent priesthood. Therefore he is able to save completely those who come to God through him, because he always lives to intercede for them."[18]

All that Jesus became for us, he remains forever! "Because I live," Christ says, "you also will live."[19]

18

The Incarnation—Truly Man, Without Sin

In this chapter we will look at five final truths about the Person of Jesus Christ—who he was and still is. We will look at the scriptural teachings that (1) he has a true human body, (2) he has a true human soul, (3) he was conceived by the Holy Spirit, (4) he was born of Mary while she was a virgin, and (5) he was born, and forever remains, sinless.

Jesus Christ Has a True Human Body

In the Book of Hebrews we read: "Since the children have flesh and blood, he too shared in their humanity so that by his death he might destroy him who holds the power of death—that is, the devil."[1]

Reference to Jesus' true human, physical body is, says Alexander Whyte, "the abiding protest of the Church against an ancient and deadly heresy."[2] The heresy is called docetism. An unabridged dictionary defines docetism accurately as the notion "that Christ's body was a mere phantom, or, if real, of celestial origin."[3]

This heresy is a denial of Christ's true humanity. It also denies the truth of the atonement, because a true body was required in order that the eternal Son of God might accomplish redemption. That is the point of the passage just quoted from Hebrews. It is of the utmost importance that Christ, the Son of God, had a true human body. If he did not, he could not have died an atoning death, and all mankind, without exception, would forever remain in sin and therefore be eternally lost.

The heresy of docetism has recurred often throughout the history of the Church. To counter a revival of docetism in the early sixteenth century, the fourth of the Thirty-nine Articles of the Church of England was formulated to set forth the real physical resurrection of Christ. In our day the reality of Christ's actual physical resurrection is still denied by many who claim to be Christians.

In New Testament times, docetism was a gnostic sect. Historian Paul Johnson says that "no one has yet succeeded in defining 'gnosticism' adequately." However, he continues,

> Gnostics had two central preoccupations: belief in a dual world of good and evil and belief in the existence of a secret code of truth, transmitted by word of mouth or by arcane writings. Gnosticism is a "knowledge" religion . . . which claims to have an inner explanation of life. Thus it was, and indeed still is, a spiritual parasite which used other religions as a "carrier." Christianity fitted into this role very well. . . . gnostic groups seized on bits of Christianity, but tended to cut it off from its historical origins. They were Hellenizing it, as they Hellenized other oriental cults (often amalgamating the results). Their ethics varied to taste; sometimes they were ultra-puritan, sometimes orgiastic.[4]

One of the worst corruptions of gnosticism Johnson describes as follows:

> The most dangerous gnostics were those who had, intellectually, thought their way quite inside Christianity, and then produced a variation which wrecked the system. The Basilides group in Egypt, and the Valentinians in Rome, though they differed on other things, both rejected the incarnation and denied that Jesus had ever been man; his body was semblance of *dokesis*.[5]

That last word is the Greek term from which *docetism* derives. The heresy was especially appealing among Greeks, because it completely removed Christianity from its Judaistic origin. If Jesus Christ was not a true human being, he obviously could not have been a true Jew. More significant than that, however, the docetic notion that Christ was only "apparently" human obviously excluded his resurrection. He would have had no body that could die and be raised. As Paul soberly reminds the Corinthians, "What I received I passed on to you as of first importance: that Christ died for our sins according to the Scriptures, that he was buried, that he was raised on the third day according to the Scriptures. . . . If Christ has not been raised, your faith is futile; you are still in your sins."[6]

Jesus Christ Has a True Human Soul

Whereas the docetists denied the reality of Christ's body, other heretics, known as Apollinarians (briefly mentioned in the last chapter), denied the reality of his human soul. They did not deny that he had a soul, but that his soul was human. They believed that the manhood of Christ consisted solely of a body. His soul, however, the place of the spirit or rational faculty, was occupied by what they called the divine Logos—making him incapable of temptation or of moral or intellectual development. As Alexander Whyte says of them,

> They accepted, without demur, the orthodox doctrine of the Incarnation as far as Christ's body went, but they could not accept it in the region of the mind. . . . Every page of the gospel narrative testifies to the reality of our Lord's humanity in His soul as well as in His body. At one time he rejoiced, and at another time He was in sorrow, and joy and sorrow are affections of a reasonable soul. He had a human will distinct from a Divine Will, for he said, 'Not my will, but Thine be done.' He spoke of what He felt when He said, 'My soul is exceeding sorrowful, even unto death.' And teaching us how to die, he said, 'Father, into Thy hands I commend my spirit.'[7]

The Mediator between man and God is himself man—the man Christ Jesus. As the writer of Hebrews tells us,

> During the days of Jesus' life on earth, he offered up prayers and petitions with loud cries and tears to the one who could save him from death, and he was heard because of his reverent submission. Although he was a son, he learned obedience from what he suffered and, once made perfect, he became the source of eternal salvation for all who obey him.[8]

Jesus Christ Was Conceived by the Holy Spirit

The third truth is that the eternal Son of God was conceived by the power of the Holy Spirit in the womb of a virgin named Mary. At the Annunciation the angel Gabriel told Mary that she would conceive and bear a son. "How will this be," Mary asked the angel, "since I am a virgin?" Gabriel explained: "The Holy Spirit will come upon you, and the power of the Most High will overshadow you. So the holy one to be born will be called the Son of God."[9] Later, when her fiancé, Joseph, learned that she was pregnant, he was troubled. An angel also appeared to him and said, "Joseph, son of David, do not be afraid to take Mary home as your wife, because what is conceived in her is from the Holy Spirit."[10]

As Matthew thought about those things, he recalled the prediction in the writings of Isaiah that a virgin would become pregnant and give birth to a remarkable child. Says Matthew, after recording the angel's reassuring remarks to Joseph, "All this took place to fulfill what the Lord had said through the prophet: 'The virgin will be with child and will give birth to a son, and they will call him Immanuel,'—which means, 'God with us.' "[11]

No statements about Christ's miraculous conception in a virgin's womb could be more direct and explicit. These, coming at the beginning of the Gospel narratives, have as much authority as any statement in Scripture. To deny their authenticity is to undermine the truth and authority of the rest of the nativity story, of the life that followed, and indeed the rest of the New Testament. Disbelief in Jesus' miraculous conception by the Holy Spirit and belief in the rest of the truths of Christianity are entirely inconsistent.

Jesus Christ Was Born of the Virgin Mary

A three hundred page volume by James Orr deals solely with the problem of Christ's miraculous conception and birth. In two concluding chapters, Dr. Orr examines the "doctrinal bearings" of the virgin birth. He sums up his argument in twenty-three statements, five of which are:

> The early Church set high value on the Virgin Birth doctrinally, as attesting (1) the true humanity of Christ, and (2) His superhuman dignity.
>
> The perfect sinlessness of Christ, and the archetypal character of his humanity, imply a miracle in His origin.
>
> The doctrine of the Incarnation of the pre-existent Son implies a miracle in Christ's origin.
>
> The miracle in Christ's origin had of necessity a physical as well as a spiritual side.
>
> The Virgin Birth answers historically to the conditions which faith postulates for the origin of Christ.[12]

W. H. Griffith Thomas covers the same ground in his book *The Principles of Theology*.[13] His conclusions are the same as Orr's—that both Christ's preexistence and his sinlessness in his earthly life demand a unique origin. Says Dr. Thomas, "It is only by the Virgin Birth that we can account for the unique earthly life of Jesus Christ. The miracle of the Incarnation is thus fitly expressed in the miraculous entrance, and harmonises with the miraculous departure in the Resurrection."[14]

The importance of Jesus Christ's being conceived by the power of the Holy Spirit and born of the virgin Mary cannot be overstated. It is far from being an optional doctrine. Says James Orr,

> The rejection of this article would . . . be a mutilation of Scripture, a contradiction of the continuous testimony of the Church from Apostolic times, a weakening of the doctrine of the Incarnation, and a practical surrender of the Christian position into the hands of the advocates of a non-miraculous, purely humanitarian Christ—all on insufficient grounds.[15]

The doctrine that Christ was conceived by the power of the Holy Spirit in the womb of a virgin is not an optional idea for believers. It is *truth*, highly important truth.

Following is a beautiful and meaningful statement by Marcus Dods:

> The same Holy Ghost who at the first creation moved on the face of the waters, when darkness was on the deep, and out of the chaos produced light, and order, and harmony, and beauty, did at the commencement of the new creation, out of the corrupted substance of the Virgin, form a human body, as perfectly separated from all corruption by the divine workmanship as the symmetry, and light, and beauty of the material world were separated from the darkness, confusion, and shapelessness of the desolate abyss. And at the moment when this body was conceived by the divine operation of the Holy Ghost, the power of the Highest united to it a soul, formed also in perfect purity and holiness. And at the same moment too were both body and soul united to the Godhead in the Person of the Son, by a personal union, never to be dissolved.[16]

It is not surprising that the angel Gabriel described the baby as "the holy offspring," or, more literally, "the holy thing begotten."[17]

What does Scripture teach about Mary herself? We will not devote any time to ideas such as her own immaculate conception, perpetual virginity, or assumption—because none of those ideas is scriptural.

Before the Annunciation by the angel Gabriel, the Bible says nothing about Mary, and there are no reliable traditions about her life before that time. But at the Annunciation several important statements about her are made: she was favored by God; she was blessed among women because she was chosen to be the mother of our Lord; having brought him into the world, she is honored by as many as honor her son; and all generations will call her blessed. The statements are given by Gabriel, by Elizabeth, and by Mary herself, as recorded in Luke 1.

How can we account for a glorification of Mary that has no basis in Scripture? Says Alexander Whyte, "The unhappy way of glorifying Mary, which has issued in such a portentous development of arbitrary dogma . . . took its rise in an orthodox interest, and with a right interest." Whyte goes on to discuss the Greek Fathers' delight in calling Mary " 'Theotokos,' the mother of Him who is God." As originally used, "This name was not at all intended to add to her honour; it was rather used as another way of vindicating the true divinity of Him who was her Son." However, "the addition of this Christological designation to the scriptural titles of Mary was speedily productive of great error and superstition."[18]

All generations will call Mary blessed; but only her Son is divine and Lord, and he alone is to be worshiped.

Jesus Christ Was Born, and Forever Remains, Sinless

Christ's sinless birth does not refer to the occasion of his birth or to the process. It refers to his nature; he was born without a sinful nature. Christ's birth was perfectly normal; the baby Jesus was born in precisely the same way as any other baby. A pregnant woman, having come to full term, gave birth to a baby boy. At the delivery only the attendant circumstances—such as the appearance of the heavenly host to the shepherds keeping watch over their flocks—were supernatural. Everything else was quite normal.

The conception that took place nine months earlier was supernatural; there was no human father. A virgin was pregnant without having been in contact with a man. Some people, for obvious reasons, find that difficult to believe, but it is a clear part of biblical teaching, and no more difficult to believe than many other truths in the Bible. It is hardly more difficult, for example, to believe in the virgin birth than in the Resurrection.

Jesus was not defiled with original sin; he was the first, and only, man ever born without sin. Article XV in the Church of England's Thirty-nine Articles sets forth the truth in these words: "Christ in the truth of our nature was made like unto us in all things, sin only except, from which He was clearly void, both in His flesh and in His spirit. He came to be the Lamb without spot, who, by sacrifice of Himself once made, should take away the sins of the world; and sin, as Saint John saith, was not in Him."

The language is quaint to our ears, but it makes the point clear that sinlessness was required for Christ's work of redemption. He was the true Lamb of God, without spot or blemish of any kind. Therefore, when he offered himself as a sacrifice for mankind's sin, he was accepted; there was no sin in himself that would have disqualified him.

19

Jesus Christ As Prophet

The redeeming work of Jesus Christ is often divided into three parts, each of which is clearly taught in Scripture. Beginning in the Old Testament, the Messiah (Christ) is spoken of in terms of prophet, priest, and king.

As early as the time of Moses, God told Israel that one day he would "raise up for them a prophet like [Moses] from among their brothers; I will put my words in his mouth, and he will tell them everything I command him."[1] While preaching in the Temple area shortly after Pentecost, Peter quoted that passage from Deuteronomy, explaining that the prophet spoken of by Moses was Jesus Christ. Peter, in fact, went on to say that "*all* the prophets from Samuel on, as many as have spoken, have foretold these days," that is, the days of the life and sacrificial death of God's Son.[2]

The Jews in Christ's times, including the disciples, found it difficult to believe that the true Messiah would be a suffering Messiah. They thought of him only in terms of glory and magnificence. Even after Jesus' three years of teaching about his purpose and work, his own disciples still did not understand what the Messiah was meant to be and do. Consequently, in our Lord's postresurrection conversation with two disciples on the road to Emmaus, he had to explain: " 'Did not the Christ have to suffer these things and then enter his glory?' And beginning with Moses and all the Prophets," Luke continues, Jesus "explained to them what was said in all the Scriptures concerning himself."[3]

Many years later, Peter explained to the young church:

> Concerning this salvation, the prophets, who spoke of the grace that was to come to you, searched intently and with the great-

> est care, trying to find out the time and circumstances to which the Spirit of Christ in them was pointing when he predicted the sufferings of Christ and the glories that would follow. It was revealed to them that they were not serving themselves but you, when they spoke of the things that have now been told you by those who have preached the gospel to you by the Holy Spirit sent from heaven. Even angels long to look into these things.[4]

This text tells us that the Spirit of Christ was in the Old Testament prophets. He was the source of their predictions. In other words, Jesus Christ was himself the Great Prophet, who spoke through all the other prophets.

At the beginning of his Gospel, John says, "No one has ever seen God, but God the only Son, who is at the Father's side, has made him known."[5] The primary function of a prophet was to make God and his will known to men. No prophet, before or since, has fulfilled that role as Jesus did. Near the end of his earthly ministry Jesus told his disciples: "I no longer call you servants, because a servant does not know his master's business. Instead, I have called you friends, for everything that I learned from my Father I have made known to you."[6] In those words, our Lord asserts that he acted as spokesman for God, telling his disciples what God wanted them to know. He was the supreme and divine Prophet.

If God had not sent the prophets, and ultimately Christ as his Prophet of prophets, how could we have known the truth about God? As God's Prophet, Christ reveals the Father and everything the Father wishes us to know about himself and his will for our salvation.

On one occasion, while praying in a public place, Jesus said, "I praise you, Father, Lord of heaven and earth, because you have hidden these things from the wise and learned, and revealed them to little children. Yes, Father, for this was your good pleasure." After prayer, he turned to his listeners and said, "All things have been committed to me by my Father. No one knows the Son except the Father, and no one knows the Father except the Son and those to whom the Son chooses to reveal him."[7]

We know about God only what he has chosen to reveal of himself. I am thankful he deigned to reveal so much! I am thankful he sent his Son, not just to be the Savior of the world—though that alone is more than enough to evoke our wonder and admiration—but also *to tell us about it.* God has taken into his confidence, so to speak, those who believe his Word and trust in his Son.

How does he tell us? In three ways: by Christ's life, by his word, and by his Spirit. Erich Sauer comments:

> From the incarnation of the Redeemer until His public appearance, the manifestation of God by Christ (John 1:18) was throughout a prophesying by means of His personality. The life of the child, the boy, the growing man revealed the holiness of God. 'He who sees Me sees the Father' (John 14:9). It displayed the divine ideal for the normal development of human life (comp. Luke 2:40, 52). The theme of this prophecy was, so to speak, 'The Man of God,' and therefore that word of the Baptist, 'I have need to be baptised by thee, and comest thou to me?' (Matt. 3:14).[8]

Christ's godly *life* was a form of witness. It was prophecy, not in the sense of prediction, but of forthtelling—telling out the divine plan for the development of human life, as seen in God's Perfect Man. That aspect of his life was, in a sense, even predictive, in that it predicted the nature of the new man who is being "renewed in knowledge in the image of [his] Creator."[9]

Second, Christ's *word* was, of course, an expression of his prophetic work. We have already seen how his teaching had a prophetic quality—that is, that he taught as God's supreme spokesman. In response to Philip's question, "Lord, show us the Father and that will be enough for us," Jesus said,

> "Don't you believe that I am in the Father, and that the Father is in me? The words I say to you are not just my own. Rather, it is the Father, living in me, who is doing his work. . . . If anyone loves me, he will obey my teaching. . . . These words you hear are not my own; they belong to the Father who sent me.[10]

Third, Christ's *Spirit* is an expression of his prophetic work. In his life in the flesh, Christ prophesied by his manner of life, and by his teaching. Now, having returned to heaven, he continues to prophesy by his Holy Spirit. As Erich Sauer explains,

> To us who are to be instructed there is now a 'coming' of the exalted Prophet by word and in spirit (John 14:18, 28). Not only do His messengers 'come'—the apostles, prophets, shepherds and teachers (Eph. 4:11), and His witnesses in general (Acts 1:8), but in them and in their message Christ Himself comes (Matt. 10:40), and from the glory continues His prophesying through the Spirit. Thus Paul says of the One crucified and risen, 'He came and proclaimed peace to you who were far off (non-Jews) and peace to those near (the Jews)' (Eph. 2:17). As the context shows, this does not speak of the preaching of Christ in the days of His life on earth before Golgotha, but of the time after His finished peace-making work on the cross, and therefore of His 'coming' in the present time, in word and spirit, to Israel and the peoples of the earth . . . His present theme is the completed redemption, with its peace and light (Acts 26:23).[11]

Thus, both in his humiliation and exaltation, Christ is God's Prophet. He speaks to the world today, as when he was on earth, by his life and word, and now also by his Spirit.

20

Jesus Christ as Priest

In addition to being the perfect Prophet, Jesus Christ is also the perfect Priest. The Old Testament refers to the Messiah as a priest. In Psalm 110 David says, "The Lord says to my Lord: 'Sit at my right hand until I make your enemies a footstool for your feet. . . . You are a priest forever, in the order of Melchizedek.' "[1]

The New Testament regards that passage from Psalm 110 as an anticipation of Christ's priesthood. In Hebrews 5, we read that "Christ . . . did not take upon himself the glory of becoming a high priest. But God said to him, 'You are my Son; today I have become your Father.' And he says in another place, 'You are a priest forever, in the order of Melchizedek.' "[2]

In several other passages in Hebrews, Christ is also seen as a priest. Christ's fulfillment of his priesthood required that he rise from the dead and return to heaven. In Hebrews 8:4 it is said of Christ that "If he were on earth, he would not be a priest, for there are already men who offer the gifts prescribed by the law." In other words, he had to return to heaven to assume the office of a priest.

In the Book of Hebrews we are also reminded that a true priest must be appointed to that office by God. "Every high priest is selected from among men and is appointed to represent them in matters related to God, to offer gifts and sacrifices for sins. . . . No one takes this honor upon himself; he must be called by God, just as Aaron was."[3]

In the Old Testament the high priest represented the entire people of Israel. When he entered the Holy Place in the Tabernacle or, later, the Temple, he wore a vestlike garment with twelve stones sewn in place, representing the names of the twelve tribes of Israel. Everything he did, whether killing an animal or sprinkling its blood, he did as the representative of the people.[4] In the same way, at

Calvary Christ functioned as a priest on our behalf. For whom did he die if not for us? Certainly not for himself! Listen to this passage from the tenth chapter of Hebrews:

> When Christ came into the world, he said: "Sacrifice and offering you did not desire, but a body you prepared for me; with burnt offerings and sin offerings you were not pleased. Then I said, 'Here I am—it is written about me in the scroll—I have come to do your will, O God.' " . . . And by that will, we have been made holy through the sacrifice of the body of Jesus Christ once for all.[5]

Christ offered himself for us. His death was vicarious. It is when we see this truth and receive it that we become Christians. Paul says, "The Son of God . . . loved me, and gave himself for me."[6] The moment a man or woman, boy or girl realizes that Christ gave himself for him or her personally, as if he or she were the only person in the universe, a human being is born from above.

Christ offered himself to God as a sacrifice *on our behalf*. He represented us, even as the Old Testament priest represented the people of Israel. But there the similarity ends and the great differences become obvious. The Old Testament priest merely killed an animal on an altar. Christ, as priest, offered himself. At Calvary he filled the dual role of priest and victim, offerer and offering. He was the High Priest who offered the sacrifice, and the spotless Lamb of God who *was himself* the sacrifice. And what he did was done on our behalf. We had nothing to offer; our souls were forfeit because of collective and personal sin. His was not; he was personally spotless. Hence, "through the eternal Spirit [Christ] offered himself unblemished to God."[7]

Christ's offering of himself began even before Calvary. It began when he said to his Father in heaven before he said it on earth, "I have come to do your will, O God."[8] His entire life was an offering of himself.

Think about a few stanzas taken from two different hymns, each pointing to the aspect of Christ's work as our Priest:

> From whence this fear and unbelief,
> If God, our Father, put to grief
>   His spotless Son for me?
> Can He, the righteous Judge of me,

Condemn me for that debt of sin
  Which, Lord, was charged to Thee?

If Thou hast my discharge procured,
And freely in my place endured
  The whole of wrath divine;
Payment God will not twice demand,
First at my blessed Surety's hand,
  And then again at mine.

Turn then, my soul, unto thy rest;
The merits of thy great High Priest
  Speak peace and liberty;
Trust in His efficacious blood,
Nor fear thy banishment from God,
  Since Jesus died for thee.[9]

The point of the hymn is clear: our peace with God depends upon the character of the High Priest who offered a sacrifice on our behalf. He offered himself, and, as the hymn says, his blood (that is, his death) was efficacious. It settled with God the accounts of all people of all time who put their trust in him. God cannot demand a second payment from those whose sins are covered by that one, perfect, and complete payment. Another hymn makes the same point:

I hear the words of love,
I gaze upon the blood,
I see the mighty sacrifice,
And I have peace with God.

I know He liveth now
At God's right hand above:
I know the throne on which He sits,
I know His truth and love![10]

He Satisfies Divine Justice

Why did Christ have to make a sacrifice for us? God's justice demanded it. As one commentator says,

> The honor of God does not permit Him to forgive sinners out of His pity; for thereby not only would the unrighteous be made equal to the righteous, and all order in His kingdom

> overthrown, but even unrighteousness itself would be put on a level with God, if, like Him, exempted from the authority of the law.[11]

In the eleventh century, Anselm, Archbishop of Canterbury, published a treatise titled *Cur Deus Homo* ("Why God Became Man"). In it he counters the very old notion that Christ's death was payment made to the devil. He also answers the question as to why it was not possible for Almighty God simply to declare man forgiven.

Anselm claims that sin consists in not giving God his due—which is perfect obedience. Sinners, therefore, are debtors to God. God could cancel the debt, but it would be inconsistent with his justice to do that. God's mercy cannot be in conflict with his justice. So the debt must be paid. But how? And who would, or could, pay it? That it *will* be paid is inferred from the improbability that God would allow his purposes in creation to be defeated.

Can the debt be paid by repentance and good works? Obviously not, since we owe these to God already. Doing good works, therefore, does not atone for past sins.

Anselm contends that since man was overcome by Satan, in order to render satisfaction to his Creator, he must overcome Satan. He must also work out a means of justification. But man is incapable either of defeating Satan or of achieving justification, which means that the case is hopeless—or would be hopeless if it were not for Christ. But now, with Christ's appearance, the hopeless case brightens. Why? Because Christ, as God, is able to render to God something greater than everything else except God. Christ is also man, and as man he is able to represent sinful man, though he himself was not sinful.

As discussed in previous chapters, Christ's sinlessness is crucial to his atonement. It is explainable only in terms of his miraculous conception, and it implies exemption from death. He was not naturally liable to death. But, Anselm points out, he voluntarily died for us, thereby rendering to God " 'something' which is of greater value than everything else except God."[12] In a comment on Anselm's work, E. A. Litton observes:

> The value of the death is to be measured by the preciousness of the life, than which nothing was more precious. God could not justly demand a life from Christ; therefore, the freewill offering in our stead redounds to our advantage. In Christ man is

> sinless, overcomes Satan, is obedient unto death, gives up his spotless life to God; here we have what we have been seeking for—full satisfaction for sin.[13]

Why should *we* benefit from Christ's death? Why should *his* death satisfy the demands of divine justice on our behalf? Anselm further explains: "The sinless sufferer [that is, Christ] justly claims a reward for what He thus, in obedience to the will of God, undeservedly underwent, and the reward which He receives is the salvation of the elect."[14]

Though the atonement is mysterious, whatever was needed, Christ supplied. God is satisfied, and if he is satisfied, why should we not be? "What, then, shall we say in response to this? If God is for us, who can be against us? He who did not spare his own Son, but gave him up for us all—how will he not also, along with him, graciously give us all things? Who will bring any charge against those whom God has chosen?"[15]

He Reconciles Us to God

Reconciliation may be defined as: "To cause to be friendly again; to bring back to harmony."[16] That is essentially how Scripture uses the term.

> Therefore, if anyone is in Christ, he is a new creation; the old has gone, the new has come! All this is from God, who reconciled us to himself through Christ and gave us the ministry of reconciliation: that God was reconciling the world to himself in Christ, not counting men's sins against them. And he has committed to us the message of reconciliation. We are therefore Christ's ambassadors, as though God were making his appeal through us. We implore you on Christ's behalf: Be reconciled to God.[17]

Again Paul tells us, "For if, when we were God's enemies, we were reconciled to him through the death of his Son, how much more, having been reconciled, shall we be saved through his life!"[18] In Ephesians 2 in a passage dealing with peace between Jew and Gentile as a consequence of Christ's death and resurrection, Paul says:

> For he himself is our peace, who has made the two one and has destroyed the barrier, the dividing wall of hostility, by abolishing in his flesh the law with its commandments and regulations. His purpose was to create in himself one new man out of the two, thus making peace, and in this one body to reconcile both of them to God through the cross, by which he put to death their hostility.[19]

As used in the Bible, reconciliation means, on our part, a change of attitude leading to a change in relationship. Whereas we were hostile to God, and estranged, we may now repent and receive the benefits of his love for us.

Who needs to be reconciled—God or man? It is a disputed question. Theologian Lewis Sperry Chafer says flatly that "the Bible never asserts that God is reconciled."[20] In his view it is man who is changed; hostile sinners are caused to be friendly again, whereas God is immutable. "He is always righteous, just, and good."[21] R. C. Trench, on the other hand, author of a book most serious Bible students consult from time to time, believes that both God and man are reconciled. Says Trench,

> It is first a reconciliation (by which God has reconciled us to Himself, laid aside His holy anger against our sins, and received us into favor), a reconciliation effected for us once for all by Christ upon His cross. . . . But it is secondly and subordinately the reconciliation (by which we are reconciled to God), the daily deposition, under the operation of the Holy Spirit, of the enmity of the old man toward God.[22]

Trench goes on to say that "All attempts to make this secondary to the primary meaning and intention of the word, rests not on an unprejudiced exegesis, but on a foregone determination to get rid of the reality of God's anger against the sinner."[23]

Certainly that was the view of the Reformers. In Article II of the Church of England's Thirty-nine Articles (issued in the middle of the sixteenth century), we read: "Christ . . . truly suffered, dead and buried, to reconcile His Father to us, and to be a sacrifice, not only for original guilt, but also for all actual sins of men."

That statement draws attention to the belief of the Reformers that Christ's death reconciled God to us. But we should fix our minds on two facts. First, whatever was needed to make God well-disposed toward us (if anything was needed at all; the need is not as obvious to some thinkers as to others) was provided by Christ's atoning death. Hence, there is no barrier on God's part to reconciliation. Second, our obvious need to be reconciled is easily met. All we need to do is come believing. "Come to me," Jesus says.[24] When we come to Christ believing, reconciliation is achieved.

As Paul says, "But God demonstrates his own love for us in this: While we were still sinners, Christ died for us."[25] However, if Christ had not died an atoning death, fellowship with God would have been impossible. Why? Because God's holiness was involved. In Thomas Boston's words, "God had a *legal* enmity against us, such as a just judge against a malefactor, whose person he may love notwithstanding (Matt. 5:25)."[26] What Boston means by his expression, "a legal enmity," is clarified by the comments of Lewis Sperry Chafer: "Before the death of Christ His righteousness demanded its required judgments."[27]

The point to remember is that whereas God yearned over fallen man, he was unable to restore man to his original state with a mere word. The Incarnation and atoning death were necessary, and that is the emphasis of all biblical theologians, who insist that God was reconciled, not man alone. The change is in his freedom, so to speak, not his attitude. As Dr. Chafer observes, "There is in the cross an outward appearance of changed attitude on the part of God; but this belongs rather to propitiation than to reconciliation. . . . It is no more Godward in its objective accomplishments than redemption. Certainly redemption is not Godward, nor, in the final analysis, is reconciliation Godward; for God is immutable. He is always righteous, just, and good."[28]

Dr. Chafer wants it known that propitiation—which deals with God's *legal* need of something to remove the barrier raised by sin—"does not infuse compassion into God." Rather it

> secures the freedom on His part to exercise His unchanging compassion apart from those restraints which penal judgments would impose. There is a truth to be recognized concerning God, that in His own being and from all eternity His holiness and His love have found adjustment concerning the sinner through the death of His Son; but this is only another approach to the same divine propitiation.[29]

In a speech before the king of Israel, a certain woman of Tekoa said, "But God does not take away life; instead, he devises ways so that a banished person may not remain estranged from him."[30] That is what reconciliation is all about: God's plan to bring banished sinners to himself.

He Intercedes for Us Before God

When he was on earth, Christ did what priests do: he offered a sacrifice. But unlike their sacrifices, his was of himself. Now, in heaven, he does what Aaron and his successors did—he intercedes on behalf of sinful people.

Christ has fulfilled the two basic functions of priesthood—sacrifice and intercession. The first function is over; having sacrificed himself at Calvary, he completed that aspect of his priestly work. The second function is continuous and continual; it never ends. As we read in Hebrews 7, "Because Jesus lives forever, he has a permanent priesthood. Therefore he is able to save completely those who come to God through him, because he always lives to intercede for them."[31] That truth is profound, and crucial to the faith.

Why does he intercede for us? Lewis Sperry Chafer explains:

> As Intercessor, [Christ's] work has to do with the weakness, the helplessness, and the immaturity of the saints who are on the earth. . . . He who knows the limitations of His own and the power and strategy of the foe with whom they have to contend, has become unto them the Shepherd and Bishop of their souls.[32]

As our Intercessor Christ does not stand like an Old Testament priest with his hands uplifted before the throne of God. He is seated at the right hand of God. The symbolism is important. Old Testament priests never sat down because their work was never finished. Day after day they offered the same kinds of sacrifices. Christ, on the other hand, offered himself once; it was a never-to-be repeated sacrifice.[33] How then does he intercede for us? By talking? By pleading with God on our behalf? As one interpreter explains,

> The Intercession of the Ascended Christ is not a prayer but a life. The New Testament does not represent Him as an *orante* standing ever before the Father, and with outstretched arms,

> like the figures in the mosaics in the Catacombs, and with strong crying and tears pleading our cause in the presence of a reluctant God; but as a throned Priest-King, asking what He will from a Father Who always hears and grants His request. Our Lord's life in heaven is His prayer.[34]

As W. H. Griffith Thomas says, "We can well be content with the thought that He is there, and that His presence with the Father is the secret of our peace, the assurance of our access, and the guarantee of our permanent relation with God."[35]

How does Christ act as our great High Priest? Among other things, by being in heaven as our Representative. Just being there on our behalf is all that is required.

21

Jesus Christ as King

Jesus Christ's third office is that of king. We read in Psalm 2:7, "I have installed my King on Zion, my holy hill." The ninth chapter of Isaiah predicts the birth of a Child on whose shoulder all government one day would rest. The ninth chapter of Zechariah is quoted by Matthew at the triumphal entry: "This took place to fulfill what was spoken through the prophet: 'Say to the Daughter of Zion, "See, your king comes to you, gentle and riding on a donkey, on a colt, the foal of a donkey." ' "[1]

From the earliest accounts of Jesus' life he was proclaimed as a king. Matthew tells us: "After Jesus was born in Bethlehem in Judea, during the time of King Herod, Magi from the east came to Jerusalem and asked, 'Where is the one who has been born king of the Jews? We saw his star in the east and have come to worship him.' "[2] In Hebrews 1:8 we read, "But about the Son he [God the Father] says, 'Your throne, O God, will last forever and ever, and righteousness will be the scepter of your kingdom.' " And from Revelation 19:13, 16 we learn that "His name is the Word of God. . . . On his robe and on his thigh he has this name written: KING OF KINGS AND LORD OF LORDS."

The passage from Matthew speaks of Christ's being the King of the Jews. The one from Revelation says he is more than that; he is King of kings and Lord of lords. The text from Hebrews takes us farther than either of the others; it says he is a divine and eternal King.

Christ Rules Us

As our Lord and King, Christ obviously rules us, or *should* rule us. Paul teaches us that "If you confess with your mouth, 'Jesus is Lord,' and believe in your heart that God raised him from the dead, you will be saved."[3] By definition, lordship means rulership.

The kingdom of God obviously is ruled by God. Paul says that God "rescued us from the dominion of darkness and brought us into the kingdom of the Son he loves."[4] God expects members of Christ's kingdom to conduct themselves as Christ's subjects.

Alexander Whyte says on the subject:

> We are not compelled, but sweetly constrained to take the law of our life in everything from His Word and Spirit. We are proud to confess that we are not our own. Things we would continually do were we our own, we do not do because we are Christ's. "Your bodies and your souls are His," says the Apostle. And every breach of the covenant in misruling the body or the soul is an act of rebellion against our heavenly King.[5]

There is great reward in keeping his commands. As Jesus promises, "Whoever has my commands and obeys them, he is the one who loves me. He who loves me will be loved by my Father, and I too will love him and show myself to him."[6]

Christ Defends Us

As our Lord and King, Christ also defends us, especially from spiritual enemies. It is a lovely subject. Who is not thrilled by the Forty-sixth Psalm, especially the first three verses:

> God is our refuge and strength,
> an ever present help in trouble.
> Therefore we will not fear, though the
> earth give way
> and the mountains fall into the
> heart of the sea,
> though its waters roar and foam
> and the mountains quake with their surging.

And who among us does not love Martin Luther's great hymn, "A Mighty Fortress Is Our God"? The second stanza emphasizes God's care in defending us from "our ancient foe."

> Did we in our own strength confide,
> Our striving would be losing;
> Were not the right Man on our side,
> The Man of God's own choosing.

Doth ask who that may be?
Christ Jesus, it is He!
Lord Sabaoth is His Name,
From age to age the same;
And He must win the battle.

It is a lovely thought, but is it true? We seem to lose so many battles to "our ancient foe," the devil, and to our other great enemies—the world and the flesh. Does Christ the King protect us? The answer is yes—on the basis both of Scripture and of experience. Says John, "You, dear children, are from God and have overcome [the antichrist], because the one who is in you is greater than the one who is in the world."[7] Jude calls for a doxology of praise "to him who is able to keep you from falling and to present you before his glorious presence without fault and with great joy."[8]

Those statements are not incompatible with passages that deal with sin in our lives or with spiritual defeat. As long as we are in the flesh we will suffer occasional defeats. We are still not completely free of our sinful nature. The world is all around us, the devil is beside us, and the flesh is within us. We will not be entirely free of those "ancient foes" until we are with the Lord in heaven. But as Luther's hymn proclaims, "Lord Sabaoth . . . must win the battle." He lets us lose some skirmishes, but the final victory is sure. God's Word guarantees it. Thomas Carlyle's translation of the last stanza of Luther's hymn make the point beautifully:

God's Word, for all their craft and force,
One moment will not linger,
But, spite of hell, shall have its course;
'Tis written by his finger.
And though they take our life,
Goods, honour, children, wife,
Yet is their profit small;
These things vanish all:
The city of God remaineth.

Who are those enemies? There are two kinds, temporal and spiritual. In most of the modern Western world we are more familiar with spiritual than temporal foes. We understand the warning of Ephesians 6:12—"Our struggle is not against flesh and blood, but against . . . the spiritual forces of evil in the heavenly realms." There are also temporal foes, of course, in the form of people who hate God. In some countries they rise to positions of great, or even total, power; and they use the authority of the state to oppose God and to persecute his people. In other places human enemies are scoffers and blasphemers and, in some cases, corrupters of society.

That evil in the world is restrained to some extent is apparent. If it went entirely unchecked, the world would be a cesspool of iniquity and a veritable hell on earth. The Psalms, as well as other parts of Scripture, note that evil men are really short-lived, and they sometimes fall into the traps they set for the righteous. For statements about those facts of life, read such Psalms as 35, 36, and especially 37.

That Satan and his minions are restrained is evident from two considerations: Scripture and observable facts. The Book of Job reveals that Satan is on a leash. The leash is much longer than we wish it were, but it is a leash; there are some bounds he cannot cross.[9] As further evidence, consider spiritual victory in the lives of people who, if Satan had his way, would spend their lives in bondage to sin. Every spiritual victory, from the initial conversion experience to victory over a bad habit, is evidence of divine restraint imposed on our ancient foes.

Christ not only restrains but conquers our foes. Their destruction is certain. John says that "The reason the Son of God appeared was to destroy the devil's work."[10] Eventually the devil himself will be destroyed. Paul says that "the God of peace will soon crush Satan under your feet."[11] Even death itself will be destroyed in due time. Says Paul, "[Christ] must reign until he has put all his enemies under his feet. The last enemy to be destroyed is death."[12]

The Book of Revelation is a source of comfort to believers troubled by evil around them or in them. Its supreme message is that Christ has overcome evil in all its forms. In due time God will make the fact plain. Meanwhile, we rest in his Word and anticipate the day when John's vision of the future will become a reality. We read that an angel, speaking as if the future had already arrived, said, "The kingdom of the world has become the kingdom of our Lord and of his Christ, and he will reign forever and ever."[13]

Hearing that proclamation, those who are in heaven worship God and thank him for destroying those who destroy the earth. The King of kings will reign in power; and when he does, he will destroy those who destroy the earth. What assurance could cheer a troubled heart more?

22

Christ's Humiliation

As he was traveling home from Jerusalem, the Ethiopian eunuch asked Philip whom the prophet Isaiah was speaking of when he wrote, "In his humiliation he was deprived of justice. Who can speak of his descendants? For his life was taken from the earth." Philip "began with that very passage of Scripture and told him the good news about Jesus."[1] In Philippians 2:8 Paul says of Jesus Christ that "being found in appearance as a man, he humbled himself and became obedient to death—even death on a cross!"

The Incarnation was an act of self-abasement, of self-humiliation. Our Lord humbled himself, and he suffered much ignominy as a consequence. From the New Testament we can see at least six aspects or steps in Christ's self-abasement: his birth; his undergoing the sufferings of earthly life; his enduring God's wrath; his death on the cross; his being buried; and his continuing for awhile under the power of death. As we think about those six downward steps the Lord took on our behalf, we are amazed at the love of God.

His Birth

For us, the birth of an ordinary child is usually an occasion of joy; and if the baby is healthy, we say he is blessed or fortunate. We assume that coming into existence and being alive is a blessing or a privilege; and few people, even among those who say it is a hard world, will challenge us. When Jesus was born, there was rejoicing, but his birth was different from all others, before or since; birth did not give him existence. He existed before birth; he was the eternal Son of God. As such, he had lived or existed (no verb is adequate) on an altogether different "level" than the level of existence he accepted at birth.

We celebrate that truth when we sing Christmas carols. One stanza of the well-known "Oh, Come, All Ye Faithful" reminds us:

God of God,
Light of light,
Lo! He abhors not the Virgin's womb;
Very God,
Begotten, not created;
Oh! come, let us adore Him,
Christ the Lord!

"Lo! He abhors not the Virgin's womb." The hymn writer understood that for the Lord, birth was an experience of considerable loss.

Many of our best hymns draw attention to the contrast between Christ as Maker of the universe and the infant in a manger. Here are lines from a hymn with a tune titled, appropriately, "Humility":

Lo, within a manger lies
He who built the starry skies,
He who, throned in height sublime,
Sits amid the cherubim.[2]

Here is a stanza from another hymn.

What led the Son of God
To leave His throne on high,
To shed His precious blood,
To suffer and to die?
'Twas love, unbounded love for us,
Led Him to die and suffer thus.[3]

All three of those stanzas point up the truth that Jesus' birth was a humiliation. It was not Christ's beginning; before the birth he occupied a throne on high, which he left when he came to earth. He left because he loved us.

Born Poor Our Lord was born into a family with humble parents. Joseph and Mary were poor. Luke says that when she gave birth to her firstborn son, "she wrapped him in cloths and placed him in a manger, because there was no room for them in the inn."[4] The inns were abnormally crowded, because many other people—like Mary and Joseph—had come to Bethlehem because of the Roman census. But there is usually room for latecomers with plenty of money. Joseph and Mary were too poor for special treatment.

Forty days later Mary went to Jerusalem to offer a sacrifice for a ritual cleansing, as was required. Normally a lamb was offered in sacrifice. However, special concessions were made for the poor; they were permitted to offer doves or pigeons, which were much cheaper.[5] It was only such a minimal offering that Joseph and Mary were able to afford.[6] Such irony! The woman who could not afford a lamb brought forth him who was himself the perfect, unblemished Lamb of God who takes away the sin of the world.[7]

We sometimes try to imagine conditions in the home in which Jesus was brought up. Certainly there were none of the luxuries we enjoy, and none of the so-called conveniences without which we think our existence would be impossible. Jesus ate simple food, wore simple clothing, slept on the floor. When he was fully grown he was still poor—poorer than foxes or birds, which have their holes or nests. Jesus had no place that he could call his own.[8]

The poverty of Jesus evidently was well-known in the early church. Matthew tells of his once having to work a miracle to pay the Temple tax.[9] Paul wrote about Jesus' poverty in order to exhort Christians in Corinth to give liberally: "For you know the grace of our Lord Jesus Christ, that though he was rich, yet for your sakes he became poor, so that you through his poverty might become rich."[10]

Paul's statement implies that poverty worked as many inconveniences for Jesus as for anyone else. True, he knew that his poverty would be relatively brief; he would soon return to the Father. Yet no one was ever more sensitive than Jesus to the true nature of poverty. No one was ever more sharply aware of the injustices underlying much of the poverty in the world. Poverty was a trial for him, as it is for everyone who experiences it. He could not endure it with cool detachment.

Born Under Law Jesus' birth also reflects his humiliation in another way. "When the time had fully come," Paul says, "God sent his Son, born of a woman, born under law."[11] Like every pious Jewish family, the one into which Jesus was born was obliged to obey the law—meaning the code given to the nation of Israel at Mount Sinai soon after the Exodus from Egypt.

Paul's statement that Christ was "born under law" reflects the genealogy given in the Gospels. In the Gospel According to Matthew, Jesus' Jewish parentage through Joseph is given, and is traced back to Abraham through the royal line of David.[12] Jesus could have claimed the throne of David; his Jewish pedigree was impeccable. In Romans 1, Paul says that the gospel concerns God's Son, "who as to his human nature was a descendant of David."[13]

Born a Jew Even a cursory reading of the New Testament reveals Jesus' Jewishness. He was born into a Jewish family, and in his lifetime he obeyed the ancient code in all its particulars. He submitted himself to the law and obeyed it perfectly. Many of the accounts and sayings in the New Testament cannot be understood apart from the fact that Jesus lived and died as a Jew.

Yet, though he was a Jew he did not belong exclusively to the Jews. In describing the privileges of the Jewish nation, Paul says:

> Theirs is the adoption as sons; theirs the divine glory, the covenants, the receiving of the law, the temple worship and the promises. Theirs are the patriarchs, and from them is traced the human ancestry of Christ, who is God over all, forever praised! Amen.[14]

Notice the distinction made in verse 5: "Theirs *are* the patriarchs," but "*from them* is traced the human ancestry of Christ." Christ was born under the law—that is, as a Jew, according to the flesh. But he is not theirs. He does not belong to them in the sense that the patriarchs (such as Abraham, Isaac, and Jacob) belong to them. He is not ours, either. But we are his, if we come to him in faith. As Paul reminds Christians, "All things belong to you, and you belong to Christ."[15]

His Suffering

From Galatians 3 we can begin to see why Jesus' being born under the law was a part of his humiliation. "Christ redeemed us from the curse of the law by becoming a curse for us, for it is written: 'Cursed is everyone who is hung on a tree.' "[16] The law pronounced a curse on everyone who failed to meet its terms. The curse meant death. Unlike all other men, Christ did not deserve being under that curse, because he was personally sinless. Not even his bitterest opponents could convict him of sin. He had no personal sentence of death. If he had so chosen, he could have lived on and on. Yet living was not his purpose in coming to earth. He came to die—as the Sin-bearer, as the cursed One—in order to redeem us from that curse. He voluntarily assumed responsibility for the sins of the world; he placed himself under the curse. Hence, in his death he was treated by God as if he were cursed.

Only in death did he become our substitute. His keeping the law in his lifetime did not help anyone. He did not keep the law for us. In dying, however, he met the law's demand that sinners must die. As Peter says, "He himself bore our sins in his body on the tree."[17] He died, and because his death was vicarious (suffered on our behalf), it satisfies the demands of the law against us. Thereby he redeemed us from the curse of the law. The law has no further claims against sinners who turn to Christ in faith.

Christ assumed responsibility for the wreck that mankind, through sinning, made of itself and of the world. The Sinless One was treated as if he were sin itself; he was treated by God as if he were cursed. Such humiliation! Such intense suffering! Such willing and loving sacrifice! We ought to fall at his feet and confess that he is Lord and Savior and altogether lovely.

As the hymn-writer puts it,

Whatever curse was mine, He bore,
The wormwood and the gall;
There, in that lone mysterious hour,
My cup—He drained it all![18]

The sufferings that Jesus experienced during his Incarnation included the internal and the external. Because he was sinless, he could not experience such things as pangs of conscience, delusions, anxiety, frustration over not having his own way, or the torment of hatred or revenge. Those kinds of suffering are due directly to sin. Yet no human being was ever as sensitive to the sufferings of others, and that element of his nature caused him great inner pain.

The Gospel writers frequently tell such things about Jesus as, "When he saw the crowds he had compassion on them, because they were harassed and helpless, like sheep without a shepherd."[19] The spectacle of suffering humanity was, for him, a source of anguish. He wept at the grave of Lazarus, and he wept over Jerusalem.[20] He was also capable of anger, or, as we would say, righteous indignation. He drove the money-changers out of the Temple because of a passionate zeal for the reverence of God's house, and the unbelief of the religious leaders of the nation often exasperated him.[21]

Jesus did suffer inwardly; but his grief and anger were not just like ours. In his grief or anger there was never sin. Our grieving is often (perhaps usually) tainted by self-pity; his was not. And our anger is often (perhaps usually) self-seeking and unreasonable, whereas his was not.

Jesus also experienced external sufferings. We are not told of his being ill or diseased in any way, but we do know that he endured the inconveniences of poverty and of political suppression in an occupied land. He was often physically weary and eventually was tortured and crucified. Indeed, Isaiah predicted that Christ, the Messiah, would be a "man of sorrows, and familiar with suffering."[22] There was no kind of suffering he did not experience, except suffering caused by his own sin or foolishness.

He endured those sufferings vicariously on our behalf. He also endured them for the sake of our instruction. Peter tells us that "Christ suffered for you, leaving you an example, that you should follow in his steps."[23]

His Enduring God's Wrath

What is the wrath of God, and how did Christ endure it? We must be sure that we understand terms such as wrath according to their use in the Bible, not their popular use. One dictionary defines wrath under the heading "anger." "Anger," the dictionary says, is "the general term for the emotional reaction of extreme displeasure and suggests neither a definite degree of intensity nor a necessarily outward manifestation." Is wrath the same as anger? Not quite. "Wrath," as the dictionary goes on to explain, "may imply either rage or indignation but suggests strongly a desire or intent to avenge or punish."[24] Elsewhere, the same dictionary defines wrath as "retributory punishment for an offense or a crime; divine chastisement."

Do those definitions of wrath square with biblical use of the word? Obviously not the first; God's wrath is not an emotional outburst. Nor is it evidence of "*a desire* . . . to avenge or punish." Judgment is God's "strange work" and his "alien task," as Isaiah says.[25]

What, then, does the Bible mean when it speaks of God's wrath? In the New Testament two common Greek words are used with reference to God's anger or wrath. The word *orgē,* used most frequently, is defined as "a settled or abiding condition of mind, frequently with a view to taking revenge."[26]

Following are three texts in which the word appears. Each of the passages says something terribly important about God's attitude toward sin and unbelief.

We are told by John the Baptist that "Whoever believes in the Son has eternal life, but whoever rejects the Son will not see life, for God's wrath remains on him."[27] In Colossians Paul advises, "Put to death, therefore, whatever belongs to your earthly nature: sexual immorality, impurity, lust, evil desires and greed, which is idolatry. Because of these, the wrath of God is coming."[28] And in his first letter to Thessalonica he tells us to "wait for his Son from heaven, whom he raised from the dead—Jesus, who rescues us from the coming wrath."[29]

God's wrath is more than a fixed attitude of hostility toward sin. It also includes his determination to avenge or punish sin at a set time. It is hard to think of a more terrible prospect than the wrath of God. Imagine living in expectation of facing an angry God! Not many people do, of course. Most of those on whom the wrath of God will fall live as if he were never in their thoughts. They do not worry about the judgment to come. Hearing of it, they often laugh.

The real pity is that no one *need* fear God's wrath. For believers in Christ Jesus, there is no wrath, and he offers his salvation to everyone. As Paul says, "No condemnation now hangs over the head of those who are 'in' Christ Jesus."[30] If, through faith, a person is "in Christ Jesus," he need not fear the wrath of God. But any person who is not in Christ has great reason to be afraid.

Christ bore God's wrath for everyone who trusts in him. Hence, for all who are linked to him by faith, bound to him in an intimate relationship, the wrath of God is a spent force. They do not fear it. They are as safe from the fury of divine wrath as Noah in the ark was safe from the pounding rain and rising waters of the Flood.

How did Christ endure God's wrath? He endured God's wrath by accepting responsibility for our sins and suffering the consequences—death on the cross. Paul says that "God made him who had no sin to be sin for us."[31] Jesus did not become sin in the sense of committing sin; he was at all times personally sinless. Nevertheless, God *treated* him as if he were sin, and dealt with him as if he were the scapegoat for the entire universe.

Our Lord's death was very painful. As one theologian says,

> The wrath of God did operate in His soul, filling it with troubles, sore amazement, heaviness and exceeding sorrow, and casting Him into an agony, even to His sweating great drops of blood, and at length bringing over it a total eclipse of all comfort, and as it were melting it within Him (John 12:27; Mark 14:33, 34; Luke 22:44; Matthew 27:46; Psalm 22:14). This was a spiritual death such as a holy soul was capable of. Now the wrath of God could justly fall upon Christ, a person perfectly innocent, inasmuch as he stood surety for sinners (Hebrews 7:22, with Prov. 6:1, 2; 2 Cor. 5:21).[32]

Was Christ's death a miscarriage of justice? Yes, in one great respect it was, because Jesus in no way deserved it. Yet at its deepest level it was a manifestation of purest justice, justice fulfilled by grace rather than condemnation. Christ agreed to come to earth to be the Savior of the world, and he could not save the world except by assuming responsibility for the sins of the world. Having assumed that responsibility, he could not escape the wrath of God against sin. Justice demanded punishment, and Jesus Christ became the representative man, the representative condemned man. God's just wrath therefore burned against him. The cross was not just a monstrous sin against an innocent man; it was the place where the holy Son of God paid the full price for man's monstrous sin. "It was the Lord's will to crush him and cause him to suffer."[33]

His Death on the Cross

In Galatians Paul teaches several sobering truths about Christ's death on our behalf. "All who rely on observing the law are under a curse," he says, "for it is written: 'Cursed is everyone who does not continue to do everything written in the Book of the Law.' " A few verses later he explains that "Christ redeemed us from the curse of the law by becoming a curse for us, for it is written: 'Cursed is everyone who is hung on a tree.' "[34]

The Jews, whose book (Deuteronomy) Paul was quoting, did not crucify people on crosses; crosses were a Roman invention. The Jews did not even hang people, except after execution by some other method. In such cases the corpses were hung on trees and the dead persons were viewed as under the curse of God. Their corpses were taken down before sunset lest the ground under the tree also be cursed.

Paul's point was that, in dying as he did—on a kind of tree (the cross)—Christ took the curse pronounced against all who do not keep the law of God perfectly and unfailingly. He was treated by God as if he were accursed, as if he were under the curse of the law. By dying himself, he removed the curse from those who trust in him. Now the law has nothing more to say to them; it can no longer curse them, because he bore that curse for them.

We sing about this awesome and marvelous truth in Philip Bliss's beautiful hymn:

> I will sing of my Redeemer,
> And His wondrous love to me;
> On the cruel cross He suffered,
> From the curse to set me free.

His Being Buried

Jesus' burial is recorded in all four Gospels and in Paul's summary of cardinal doctrines in 1 Corinthians 15. His burial is implied in every scriptural reference to the Resurrection. It is also part of the Apostles' Creed: "I believe . . . in Jesus Christ . . . who was . . . crucified, dead and buried."

Was it necessary that Jesus be buried? Yes, for at least two reasons. First, it gives evidence that Christ died; he did not just faint, later to be resuscitated. Second, the burial completed his sacrifice of himself as an offering for sin. As someone has observed,

> He went into the tomb a sin offering sacrificed unto death. He came out completely unrelated to the burden of sin. Such is the doctrinal significance of the words (in the Apostle's Creed), "and . . . was buried." There could be no tracing of the disposition of sin achieved in the tomb, as there was never tracing of the further life and existence of the scapegoat after it was released in the wilderness. In that burial which was an aspect of Christ's undertaking in behalf of the believer's sin nature, too, there is also evidently a disposition of those judgments which duly fell upon him. . . .[35]

His burial was an essential part of Christ's humiliation. It completed the sacrifice accomplished on the cross.

His Being for Awhile Under the Power of Death

The final aspect of Christ's humiliation was his continuing under the power of death for a time. He spent three days and three nights in the grave. In his first sermon Peter proclaimed Christ's resurrection: "God raised him from the dead, freeing him from the agony of death, because it was impossible for death to keep its hold on him."[36] Christ could not be held indefinitely in death's power. Yet it was necessary in God's plan of redemption that he be held briefly in its grip—for three days and three nights.[37] The Author of Life allowed himself to be put to death, buried, and held in the power of death.[38]

In two important respects Jesus Christ did not share the totality of mankind's experience: he did not lose communion with God (except during the hours at Calvary when he was under the curse), and he did not endure the pains of hell forever. Just before commending his spirit to God and dying, he said, "It is finished."[39] His sacrifice and his sufferings were ended. As he himself said through the words of the prophet, "Therefore my heart is glad and my tongue rejoices; my body also will live in hope, because you will not abandon me to the grave, nor will you let your Holy One see decay."[40]

Now and throughout all eternity he is the risen and exalted Lord and Savior.

23

Christ's Exaltation

We will be looking at four aspects of Christ's exaltation: his resurrection, his ascension, his being seated at the Father's right hand, and his coming again. These events or activities reverse the steps taken in his humiliation (primarily his experiencing birth, death, burial, and the power of death), which we considered in the previous chapter.

In his humiliation Jesus was born as a man; in his exaltation he ascended to heaven. In humiliation he suffered and endured God's wrath as penalty for our sin; in exaltation he is now seated at the right hand of his Father. In his humiliation he was buried; in exaltation he was resurrected. In his humiliation he bore the curse of sin by enduring death for awhile; in his exaltation he will come again to judge the world.

Resurrected

The apostles proclaim Christ's resurrection in terms that hardly need interpreting. His rising from the dead was literal, not figurative. His body came out of the tomb in which it had been buried, and the risen Christ talked with his disciples, ate with them, and let them handle him.

Alexander Whyte mentions four ways in which Paul deals with the fact of Jesus' resurrection:

> First, the resurrection is spoken of as an outward fact, of which there were many witnesses. Secondly, as an idea or doctrine, forming a part also, or aspect of, the inner life of the gospel. Thirdly, as the figure, or condition, almost the cause, of the resurrection of believers, which is identified with the resurrection of Christ as the Christian himself is with Christ. Fourthly, as the figure, or condition, or principle of spiritual resurrection.[1]

No truth is more essential to the gospel than the Resurrection. "And if Christ has not been raised," Paul explains, "our preaching is useless and so is your faith. More than that, we are then found to be false witnesses about God, for we have testified about God that he raised Christ from the dead. . . . And if Christ has not been raised, your faith is futile; you are still in your sins."[2] The literal, bodily resurrection of Jesus Christ is the heart of the gospel. Without it there is no gospel.

Ascended

Christ's ascension is described in two of the Gospels and in Acts. Mark says that "After the Lord Jesus had spoken to them, he was taken up into heaven and he sat at the right hand of God."[3] Luke says simply that "while he was blessing them, he left them and was taken up into heaven."[4] In Acts, which was also written by Luke, we read that Jesus "was taken up before their very eyes, and a cloud hid him from their sight."[5] The disciples kept looking up, gazing at the sky, as if to keep him in view as long as possible. His departure was, among other things, E. A. Litton points out, "an infringement on the law of gravity."[6] No one who accepts the reliability and authority of Scripture can question the reality of Christ's ascension.

The disciples should not have been surprised by the Ascension. Jesus had told them he would go back to heaven: "I came from the Father and entered the world; now I am leaving the world and going back to the Father."[7] In the same discourse in which that statement appears, the Lord linked his departure with the coming of the Holy Spirit.

What is the significance of the Ascension? For one thing, without it Christ could not have fulfilled his promise to be with us. Before leaving the disciples he said,

> All authority in heaven and on earth has been given to me. Therefore go and make disciples of all nations, baptizing them in the name of the Father and of the Son and of the Holy Spirit, and teaching them to obey everything I have commanded you. And surely I will be with you always, to the very end of the age.[8]

If Christ had not ascended, he could not have fulfilled that promise. Even in his resurrected body, he could not have been with all his people at every moment. He could only have been one place at a time.

The Ascension also enabled Christ to give gifts to his Church, the point Paul makes in a fascinating passage in Ephesians 4. Paul quotes a line or two from Psalm 68, which says, "When you ascended on high, you led captives in your train; you received gifts from men."[9] Before Christ ascended, no one really knew what the Psalm meant. Interpreting that Psalm, Paul says:

> (What does "he ascended" mean except that he also descended to the lower, earthly regions? He who descended is the very one who ascended higher than all the heavens, in order to fill the whole universe.) It was he who gave some to be apostles, some to be prophets, some to be evangelists, and some to be pastors and teachers, to prepare God's people for works of service, so that the body of Christ may be built up.[10]

Paul makes it clear that the Ascension was required for the building up of the Church.

Several passages in Hebrews link Christ's ascension and his present work as a priest:

> Therefore, since we have a great high priest who has gone through the heavens, Jesus the Son of God, let us hold firmly to the faith we profess.[11]
>
> [Heaven is] where Jesus, who went before us, has entered on our behalf. He has become a high priest forever, in the order of Melchizedek.[12]
>
> Such a high priest meets our need—one who is holy, blameless, pure, set apart from sinners, exalted above the heavens.[13]
>
> Christ . . . entered heaven itself, now to appear for us in God's presence.[14]

Seated at His Father's Right Hand

The New Testament speaks numerous times of the ascended Christ sitting at the right hand of God the Father.[15] As Calvin explains, Christ

> is installed in the government of heaven and earth, and formally admitted to possession of the administration committed to Him, and not only admitted for once, but to continue until He

> descend to judgment. . . . All that the apostles intend, when they so often mention His seat at the Father's right hand, is to teach that everything is placed at His disposal.[16]

Christ not only is risen from the dead, he is the ascended Lord who is now very busy in heaven on our behalf. What is he doing in heaven? Following are some of the things he did either immediately after returning to heaven or is now doing: first, he sent the Holy Spirit into the world on the day of Pentecost; second, he added disciples to the Church, and is still adding them; third, he accompanied the apostles as they went forth preaching, and he still works with his servants in their work for him; fourth, just as he healed a lame man, there is ample reason to believe he still heals miraculously when it pleases him to do so; fifth, he stood up to receive the first martyr, Stephen; sixth, he appeared to Saul of Tarsus.

Those activities are all mentioned in the Book of Acts. Two of them—namely, the sending of the Holy Spirit at Pentecost and the appearing to Saul of Tarsus—were done once for all. The rest were probably the first instances of postresurrection activities in which he is still engaged.[17]

That is not a complete list of his activities at the Father's right hand. The New Testament notes other things, most of which may be subsumed under his priestly duties, which were touched on in the discussion of the Ascension.

One of Christ's most important present heavenly works on our behalf is his advocacy. "My dear children," John writes, "I write this to you so that you will not sin. But if anybody does sin, we have one who speaks to the Father in our defense—Jesus Christ, the Righteous One."[18] Christ is not just *there* at his Father's right hand; he is there *on our behalf*. As an outstanding theologian has written, "We can well be content with the thought that He is there, and that His presence with the Father is the secret of our peace, the assurance of our access, and the guarantee of our permanent relation with God."[19]

Coming Again

The fourth aspect of Christ's exaltation, his coming again, will involve two distinct works: his coming to bless and his coming to judge.

The New Testament teaches a great deal about the return of Christ, and in such a way that its importance cannot be overstated. By comparison, church ordinances are treated almost casually. Baptism, for example, is mentioned nineteen times in seven of the epistles, and in fourteen epistles is not mentioned at all. The Lord's Supper (or Communion) is dealt with in only one of the twenty-one epistles. The Second Coming, on the other hand, is mentioned more than three hundred times—working out to one verse in every thirteen in the entire New Testament, or one in every ten verses in the epistles. Unfortunately, in our treatment here we can only take notice of a few of those many passages.

Coming to Bless In John 14:3 Jesus said, "And if I go and prepare a place for you, I will come back and take you to be with me that you also may be where I am." At the Ascension, as they stood by to reassure the grieving disciples, the two angels said, "Men of Galilee, why do you stand here looking into the sky? This same Jesus, who has been taken from you into heaven, will come back in the same way you have seen him go into heaven."[20]

Inevitably the apostles taught Christians in the early church to wait for God's Son from heaven.[21] The expectation of his return became (and still is) "the blessed hope" of faithful Christians.[22] His coming will be "the climax and culmination of His work of redemption, when the Body of Christ, the Church, will be completed, and the Lord will usher in that Kingdom which will eventually result in God being all in all (Ephesians 1:14; Romans 8:19-23; 1 Corinthians 15:23-28)."[23]

Coming to Judge The New Testament distinguishes several future judgments. First, there will be a judgment of the life and work of each believer. Our Lord assures us that, having received him, we shall never be condemned for our sins.[24] Paul reiterates that truth in his letter to Rome: "There is now no condemnation for those who are in Christ Jesus."[25] But our lives as Christians—meaning the service we render him—will be evaluated at the judgment-seat of Christ. Though we will not suffer loss of salvation, we may suffer loss of reward.[26]

The second and third future judgments respectively will fall on the nation of Israel and the other nations that emerge from the Great Tribulation. Key passages that deal with those judgments are Ezekiel 20:33-44 in the Old Testament and Matthew 24, 25 in the New.

The final judgment is described in Revelation 20:11-15 and is usually termed the judgment of the Great White Throne. The description in Revelation 20 is one of the most frightening passages in the Bible. It speaks of God's final dealing with the wicked of all history. Everyone who appears at that judgment is eternally lost. Evidently the objective of the judgment is to pronounce a verdict on each person, according to the degree of his or her personal wickedness. It is a frightening passage, and unutterably sad.

The Great White Throne judgment is also tragic, because no one need appear there. Jesus came into the world to seek and to save the lost, not to condemn them. After telling his listeners that the Father had committed all judgment to the Son—that is, to Jesus himself—Jesus said, "I tell you the truth, whoever hears my word and believes him who sent me has eternal life and will not be condemned; he has crossed over from death to life."[27]

The Judge himself made that offer! So if a person is eternally lost, whose fault will it be? Clearly not God's. He wanted (and still wants) to save, not condemn.

Scripture states categorically that God will punish evil. Paul says that God "has set a day when he will judge the world with justice."[28] God's holiness demands an accounting for offenses against it. "But if our unrighteousness brings out God's righteousness more clearly," Paul says in another place, "what shall we say? That God is unjust in bringing his wrath on us? (I am using a human argument.) Certainly not! If that were so, how could God judge the world?"[29]

In that verse Paul assumes the necessity of divine judgment of the world. In another passage he says:

> All this is evidence that God's judgment is right. . . . God is just: He will pay back trouble to those who trouble you. . . . He will punish those who do not know God and do not obey the gospel of our Lord Jesus. They will be punished with everlasting destruction and shut out from the presence of the Lord and from the majesty of his power.[30]

Those are frightening passages; they unmistakably set forth the truth that God not only will judge the world, but that his nature requires it. It is only just that he exercise judgment. The prospect of judgment settles the mind that is troubled by the presence of apparently unpunished sin in the world. Crooks and killers and tyrants do not really get away with it.

Yet, for all who put their trust in Christ the menace is gone. For them there will be no condemnation. That is the promise of the Lord himself.

24

The Holy Spirit's Work in Redemption

The salvation that was secured for us by Jesus Christ is now administered in and through us by his Holy Spirit. Believers are living evidence of the Spirit's work. The following passage from Paul's Epistle to Titus is so plain that it needs no explanation:

> It was not because of any good works that we ourselves had done, but because of his own mercy that he saved us through the washing by which the Holy Spirit gives us new birth and new life. God abundantly poured out the Holy Spirit on us, through Jesus Christ our Savior, that by his grace we might be made right with God and come into possession of the eternal life we hope for.[1]

Technically the terms *salvation* and *redemption* are distinct, redemption being one of several aspects of salvation. Often, however, they are used interchangeably, and that is how we are using them here. They are two ways of describing the same work of Christ, who is called in Scripture both Savior and Redeemer. Salvation implies lostness, whereas redemption implies bondage.

A redeemer redeems out of bondage, not by intrigue or force, but by payment. The verb *redeem* means to regain possession by repurchase or by payment of what is due. That is the idea set forth in Scripture. Fallen mankind is shown as being in a state of bondage. Salvation requires redemption out of that bondage. Hence, our Lord said that he, the Son of Man, came "to give his life as a ransom for many."[2] Nothing less than his life could ransom—that is, redeem—enslaved mankind. God wants us to remember that fact. Says Paul, "You are not your own; you were bought at a price. Therefore honor God with your body."[3] The apostle does not indicate the nature of the price; he assumes that his readers know what the price was. Peter, on the other hand, draws attention to the price: "For you know that it was not with perishable things such as silver or gold . . . but with the precious blood of Christ, a lamb without blemish or defect."[4]

The redemption of mankind did not come cheap; it cost the precious blood of Christ. It costs the redeemed nothing, but it cost the Redeemer everything. He purchased our redemption with his own blood. The Lord wants us to remember that wonderful but sobering truth whenever we are tempted to live carelessly or godlessly.

How is Christ's work of redemption made effective for the salvation of the lost? Salvation has been provided by Christ's atoning sacrifice. The question is, how does it come to us? Has God simply declared that everyone is saved, so that we need not worry about it; or is salvation granted to some and not to others; and if so, on what basis?

The Holy Spirit of God applies Christ's work to us individually as we trust in what Christ has done. As Paul says, "[God] saved us, not because of righteous things we had done, but because of his mercy. He saved us through the washing of rebirth and renewal by the Holy Spirit, whom he poured out on us generously through Jesus Christ our Savior."[5] Salvation is entirely God's work. The Father sent the Son, the Son provided a righteous basis for salvation, and the Holy Spirit makes the saving work effective in all who believe the gospel.

Could we have become a Christian without help? To put the same question differently, before we became a believer did we have within ourselves an innate, natural desire to seek the Lord and find him? Or did we need help from the Holy Spirit of God even to believe in Christ?

The question has aroused controversy for many centuries. Following are brief summaries of the two major attempts across the centuries to answer the question. They are given here in their extreme forms.

At one end of the spectrum, some interpreters believe that no one needs supernatural help to find God. Having been made in the image of God, man aspires Godward. These people make much of the freedom of the will. We often speak loosely of choosing according to our own free will. But as used theologically, the concept of the freedom of the will is a technical one. It implies that the choices people make are not imposed upon them either by inner or divine necessity.

It seems as if that would be nice if it were true. But it is not. That sort of freedom of the human will is an illusion. With the rest of human nature, the human will is also flawed by sin. Says Jeremiah, using "the heart" to stand for the whole of human nature, "The heart is deceitful above all things and beyond cure."[6] Paul says, "I know that nothing good lives in me, that is, in my sinful nature."[7] Hence, the choices we make are influenced by indwelling sin. How then can they be truly free?

At the other end of the spectrum are thinkers who say that God does everything that must be done for salvation. In their view, sinners are so seriously affected by sin that they can neither take the initiative, nor respond to divine initiative. Hence, God must *compel* them to believe. He approaches sinners whom he chooses with irresistible grace.

There are also serious problems with that view. First, it ignores biblical teaching about human response to the Word of God. If you read the Bible inductively, you will probably conclude that whatever limitations sin may impose on the freedom of the will, people are free to accept or reject God's offer of mercy. In spite of sin, *some* freedom remains. Second, that view raises serious questions about the moral nature of God. Proponents often answer questions about the moral implications of their view by quoting Romans 9:20—"But who are you, O man, to talk back to God?" No sane person argues with God; the argument is with people who presume to speak for God. I do not question anything God says or does; but I do question *theories,* including my own, *about* what he says or does.

According to the first extreme view mentioned above, man enjoys perfect freedom of the will. According to the second, he is so totally depraved that he must be compelled to respond to the gospel. Neither position does justice to the Bible.

Two better views are those held respectively by Arminians and Calvinists. These positions differ in that Arminians hold that through what they call common grace, sinful people can respond to the message of the gospel. Calvinists, on the other hand, hold that without initial help from the Holy Spirit, no one can respond to the gospel. Arminians and Calvinists agree that the work of the Holy Spirit is necessary. Without the Holy Spirit, there is neither regeneration nor the power for a holy life. Where they disagree is on the point at which the Holy Spirit's help becomes necessary. I have oversimplified the two positions, but that is their essential distinction.

As far as what is required of us, however, the process is not terribly important. Believing in Jesus Christ is all that we *can* do and all that we *must* do for salvation. If we are Christians, we have already done that. If we are not believers in Christ and want to become such, we need not ask where the desire comes from. All we have to do is believe. Because God has told us to believe, we know that we *can* believe. "Believe in the Lord Jesus, and you will be saved."[8] In different words, that call is given many times in the New Testament.

The Agent of Salvation

All that we must believe (and in this nearly all thoughtful Christians agree) is that at some point the Holy Spirit of God gives whatever help is necessary in order for a lost soul to be saved. Apart from his gracious work, none of us would, or could, have the experience of regeneration or the power for a holy life.

The Holy Spirit, the third Person of the Godhead, is the agent of salvation. The Father sent the Son, and the Son, by his obedience to the Father in offering himself as a sacrifice, made salvation possible. The Holy Spirit applies that work to those who believe. Therefore, no one can be saved apart from the work of the Holy Spirit of God. All of the Trinity is involved in the redemption of the world.

But how does the Holy Spirit apply redemption to those who are saved? His activity involves his working faith in us and his uniting us in Christ.

He Works in Us First, what is the scriptural basis for the Holy Spirit's work of faith in us? Theologians usually quote Genesis 6:3—"My Spirit will not contend with man forever," which implies that the Spirit deals with men and women at some time in each person's lifetime. A second passage is John 16:8-11, which reads:

> When he comes, he will convict the world of guilt in regard to sin and righteousness and judgment; in regard to sin, because men do not believe in me; in regard to righteousness, because I am going to the Father, where you can see me no longer; and in regard to judgment, because the prince of this world now stands condemned.

A third passage is 2 Corinthians 4:13. "It is written: 'I believed; therefore I have spoken.' With that same spirit of faith we also believe and therefore speak."

None of those texts states explicitly that the Holy Spirit works faith in us. In the third text, it is not even certain that the word *spirit* should be capitalized, in that way standing for the Spirit of God. Then why the contention that the Holy Spirit works faith in us?

There are two possible explanations. First is the assumption that human nature is too depraved to believe in God unless God himself helps. Second, and much more importantly, are the many Scripture texts that teach that the Holy Spirit is clearly active in the regeneration of a human soul. The Holy Spirit activates in us the faith that begins the whole process.

It is difficult to determine the extent of the purely human response, but that the Holy Spirit is involved from the beginning is also evident from numerous other Scripture passages. Paul tells us that "No one who is speaking by the Spirit of God says, 'Jesus be cursed,' and no one can say, 'Jesus is Lord,' except by the Holy Spirit,"[9] and that "we know that he has chosen you, because our gospel came to you not simply with words, but also with power, with the Holy Spirit and with deep conviction."[10] Luke reports that "Lydia . . . was a worshiper of God. The Lord opened her heart to respond to Paul's message."[11]

He Unites Us with Christ Following his working faith in us, the Spirit unites us with Christ. When the Holy Spirit unites us with Christ, we are from that moment said to be "in Christ"[12] and Christ is said to be "in" us.[13] In uniting us with Christ, the Holy Spirit regenerates us, and he also becomes the seal or pledge of our salvation. "[God] saved us through the washing of rebirth and renewal by the Holy Spirit, whom he poured out on us generously through Jesus Christ our Savior."[14] In his letter to Ephesus Paul describes the same basic truth, giving us the sequence of the Spirit's activities: "You also were included in Christ when you heard the word of truth, the gospel of your salvation. Having believed, you were marked in him with a seal, the promised Holy Spirit, who is a deposit guaranteeing our inheritance until the redemption of those who are God's possession—to the praise of his glory."[15]

First, we must hear the gospel; second, we must believe it. When we believe, at that moment we are (1) included in Christ—

which is one way of saying united to Christ, and (2) we are given the Holy Spirit as a seal or pledge guaranteeing all that God has for us—namely, completed redemption.

It is the Holy Spirit who unites us to Christ. He is the divine agent of "the washing of rebirth." When he unites us with Christ, he also becomes part of us. We are marked with a seal, the promised Holy Spirit, who is a deposit guaranteeing our inheritance until everything is finally and fully realized in heaven.

John 15 and Romans 6 are important passages that set forth the fact of our union with Christ. Many others state or imply the same truth. Christ himself tells us that as believers we are in him, and he is in us. The relationship is as vital as the connection between a vine and its branches[16] or a body and its various members.[17]

In Romans 6 Paul makes our union with Christ the basis of an appeal for us to live as Christians—that is, to model our lives after Christ's. We are accustomed to think of Christ's death on our behalf, that he died *for* us. In Romans 6, Paul teaches us to think also of ourselves as having died *with him*. That is one of the implications of union with Christ. That truth has very practical implications, as I. Howard Marshall explains:

> [Christ's] death can be described as a death to sin, or a death as far as the power of sin is concerned. When Jesus died, he passed out of the sphere in which sin can exercise dominion over men, . . . since sin can exercise no claims over a dead man, and temptation can no longer entice the person who is dead to its attractions.[18]

Christ's death is viewed as if it were also ours. Marshall explains the implications of Paul's point:

> Paul goes on to teach that the Christian may be said to have died with Christ—a fact that he possibly saw illustrated in the symbolism of 'burial' in baptism by immersion. . . . When this happens, the believer need no longer be under the power of sin (Rom. 6:3, 6, 7). His old selfish nature, which was the base of operations of sin, has been crucified with Christ, and he no longer needs to obey it.[19]

We begin to see the practical significance of union with Christ. Thinking about our union with him—in his death and in his resurrection and in his life as the ascended Lord—to the extent that we take it seriously, we are enabled to win victories over the power of sin. Someday—when we enter the presence of God—we will be completely victorious over sin. Meanwhile, having the prospect in mind, and knowing that even now we are linked with Christ—as vitally linked as branches to the vine or limbs to the body—we have strong incentive to live purely and righteously in this present evil age.

He Calls Us Effectively

It is obvious that when the gospel is preached, reaction to it is not uniform. Some believe the message, whereas others—throughout history the majority—do not believe. Why? Only two explanations are possible: either those who hear are themselves fundamentally different, or the message is charged with supernatural power in some cases. Theologians who use the expression "effectual calling" choose the second of those alternatives; in their view, a positive response to the message is evidence of a special working of divine grace accompanying the preaching of the Word. In other words, God overcomes the natural inclination of some to disregard the message. This special outpouring of grace—over and above so-called "common grace" available to all men—is, in the thinking of those theologians, the "effectual calling."

In support of their position, they quote passage such as "[God] . . . has saved us and called us to a holy life—not because of anything we have done but because of his own purpsoe and grace,"[20] and "From the beginning God chose you to be saved through the sanctifying work of the Spirit and through belief in the truth. He called you to this through our gospel, that you might share in the glory of our Lord Jesus Christ."[21]

We need not drag into our treatment the age-old questions about the apparent conflict between man's free will and divine election, which already has been discussed briefly. The Bible does not talk about nonelected people, and there is no reason to think that anyone who has ever lived could not have believed, or if now living cannot now believe. The Holy Spirit is in the world, convicting *the world* of sin and of righteousness and of judgment to come.[22]

The Holy Spirit wants to lead everyone to Christ. If a person does not come, whose fault can it be? Neither that person nor anyone else can blame God or say that the Holy Spirit did not accompany the message with power. If a person does not come to Christ, the indictment leveled against the ancient people of Israel applies equally to him. "Let us be careful that none of you be found to have fallen short of [God's rest]. For we also have had the gospel preached to us, just as they did; but the message they heard was of no value to them, because those who heard did not combine it with faith."[23]

The writer does not ask God to combine the message with an extra measure of grace; he asks the would-be-believer to combine it with faith. If the call does not bring a positive response, no one can charge God with an ineffective calling.

In order to persuade us to want to believe, and then enable us to believe, the Holy Spirit must first convict us of our sin and need, then enlighten our minds, and finally renew our wills.

He Convicts Us of Sin What we think about our sinfulness and our need for salvation will obviously determine whether we come to Christ in faith or turn from him in unbelief. A person who sees no sin in his life will see no need for help and therefore no need for salvation. As Alexander Whyte comments,

> The Holy Ghost . . . frames an indictment, and carries a conviction in their consciences against sinners. . . . if He is to enter our hearts effectually as the Spirit of grace and salvation, he must begin his work in truth. And the first stage of his work is finished when our mouth is shut under a sense of guilt and shame.[24]

He Enlightens Our Minds The second aspect of the Spirit's effective calling of persons to Christ is his work of convincing or persuading. The mind must know and be persuaded of the truth of the gospel, and the will must be persuaded to trust in it.

In a dialogue with some men who were challenging his authority, Christ made a remarkable connection between the mind and the will. "If anyone chooses to do God's will," he said, "he will find out whether my teaching comes from God or whether I speak on my own."[25] Jesus seems to say that right spiritual knowledge proceeds from a right will.

That an unconverted mind needs to be enlightened is clear from several texts in the New Testament. For example, Jesus said, "For judgment I have come into this world, so that the blind will see."[26] Paul said, "If our gospel is veiled, it is veiled to those who are perishing. The god of this age has blinded the minds of unbelievers, so that they cannot see the light of the gospel of the glory of Christ, who is the image of God."[27]

Paul also says that the Gentiles of his times were "darkened in their understanding and separated from the life of God because of the ignorance that is in them due to the hardening of their hearts."[28] These and other texts support Whyte's statement:

> Darkness and light are terms which continually occur to describe a state of nature and a state of grace in the Scriptures. Heathenism is a life of darkness; Judaism, if not darkness, has its eyes under a dense veil; while an unregenerate state in Jew and Gentile is slavery in a kingdom of darkness. Believers alone are children of light and of the day. They are light in the Lord. Nay, they are the light of the world.[29]

But how does the Holy Spirit enlighten darkened minds? Paul describes unbelieving Gentiles as "darkened in their understanding . . . because of the ignorance that is in them."[30] We see the connection between ignorance and darkness. Spiritual ignorance *is* spiritual darkness. Spiritual knowledge, on the other hand, brings light. Therefore, to enlighten our darkened minds, the Holy Spirit brings us the knowledge of Christ.

The Holy Spirit bring us the knowledge of Christ in two ways: first, through the written Word of God, and second by bringing his influence to bear on our minds. That is precisely the way in which the Holy Spirit achieves the earlier step of convincing and convicting us of sin. Says Paul, "Through the law we become conscious of sin."[31] The law, as used here, is the Old Testament, specifically the parts, such as the Ten Commandments, that deal with conduct.[32] The written Word reveals God's truth. The Holy Spirit brings his influence to bear on a person's mind, so that one responds to the written Word, acknowledging his sin and guilt before God.

In Romans 7 Paul describes his personal response to the law's convicting power. His response was prompted by the Holy Spirit, as the next chapter reveals. That is how the Holy Spirit enlightens minds in the knowledge of Christ. As Paul explains, "Faith comes from hearing the message, and the message is heard through the word of Christ."[33] In another place, the apostle says virtually the same thing, but he gives additional information about what may be termed the process of enlightenment. "And you also were included in Christ when you heard the word of truth, the gospel of your salvation. Having believed, you were marked in him with a seal, the promised Holy Spirit."[34]

We see what happens. First, the message is preached or is read in the Bible. Whether listening or reading, we hear the message. It comes to us, as Paul tells his friends in Thessalonica, not in word only, but also "with power, with the Holy Spirit and with deep conviction."[35] Thus, in some cases at least, conviction and enlightenment in the knowledge of Christ are simultaneous. In every case they result from a combination of two things: exposure to the Word of God and the power of the Holy Spirit of God.

If a person is not yet a believer, talk about the Holy Spirit is of no interest to him, except perhaps as a source of encouragement. But if one finds it hard to believe the gospel, he should ask God to help. He will send his Holy Spirit to bring conviction of sin *and* enlightenment. The Spirit will make the knowledge of Christ a personal thing in that person's life.

He Guides Our Wills The third of the three works or operations of the Holy Spirit in effectively calling people to Christ Jesus is that of his guiding the will. The fact that our wills need guidance and assistance—or as some theologians term it, renewal—implies that the will is not capable in itself of deciding as it should. At the Fall the human will, along with every other aspect of man's nature, was corrupted. As one theologian explains:

> Sin is defiance, revolt, and implies a deliberate, voluntary breaking away from the Divine will and a violation of the Divine order. . . . sin at its deepest is the rejection of God and disobedience to His will. . . . Man's self-will has been exercised in opposition to the will of his Creator, and this constitutes the Fall, the marring of God's creative work and the thwarting of His Divine purpose. . . . [man] has fallen from a primeval condition of innocence by reason of his self-will.[36]

Man's self-will is now, by nature, opposed to God's will. It may be said that the self-will which led to the original act of disobedience was in itself sin, and self-will is also an effect of disobedience. Self-will, therefore, is both the cause and an effect of the Fall. Man's will, with every other part of his being, has been seriously damaged by that initial act of self-will.

Another theologian helpfully comments:

> All the parts of man's nature have suffered each their own peculiar injury by the catastrophe of the Fall, but it is those parts that have more immediately to do with God and His revealed will that have suffered most. And no part has suffered such a shock and hurt as the will. It is now by nature and in every unregenerate man turned away from God, and in bondage to sin and evil.[37]

That is the plight of man's natural will—fallen and in bondage to sin and evil. The bondage of the will means, as Whyte says further, that "It is not that man would do good, would return to God if he could; it is not that he cannot; he *will not*."[38]

Only the Holy Spirit can renew the will, which *must* be renewed if man is going to return to God and serve him. What keeps a person at a distance from God if not his will? "You refuse to come to me to have life," Jesus told some of his opponents.[39] That is the explanation, from the lips of the Savior himself, of all unbelief.

Obviously a renewed will is not returned to its state before the Fall. If Adam sinned through self-will, why think that a person today with a will of the same sort would not repeat the sin? Philippians 2:13 says, "For it is God who works in you to will and to act according to his good purpose," asserting clearly that God *enables* regenerate people to will and to do what is right.

The Westminster Confession of Faith gives two helpful paragraphs on the will. The first is:

> When God converts a sinner, and translates him into the state of grace, he frees him from his natural bondage under sin, and by his grace alone enables him freely to will and to do that which is spiritually good; yet so as that, by reason of his remaining corruption, he does not perfectly nor only will that which is good, but does also that which is evil.[40]

Yet, even after we are saved we are still sinful, and therefore we can still will to do what is evil. Romans 7 elaborates on this truth: "I find this law at work," Paul says. "When I want to do good, evil is right there with me."[41]

How long will this sad state continue? A second quotation from the Westminster Confession says, "The will of man is made perfectly and immutably free to do good alone in the state of glory only."[42]

Only in heaven will we be totally free from sin, no longer under its dominion or in its presence. Only in heaven, therefore, will there be no possibility of choosing evil. Having willed by choosing Christ to be where no evil exists, we shall finally reach a state in which it is no longer possible to sin. As a theologian in the nineteenth century said, "[A Christian in heaven] cannot look upon sin, for he looks only on Him in whom is no sin; he cannot will to do evil, for he has willed that evil be shut out forever."[43] Just thinking about it should make us long for the day!

God's gracious Spirit is at work in the world, convincing of sin and need, enlightening minds in the knowledge of Christ, and renewing wills. Even in the ancient Roman Empire there were those who sought the Lord. Paul's first convert was a woman described as "a worshiper of God." When she heard Paul's message, she believed. Why? Because the God whom she imperfectly worshiped opened her heart by his Spirit. He had acted on her heart before Paul's arrival, and he continued to act on it while Paul was preaching.[44]

The Spirit's objective is to persuade and enable men, women, and children to embrace Jesus Christ, to cling to him in faith. The Holy Spirit of truth bears witness of Christ, as Jesus said he would, in order to bring people to the Lord as believers.[45]

The Spirit does not restrict his work to a select few. He is convincing *the world*—to the extent that the world is willing to be convinced or convicted. As Charles Hodge says,

> The gospel call is universal in the sense that it is addressed to all men indiscriminately to whom the gospel is sent. . . . If therefore anyone holds any view of the decrees of God, or of the satisfaction of Christ, or of any other scriptural doctrine, which hampers him in making the general offer of the gospel, he may be sure that his views or his logical processes are wrong. The apostles were not thus hampered, and we act under the commission given to them.[46]

Jesus Christ freely offers the gospel. Those are lovely words. How reassuring to know that the Spirit of Christ is here, working to persuade men to believe that Jesus is the Christ and, in believing, to have life in his name.

25

Justification

What is justification? We often use the word in ordinary conversation. Suppose I go to an auto show and am carried away with desire for a new car. I do not need a new car; the one I have runs well and looks more or less decent. But I want a new one. My argument in defense of trading in the old car on a new one is my "justification" for buying a new car. What my wife may term a silly excuse, I term justification.

Legally the word has a slightly different meaning. It means to be found without offense or to be cleared of charges. You know the story of Captain Alfred Dreyfus, a French Jew whose fellow military officers framed him and sent him to Devil's Island. Under pressure from people like Emile Zola, the French government pardoned Dreyfus. To the government's amazement, Captain Dreyfus was outraged by the pardon and refused to take it. He demanded exoneration, which he eventually received. To have accepted a pardon would have been to admit guilt. Dreyfus wanted to be declared innocent, to be justified.

That is much closer to the theological meaning of the word. My desk dictionary gives a rather good theological definition of justification: "being accepted by or made acceptable to God, as righteous or worthy of salvation—chiefly in phrases giving grounds of such acceptance, as justification by faith."[1] That definition is accurate and concise.

Before we go further, it might be well to establish what justification is not. It is not a state of righteousness. A justified person is essentially no more righteous than before conversion. But he is *declared* to be righteous. And since it is God who declares it, the declaration is as good as the fact. Justification is an act of God, by which he pardons all our sins.

When we are justified, we are accepted by God. He accepts us willingly and gladly, not grudgingly, as if his love overcame his holiness but left him uneasy, so to speak. We know he accepts us cheerfully, because he himself has made us acceptable in his sight—not slightly acceptable, but so overwhelmingly acceptable that he regards us as justified. Because of faith in Jesus Christ, we are justified, which means that we have been cleared of all charges against us. God himself can no longer find anything objectionable in us.

A Christian who claims to be justified is not boasting; instead, he is simply recognizing what God has done for him. He is also saying that God's action was prompted by free grace. What is free grace? The least that can be said about it is that it is God's disposition to do something for us apart from our having earned it or being worthy of it. Paul says that God justifies the ungodly—not ungodly people who struggle to improve themselves and having improved themselves may then be counted worthy, but ungodly people whose only contribution to their justification is belief in Jesus Christ. Says Paul, "to the man who does not work but trusts God who justifies the wicked, his faith is credited as righteousness."[2]

God knows that even though we are believers in his Son, we are still sinful. Nevertheless, in his free grace he has pardoned all our sins, and we are immeasurably blessed. As David says, "Blessed [that is, favored and happy] are they whose transgressions are forgiven, whose sins are covered. Blessed is the man whose sin the Lord will never count against him."[3]

The beautiful hymn "Accepted in the Beloved" reminds us:

In the Beloved, accepted am I,
  Risen, ascended, and seated on high;
Saved from all sin through his infinite grace,
  With the redeemed ones accorded a place.

In the Beloved, I went to the tree,
  There, in His Person, by faith I may see
Infinite wrath rolling over His head,
  Infinite grace, for He died in my stead.[4]

The "Beloved" is, of course, our Lord Jesus Christ. The hymn echoes two verses in Ephesians 1, where we read that God has made us "accepted in the beloved, in whom we have redemption through his blood, the forgiveness of sins, according to the riches of his grace" (vv. 6, 7, KJV). The last few words in the refrain of the hymn make the meaning very clear: "God sees my Savior and then He sees me, 'In the Beloved,' accepted and free."

In Christ, God accepts us as righteous in his sight. How can he do it? Is he not a holy God, and are we not sinful? Yes to both questions. He accepts us because through faith we are "in Christ." We may not *feel* intimately related to Christ, but the relationship exists. Once we turn to him in faith, we enter into a relationship thicker than blood. We are *in Christ.* As such, we are accepted by God.

Justification is an act of God wherein he does two things: he pardons all our sins, and he accepts us. But how can he do that without violating his own holiness and justice? As we have discussed previously, he does it because of the sacrifice of his perfect, sinless Son, Jesus Christ. Because Christ died for us—that is, in our place—God cannot demand payment from us.

God accepts us as righteous *because of Christ's work on our behalf.* In doing so, he declares us to be righteous; he credits or imputes righteousness to us.[5] Justification is an act of God in which he pardons our sins and accepts us as righteous. He does so by crediting us with the values of Christ's death. His righteousness is imputed to us; it is credited to our account. That does not mean that we are actually holy as God is holy; it does mean that having been cleared of all charges by virtue of our blessed substitute's death, we are now regarded as righteous.

In the sixteenth century Martin Luther and his followers proclaimed the truth that salvation is not at all by works but completely by faith. That stand aroused a great deal of opposition because then, as now, there were people who refused to believe that salvation is free. They wanted to work for it. They wanted to earn merit of some kind. Consequently they taunted Luther and his friends, calling them *solifidians,* a Latin term that could be literally translated as "faith-alone-ians."[6] Luther did not mind; in fact, he gloried in the name, since the Bible plainly declares that salvation is by faith alone, not by faith plus works.

In Ephesians Paul declares, "For it is by grace you have been saved, through faith—and this is not from yourselves, it is the gift of God—not by works, so that no one can boast."[7] In Romans he gives the truth just as plainly: "Now when a man works, his wages are not credited to him as a gift, but as an obligation. However, to the man who does not work but trusts God who justifies the wicked, his faith is credited as righteousness."[8] Salvation cannot be earned by good works; it is given to those who believe. We see why Luther insisted on faith alone, not faith plus good works as the way to be saved.

Salvation is not for sale; it is God's gift. A gift cannot be earned; it can only be accepted or rejected. Accepting the gift is an act of faith; it expresses confidence in the giver, especially when the giver does not force it on you but simply offers it. God offers salvation freely. All those who believe that he means what he says will receive what he offers. Their faith, Paul says, is credited as righteousness—which means that they now stand before God as acceptable, as justified.

A certain type of human perversity enables men, or drives them, to twist the Word of God. The Bible teaches plainly that salvation is by grace, which means it is given freely, without price or the need to offer anything to God. We have referred to passages in Romans 4 and Ephesians 2 that make this truth unmistakably clear. Another important text is Galatians 2:16—"So we, too, have put our faith in Christ Jesus that we may be justified by faith in Christ and not by observing the law, because by observing the law no one will be justified." We are justified by faith alone—not by works, and not by faith plus works or by works plus faith.

People react in different ways to this great truth. Some try to turn the grace of God into license. They reason that if salvation is free, they can sin all they want and then return for forgiveness any time they please. But both the logic and the motivation of such thinking are perverted, and Paul says that the condemnation of such people is just.[9] Others are offended by the truth of justification by faith alone. They fear it ignores Scriptures calling for obedience to the will of God. They fear it conflicts with such texts as the following from the Epistle of James: "What good is it, my brothers, if a man claims to have faith but has no deeds? Can such faith save him?"[10]

That is a vital question, the answer to which is no—that sort of faith cannot save him, because it is not genuine faith. Says James, "Faith, if it is not accompanied by action, is dead." It is that kind of faith, dead faith, faith that does not carry a commitment, that prompts James to say that "a person is justified by what he does, and not by faith alone."[11] So we see that there is no conflict between faith as Paul uses the word, and faith as James uses it. The conflict is between Paul and James on the one side and people who misunderstand or misuse the Bible on the other.

As the Reformers taught, genuine faith never exists without works, although it justifies without works.

26

Adoption

In the New Testament, only Paul speaks of adoption in a theological sense, and in only five places. Nevertheless, in those five places he sets forth a lovely doctrine. In Romans 8 he says, "For you did not receive a spirit that makes you a slave again to fear, but you received the Spirit of sonship. And by him we cry, '*Abba,* Father!' "[1] Some translations say, "a spirit of adoption," others "the Spirit who makes you sons." The Spirit of God makes us sons. That is the meaning of adoption. Later in the same chapter Paul says, "Not only so, but we ourselves, who have the firstfruits of the Spirit, groan inwardly as we wait eagerly for our adoption as sons, the redemption of our bodies."[2]

The second verse *seems* to contradict the first. In the second one adoption is not spoken of as the Spirit's work of having made us sons, but as something for which we are still waiting. But there is no contradiction. The second verse displays a completed, final aspect of adoption. We *are* the sons of God by faith, and we *are waiting,* as Paul explains, for the future manifestation of our adoption as sons—the redemption (that is, the resurrection and transformation) of our bodies. Meanwhile, we thank God that "in love He predestined us to be adopted as his sons through Jesus Christ."[3]

Those whom God adopts as sons are believers in Jesus Christ. As Paul says, "You also were included in Christ when you heard the word of truth, the gospel of your salvation. Having believed, you were marked in him with a seal, the promised Holy Spirit, who is a deposit guaranteeing our inheritance until the redemption of those who are God's possession—to the praise of his glory."[4]

As we saw in the last chapter, justification is an act of God's free grace in which he does something in our behalf. Similarly, adoption is an act of God's free grace in which he does something else in our behalf—he receives us into the ranks of the sons of God, and he confers on us all the privileges of the sons of God. That was stated as if it were two distinct acts, whereas actually it is one act. Adoption means placing us as sons of God, with all the privileges of divine sonship.

There is a distinction between regeneration, whereby we become children to God, and adoption, whereby we are placed as sons. We become children of God by the new birth; we become sons of God by adoption. The term *children,* which the Apostle John prefers, refers to our nature as born of God. The term *sons,* which Paul prefers, refers to our place and rights as sons of God.[5]

Two questions may come to mind. First, when does that transaction take place; and second, are there evidences that it has taken place? The answer to the first question is: at the moment of conversion, or the new birth. As Paul says, "You are all sons of God through faith in Christ Jesus."[6] Several transactions related to salvation take place simultaneously, not in series. But we can understand salvation more easily if we consider them separately.

The answer to the second question is found in Romans 8:14—"Those who are led by the Spirit of God are sons of God." It is not good enough to claim to belong to God unless there is some response to the Holy Spirit. He speaks to us in the Bible, and if we are God's sons, we will respond. If not, what right have we to the name Christian? And who will believe us if we say we are sons of God?

27

Sanctification

Sanctification is the noun form of "to sanctify," which means "to set apart to a sacred office or to religious use or observance; to hallow."[1] That definition agrees well with the Bible's use of the word. The word *hallow* is related to the word *holy*, and there is no basic difference in meaning between "to make holy" and "to sanctify," or between "holy" and "sanctified." The difference is in the origin of the English terms. *Sanctify* and its related words come to us through Latin, while *holy* and its related terms come through Anglo-Saxon.

Sanctification is an unusually complex subject in the Bible. It is also unusually important, as indicated by Paul's simple but forceful statement, "It is God's will that you should be holy."[2] God wants his people to be holy, and it is his plan to make us holy. In Christ, God has not left us on our own, but has claimed us for his own. He has marked us out as distinct from the rest of the world. That is what sanctification means. When we became Christians, we were dedicated to God in Christ Jesus and claimed by him as his own. In short, we were sanctified. That is when our sanctification began, but it is not when it ended.

Scripture speaks of two kinds—or, better, two aspects—of holiness or sanctification. They are commonly referred to as positional sanctification and practical sanctification.

Sanctification Is Positional

The root idea of *holy* and *sanctified* is "set apart." In the Old Testament persons and things alike were sanctified. Aaron's sons were sanctified, Mount Sinai was sanctified, the Tabernacle and Temple were sanctified, and often even houses and fields were sanctified.[3] Obviously none of those things was made holy in the sense of moral or spiritual purity or righteousness. They were called holy because they were set apart for God's purposes and service. A man's house or his field could be set apart for the Lord's use, and a man himself could be set apart for the Lord's use.

In that sense, therefore, it is possible for a person in this present earthly life to be completely sanctified, completely set apart for God. In that sense, every Christian is completely sanctified. Whether he is faithful and obedient or not, he has been set apart completely for God because of his relationship to Jesus Christ. That is what Peter meant when he spoke of "the sanctifying work of the Spirit." In the same chapter he reminds us that we were not redeemed with perishable things such as silver and gold, but with the precious blood of Christ.[4] At the time we are redeemed by Christ's blood, we are also—by virtue of that costly price—set apart for God. We belong to him. We are sanctified.

Two other texts make the same point. In the Book of Hebrews we read that Christ "by one sacrifice . . . has made perfect forever those who are being made holy," and in 1 Corinthians Paul addresses the believers to whom he is writing as "the church of God in Corinth, . . . those sanctified in Christ Jesus and called to be holy."[5]

That sanctification is positional. Since we belong to Christ, since we are *in* Christ, as Paul says, we are sanctified. We have been set apart for God. Our relationship with him constitutes our sanctification. Because we are in him, and because being in him gives us a position of acceptance before God, we are set apart for God—which is the meaning of positional sanctification.

Sanctification Is Practical

The text from 1 Corinthians just mentioned also alludes to the second aspect of sanctification—the practical. "To the church of God in Corinth, to those sanctified in Christ Jesus and *called to be holy*."[6] "Sanctified," and "called to be holy" represent positional and practical sanctification respectively. Since we *are* set apart for God, we are called to *live* as godly people.

Christians living in Corinth had failed quite miserably in that regard, as Paul reminds them throughout his first letter to them. They were still involved in every sort of wickedness and sin. Yet Paul addressed them as "sanctified in Christ Jesus." By virtue of their relationship to Christ through faith, they were sanctified. But they were not living like sanctified people, which is what prompted Paul's letter. It was a rebuke and a reminder that they were called to live out their positional sanctification in practical obedience to God.

The practical aspect of sanctification is concerned with the manner of life appropriate to those whom God claims as his own. It is not, of course, easy to live consistently as a person set apart to God. Hence the warnings and exhortations in the New Testament for us to shape up as Christians. Says Paul, "Just as you used to offer the parts of your body in slavery to impurity and to ever-increasing wickedness, so now offer them in slavery to righteousness leading to holiness. . . . But now that you have been set free from sin and have become slaves to God, the benefit you reap leads to holiness, and the result is eternal life."[7] Twice in the same paragraph Paul speaks of holiness, or sanctification, as a way of life.

Neither Paul nor any of the other apostles speaks of sanctification in abstract terms. In 1 Thessalonians 4 Paul says, "It is God's will that you should be holy; that you should avoid sexual immorality; . . . For God did not call us to be impure, but to live a holy life."[8]

Careful study of the New Testament will show that practical sanctification is just that—very practical. God gets down to brass tacks, so to speak. Consequently, sanctified people are not those with their heads in the clouds; they are those who know the difference between evil and good and seek, with God's help, to avoid evil and to do good—which they know is the will of God for them. Nothing could be more practical.

Practical sanctification is progressive. We are made positionally sanctified, completely and instantaneously, when we accept Jesus Christ as Savior. Practical sanctification, on the other hand, is a continuous process as long as we are on earth. God expects our Christian living to continuously improve. In the Book of Hebrews we are called to "make every effort to live in peace with all men and to be holy; without holiness no one will see the Lord."[9] Positionally we are completely sanctified the moment we first trust Christ. But practically all of us have a long way to go. Striving to be like Christ—in other words, to be holy in our living—is the essence of Christianity. Ideally we get better at it the longer we live. John Bunyan did not title his book *The Pilgrim's Progress* just because he thought it was a pretty title. Spiritual progress is what Christian living is all about.

Ironically, however, the holier a person becomes, the less conscious he may be of spiritual growth. The closer a person walks with Christ, the more aware he becomes of God's perfect holiness, and the more aware he becomes of his own imperfect holiness. It is also possible, unfortunately, for a genuine Christian *not* to progress, and to be unaware of his spiritual stagnation. In at least two epistles believers are rebuked for spiritual shallowness. The Christians in Corinth were pathetically worldy and immature. Paul called them spiritual infants.[10] The believers to whom the Book of Hebrews was addressed were also immature. The writer of that epistle said they needed milk, not solid food, and he suspected them of being lazy.[11]

No doubt with more mature believers in mind, John wrote, "Dear friends, now we are children of God, and what we will be has not yet been made known. But we know that when he appears, we shall be like him, for we shall see him as he is."[12] In a similar vein Paul exhorted the believers in Rome: "Do not conform any longer to the pattern of this world, but be transformed by the renewing of your mind."[13] He explained to the Christians in Colosse: "You have taken off your old self with its practices and have put on the new self, which is being renewed in knowledge in the image of its Creator."[14]

Those passages make clear that renewal of the mind is part of the sanctifying process. To the extent that we allow the Word of God, under the influence of the Holy Spirit, to mold our minds, they will be brought into alignment with God's will. Through his Word we know what God expects of us; we know what his will is. For all of us this renewal of the mind is a radical process, but for some it is more obviously so than for others. In every case, however, the renewal is a necessary part of the sanctifying work of the Holy Spirit. It is his answer to our Lord's prayer when he prayed for his disciples, including us, "Sanctify them by the truth; your word is truth."[15]

On a visit home to his native Scotland, Fred Stanley Arnot, a pioneer missionary to Africa, was asked to write his favorite verse in a friend's Bible. Arnot wrote Psalm 23:3, and his friend was surprised by the missionary's choice of texts. If he had written Psalm 23:1 the friend would not have been surprised, because that verse is a great affirmation of faith: "The Lord is my shepherd; I shall not want" (KJV). Verse 3 is, "He restoreth my soul: He leadeth me in the paths of righteousness for his name's sake." Why did the missionary list that verse as his favorite? Probably because he had lived long enough to experience the deep need felt by all mature believers for forgiveness—not forgiveness of sins committed *before* conversion, but forgiveness of sins committed *after* conversion. For sins committed before conversion, we needed forgiveness and its attendant salvation. For sins committed after conversion, we need continuing forgiveness and its attendant restoration.

David felt the need of *restoration to God,* and he rejoiced in its satisfaction. "When I kept silent [about my sin]," he said, "my bones wasted away through my groaning all day long" (Ps. 32:3). After David turned to the Lord, he said:

> Then I acknowledged my sin to you
> and did not cover up my iniquity.
> I said, "I will confess
> my transgressions to the Lord." (v. 5a)

What happened next? David tells us. In prayer he continues: "and you forgave the guilt of my sin" (v. 5b). David began the Psalm by rejoicing in the blessedness of sins forgiven: "Blessed is the man whose sin the Lord does not count against him" (v. 2). With forgiveness comes reconciliation and restoration. Later in life David wrote the Twenty-third Psalm, which included Fred Arnot's favorite verse, "He restoreth my soul" (v. 3).

Restoration is part of the sanctifying process. Sanctification is progressive, but all of us fail many times. We need frequent forgiveness, and we need restoration. The good news is that God does restore our souls. He gives us the spiritual lift we need. Moreover, he "dusts us off"; he cleanses us. When John says, "If we confess our sins, he is faithful and just and will forgive us our sins and purify us from all unrighteousness,"[16] he echoes David.

In Psalm 23:3 David says that the Lord both restores his soul *and* "guides [him] in paths of righteousness for his name's sake." For the Lord's name's sake? Yes, for the Lord's own name's sake. God has a stake in his children. What is his initial sanctifying work if not his claiming us for himself? He has a stake in us, and he will not forsake us or discard us. When we come confessing our sins, he will restore us, cleanse us, and lead us in righteous paths, just as he did David.

Paul asks, "We died to sin; how can we live in it any longer?"[17] A few verses later he says that "our old self was crucified with him [Christ]."[18] Paul does not set forth death to sin as a process but as an accomplished fact. "We *died* to sin" and "our old self *was* crucified." The tenses help us understand the apostle's meaning. Furthermore, in statements at the end of the paragraph Paul makes it very clear that his use of the death metaphor is not intended to indicate a process, but an act accomplished completely at the time. "The death [Christ] died, he died to sin once for all; but the life he lives, he lives to God. In the same way, count yourselves dead to sin but alive to God in Christ Jesus."[19]

Since Christ had no sinful inclination or actions, what did Paul mean in saying that Christ died to sin? Christ's death to sin was his death on the cross. Paul was not speaking of death in the sense of being insensitive to sin, but of being unresponsive to sin. Christ never responded to sin. His "death to sin" was his bearing sin's penalty for us at Calvary. Sin demands the death of every sinner. In accepting responsibility for the sins of mankind, Christ made himself vulnerable to death. As the bearer of sins, he had to die. When he died, he satisfied sin's claims; sin now has no more claim on him, so that it may be said that he died to sin. In dying for our sins, he died to sin.

That is the meaning of *our* death to sin. True, neither you nor I have yet died. Nevertheless, in Christ we *have* died to sin. What he accomplished is credited to our account, so that we are viewed by God as having paid the penalty. "One [that is, Christ] died for all, therefore all died [in him]."[20]

It is comforting to know that whatever claims sin had on us were taken care of at Calvary. Sin said the sinner must die. But Christ died for the ungodly—that is, for sinners. Therefore sin has nothing more to say to the sinner who trusts in Christ. He has died to sin's claim. His penalty has been paid by his Lord.

Christ died to sin by suffering and dying on the cross, and he did it once for all. We also died to sin once for all, not by experiencing literal death, but by becoming—through faith—part of him. We are *in Christ,* and *in him* we died to sin once for all.

We are not talking about a legal standing before God. Response to sin is not the issue in Romans 6, in which the expressions, "dead to sin" and "alive to God" occur (v. 11). The issue there is our *standing* before God. Many Christians, failing to understand this truth, think that the passage teaches that Christians are no longer able to respond to sin. Yet they know they *can.* They feel the force of temptation and, like everyone else, often fall into sin. They become miserable in their futile striving to attain what can never be attained.

But "dead to sin" does not mean immunity to temptation and sinful actions. The old nature will not die until our bodies die. Not until we expire will we cease to feel the force of temptation. But God tells us to *count* ourselves to be dead to sin and alive to God in Christ Jesus.[21] He tells us to live *as if* sin had no more claim or power in our lives. That is not easy to do, of course, but by God's help and with practice and self-discipline it becomes easier.

As Paul told believers in Galatia, "Those who belong to Christ

Jesus have crucified the sinful nature with its passions and desires."[22] The Epistle to the Colossians makes the truth perhaps even plainer:

> Put to death, therefore, whatever belongs to your earthly nature: sexual immorality, impurity, lust, evil desires and greed, which is idolatry. . . . you must rid yourselves of all such things as these: anger, rage, malice, slander, and filthy language from your lips. Do not lie to each other, since you have taken off your old self with its practices and have put on the new self, which is being renewed in knowledge in the image of its Creator.[23]

Christ wants us to be different from what we were when we were first saved. He wants us to lay aside evil habits and to form new habits appropriate to those whom God calls to his kingdom and glory. It is a lifetime process, and through it all we have the help of the Sanctifier, the Holy Spirit of God.

28

Present Blessings of Believers—Assurance, Peace, Joy

The primary and foundational benefits of salvation are justification, adoption, and sanctification—the truths discussed in the previous three chapters. These benefits describe the new relationship we have with God through faith in Jesus Christ. Yet we cannot feel them or experience them in the usual sense of these terms. We know about them because God's Word teaches them and explains them.

Other benefits of salvation, however, flow from those three. These "secondary" benefits or blessings we experience more directly and consciously. They are secondary in the sense that they flow from the primary benefits and that in some respects they are not as crucial. Without justification, for example, a person is lost. But a person who is justified may go through life without assurance of God's forgiveness and love, yet still be forgiven and loved.

Assurance

Many saved people are not sure they are saved. They *hope* they are saved, but they do not *know* they are saved; they have no assurance of salvation. When they get to heaven, they will realize that their anxiety on earth about salvation was unnecessary and unhelpful.

Assurance is certainty. Not many of us could stand the strain of perpetual doubt about something so important as salvation. If we did not have some assurance that we would reach our heavenly destination in spite of many failures in this life, we would probably give up. A person who is assured of salvation is confident that he is saved, positive that he will get to heaven. He says he *knows* he is saved, not *hopes* he is saved.

Some people, including some Christians, believe such certainty is no more than presumption. But the Bible gives ample reason for a believer in Jesus Christ to be entirely confident that he is saved.

At this point we should distinguish between security and assurance. A person may be eternally secure, yet have no assurance that he is in fact safe and secure. Another person may be brimming with assurance, confident that he is on the road to heaven, when in fact he is on the road to hell. Our Lord told some of the most religious people in the world—who even belonged to God's specially favored people, Israel—that they were doomed. They were furious, because they thought they were guaranteed entrance into heaven. They had plenty of assurance, but their assurance was deceptive.[1]

Security, or eternal security, is an expression used to denote the doctrine that salvation is irrevocable, permanent. It is the doctrine reflected in the common expression,"once saved, always saved." If that doctrine is true, a saved person may have assurance—valid, biblical assurance—that he is eternally secure. But if the Bible does not teach the eternal security of a saved person, assurance is out of the question; nobody could know for sure until after he dies.

But Scripture *does* teach the doctrine. In fact, it teaches this great truth in at least three ways: by the use of terms (such as *eternal life*) that require permanence; by direct statements regarding security; and by strong implications.

Taught by the Use of Terms That Require Permanence The New Testament makes at least thirty references to eternal life. Among those are, "Just as Moses lifted up the snake in the desert, so the Son of Man must be lifted up, that everyone who believes in him may have eternal life,"[2] and "For the wages of sin is death, but the gift of God is eternal life in Christ Jesus our Lord."[3]

The point of those verses is obvious: the life offered to persons who believe in Jesus Christ is *eternal*. This greatest and most undeserved blessing of God, given to every person who believes in his Son, is everlasting life. The gospel does not simply offer temporary blessings; it offers *eternal* life. If the gift could be lost or withdrawn for any reason, it would not be eternal. The phrase *eternal life*, which, with its synonyms, the Bible uses so frequently, not only would be inappropriate but inaccurate.

By itself, that line of evidence is not always convincing. Some believers, who hold to the complete accuracy and reliability of Scripture, agree that the gift is eternal life, but contend that it is granted conditionally. Unless a person possesses the gift at the moment of death, they argue, he does not enter into eternal life—no matter how long he may have possessed the gift before that time.

Taught by Direct Statements The fact that God's offer is *eternal* life is not the only line of evidence proving the reality of eternal security. God's Word gives direct statements guaranteeing our salvation.

Jesus said, "I tell you the truth, whoever hears my word and believes him who sent me has eternal life and will not be condemned; he has crossed over from death to life."[4] He also said, "My sheep listen to my voice; I know them, and they follow me. I give them eternal life, and they shall never perish; no one can snatch them out of my hand."[5] Both of those assurances not only speak of "eternal life"—by definition meaning life that *cannot* end—but emphasize the point by saying, in the first passage, that those who believe in Christ "*will not* be condemned," and in the second passage that "they *shall never* perish" and that "*no one* can snatch them out of [the Lord's] hand."

Paul was "convinced that neither death nor life, neither angels nor demons, neither the present nor the future, nor any powers, neither height nor depth, nor anything else in all creation, will be able to separate us from the love of God that is in Christ Jesus our Lord."[6] The apostle ruled out every possibility—angelic and demonic, heavenly and earthly, present or future—of a believer's ever losing the gift of life he has in Christ. He assured the Christians at Philippi that "he who began a good work in you will carry it on to completion until the day of Christ Jesus."[7]

Without qualification Paul taught that trust in Jesus Christ secures an irrevocable gift—eternal life. Nothing can separate us from the love of God, Paul insisted. Having begun a work in us, God will continue it until it is done. God will no more let us go than he will let his own Son go, because we are now *in his Son*. "Once saved, always saved" is not a wishful cliché, but a glorious truth.

The Bible teaches that salvation, once it is granted, is permanent. It is an irrevocable gift. Irrevocable! God promises that he *will not* take it from us and that nothing else or no one else *can* take it from us. Christ "is able to save *forever* those who draw near to God through him, since he always lives to make intercession for them."[8]

Taught by Implication The specific teachings about eternal security given above should need no supplement. Other passages like them are so numerous and clear that it is difficult to understand how a believer who knows those texts could still be in doubt about his salvation. But God gives still further evidence in his Word.

The very nature of salvation offers us assurance. Salvation is not just a gift; it is a state of being that cannot be altered. It is a fixed standing before God that he himself creates and legislates into existence when a person trusts in his Son.

When a man believes the gospel, irreversible things happen. One of these irreversible things is indicated in a text quoted above. Jesus said, "I tell you the truth, whoever hears my word and believes him who sent me has eternal life and will not be condemned; he has crossed over from death to life."[9]

That is a powerful statement. Its use of the present tense (*has* eternal life) indicates that eternal life is received immediately upon believing. Its reference to crossing from death to life indicates the irrevocability of the gift. When God gives eternal life, something happens to the receiver. He not only receives eternal life—he passes from one standing to another. He no longer stands under judgment of God; he has crossed from death to life.

In his Epistle to the Colossians, Paul echoes our Lord's words. Speaking of the Father's activity in saving us, he says, "He has rescued us from the dominion of darkness and brought us into the kingdom of the Son he loves, in whom we have redemption, the forgiveness of sins."[10] We have crossed over from death to life, and we have been delivered from the kingdom of darkness and brought into the kingdom of God's beloved Son. That is irreversible.

Another irreversible aspect of God's work in saving us is the gift of the Holy Spirit. After telling believers in Ephesus that they were included in Christ, Paul explains how it happened. "Having believed, you were marked in him with a seal, the promised Holy Spirit, who is a deposit guaranteeing our inheritance until the redemption of those who are God's possession—to the praise of his glory."[11]

Here, then, is one of the strongest proofs of the security of every true believer: the nature of salvation. It is a work of God. We are included in Christ when we believe the gospel. When we believe, we are marked with a seal, the promised Holy Spirit. The Holy Spirit in us is a divine *guarantee* that we will get everything God promises to believers. The Holy Spirit is also evidence that we *now* belong to God, that we are already his possession. In that great truth we *are* secure and should *feel* secure. God does not let anyone snatch his possessions out of his hand. Who could be more secure than a child of God!

Seeming Disproofs Some Bible texts, however, *seem* to contradict the doctrine of eternal security, and therefore of assurance of salvation. In the Book of Hebrews, for example, we read, "It is impossible for those who have once been enlightened, who have tasted the heavenly gift, who have shared in the Holy Spirit, who have tasted the goodness of the word of God and the powers of the coming age, if they fall away, to be brought back to repentance, because to their loss they are crucifying the Son of God all over again and subjecting him to public disgrace."[12]

Of that and similar texts, William Evans writes, "Passages which seem, to some, to contradict the doctrine of security are found to be related to rewards, chastisement, and the fact that an absence of good works reveals a lack of genuine faith, Phil. 2:12, 13; 2 Peter 3:9-17."[13]

Evans is right. If we examine every text according to recognized principles of interpretation of any kind of document, whether secular or biblical, we are led to the conclusion that verses that seem to raise the possibility of loss of salvation do not in fact do so. In most cases they raise questions about the true salvation of so-called believers. They ask readers to consider whether they have ever sincerely believed.

The troublesome passage in Hebrews 6, for instance, can be properly understood only in context—which includes the spiritual condition of its readers and the particular temptation to which they were exposed. They were a mixed group of Jews, composed of genuine believers and others who, under severe pressure from enemies of the faith, proved that they were not genuine believers. They renounced Christ and returned to their old religion of Judaism.

By renouncing Christ, they proved that they never knew him. Renouncing him also proved that they had made a final decision to reject him. They would *never* believe sincerely. Hence, it was impossible for them "to be brought back to repentance." They had made a *final* choice.

That passage cannot be applied to mere backsliders. It says too much to be applied to Christians who become careless or who yield to sin, including serious sin. It says there is no hope, no possibility of turning again to God. A backslider *can* be restored; a gross sinner *can* come confessing, in repentance, and find forgiveness. Speaking to his fellow-Christians, John wrote, "If we confess our sin, he [Christ] is faithful and just and will forgive us our sins and purify us from all unrighteousness. . . . My dear children, I write this to you so that you will not sin. But if anybody does sin, we have one who speaks to the Father in our defense—Jesus Christ, the Righteous One."[14]

The Hebrews 6 passage deals with the apostasy of pseudo-believers who experienced the benefits of life within a believing community and knew all that Christ stands for; but with eyes wide open they renounced their outward association with Christ. They in fact denounced him as a fraud, worthy of the death he died. In so doing they crucified him all over again. They were apostates, not backsliders, and for apostates there is no possibility of spiritual renewal.

The arguments can be summed up in this statement: eternal security rests on Christ's work for us. He died for us, and the value of his death is such that all who are *in him* are eternally secure. When we believe in Jesus Christ, which is all we can ever do to be saved, God himself takes charge of our spiritual destiny, assuming full responsibility for our salvation. He will not even listen to accusations telling him his people are a bad lot. As Paul says, "If God is for us, who can be against us? . . . Who will bring any charge against those whom God has chosen? It is God who justifies."[15]

Eternal security rests on God's work on our behalf—the work of Christ in dying for us, and the work of the Holy Spirit in uniting us to Christ. Assurance of salvation, however, depends on two other things as well: first, knowing what the Bible teaches, and second, believing its teaching. No doubt many genuine believers have no assurance of salvation. They go through life wondering whether they will get to heaven. In every case, the problem is ignorance of the full nature of salvation.

Such ignorance is their own fault. Paul repeatedly says that he wants believers to *know* something, or that he does not want them to be ignorant about such and such a truth. A major theme of John's first letter is knowing God's truth and knowing our relation to God through Christ. No passage of Scripture more directly states the truths of eternal security and of the believer's assurance than this one from chapter 5: "God has given us eternal life, and this life is in his Son. He who has the Son has life; he who does not have the Son of God does not have life. I write these things to you who believe in the name of the Son of God so that you may know that you have eternal life."[16]

Correct knowledge of God's Word is closely associated with assurance of salvation. In the passage just cited, John makes a series of statements, culminating in the assertion that a person who has the Son of God has life. Then he explains why he wrote as he did: that his readers might *know* that they had eternal life, that they would have assurance of salvation and the confidence that can only come with that assurance.

If we examine every passage that seems to set forth the possibility of losing salvation, we will see that in context the text does not deny the truth of eternal security. This is a repeated and clearly established truth of Scripture, and properly used is a truth that should greatly encourage God's people to holy living. What could be more inspiring and motivating then the fact that we are God's "forever people"?

Peace of Mind and Conscience

Peace of mind and conscience is the second of five secondary blessings of salvation. Paul links peace closely with justification,[17] but in at least one important passage he implies that peace is also tied to adoption and sanctification: "Do not be anxious for anything, but in everything, by prayer and petition, with thanksgiving, present your requests to God. And the peace of God, which transcends all understanding, will guard your hearts and your minds in Christ Jesus."[18] The prayer and thanksgiving of which Paul speaks here could only come from minds and hearts that are aware of their relationship to God as sons, and who live accordingly. Paul says, "Because you are sons, God sent the Spirit of his Son into our hearts, the Spirit who calls out, 'Abba, Father.' "[19] Knowing that we are his sons, we call upon God as "Our Father who art in heaven." In so doing, we find peace.

Those who know they are forgiven no longer let their consciences trouble them about past sins. Paul speaks about this kind of peace in his letter to the Romans—"Therefore, since we have been justified through faith, we have peace with God through our Lord Jesus Christ."[20] Lest anyone misunderstand, a forgiven person should have a more sensitive conscience than he did before conversion. But when he first trusts God, he learns to shift the guilt of sin to the only One capable of bearing it, Jesus Christ our Lord. He accepts forgiveness, and his conscience rests.

But the rest that we find in forgiveness is not that of inactivity. Long after he had made peace with God, Paul said that he did his best "to strive always to keep [his] conscience clear before God and man."[21] But his conscience did not trouble him about sins committed in the past, nor about more recent sins which he had confessed and from which he had turned. All those sins were forever forgiven, and they no longer troubled him. There are few, if any, sweeter benefits of salvation than that kind of peace in God.

Through Christ we not only have peace *with* God but peace *in* God. A continuing work of grace is ours. As Edward H. Bickersteth says in his lovely hymn,

> Peace, perfect peace, in this dark world of sin.
> The blood of Jesus whispers peace within.[22]

That is the source of our peace with God and our continuing peace in him—the blood of Jesus. Believing that wonderful truth, who could not have a conscience at rest?

The Lord himself assures all of his disciples: "Peace I leave with you; my peace I give you. I do not give to you as the world gives. Do not let your hearts be troubled and do not be afraid."[23] Jesus promises his followers an inner peace of mind, freedom from disquieting and oppressive thoughts or emotions.

The greetings in almost every one of Paul's letters include the prayerful desire for the peace of those to whom he wrote: "Grace and peace to you from God our Father and from the Lord Jesus Christ."[24]

For some Christians, unfortunately, that kind of peace—the freedom from disquieting or oppressive thoughts or emotions—is as elusive as the freedom from war and civil disturbances that the world longs for. Why should this be true? Why should not all God's people enjoy the peace that he wishes them to have? As with lack of assurance, the explanation is found in ignorance of God's Word, refusal to believe that God means what he says in his Word, or a combination of both. In his well-known study of Greek words, W. E. Vine notes that peace is "the harmonized relationships between God and man, accomplished through the gospel," and is also "the sense of rest and contentment consequent thereon."[25] Paul says that Christ "came and preached peace,"[26] the peace that he gives to everyone who believes in him.

Joy

On my wall at home is a plaque that reads, "Joy is the most infallible sign of the presence of God." For Christians, irritability is always evidence that we are out of sorts and not as consciously aware of

God's presence as we should be. Joy is indeed an infallible sign of the presence of God. To be more exact, it is an infallible sign of *consciousness* of his presence. Since Jesus said that he would never leave us, and since our bodies are temples of the Holy Spirit, God is always present with believers. But we are not always aware of his presence. Hence our emotional self-indulgence, the giving way to crabbiness, gloom, or self-pity.

A Christian's joy or depression, contentment or anger, are not mere matters of temperament. Some people are perhaps "naturally" cheerful and others grouchy, especially early in the morning. But the Bible says joy is a gift. "For the kingdom of God is not a matter of eating and drinking, but of righteousness, peace and joy in the Holy Spirit."[27] Joy is one of the gifts God offers *every* citizen of his kingdom, which is every person who belongs to the King, Jesus Christ. Paul can urge us to "rejoice in the Lord always"[28] because joy "has its source outside mere earthly, human joy. It is joy . . . in the Lord, and therefore outside ourselves."[29]

We read of, hear about, and perhaps know depressed Christians. They are, of course, joyless, unhappy people. Many are perfectionists whose dissatisfaction with their personal performances affects their view of God. They assume that he also is dissatisfied with them. Hence they get depressed and have no joy.

But joy does not come from what we accomplish, anymore than salvation comes from what we accomplish. Joy is a fruit of the Holy Spirit.[30] Joy is not genetic, a temperamental quality some are born with, others not. When reminding his friends in Thessalonica of their conversion experience, Paul told them, "You welcomed the message with the joy given by the Holy Spirit."[31]

If joy is given by the Holy Spirit, why are so many Christians miserable? Why do they live joylessly? Because the gift of joy is contingent. It isn't forced on us. God wants us to be joyful, even as he wants us to manifest the other fruits of the Spirit. But nobody instantly and automatically manifests love, peace, patience, kindness, goodness, faithfulness, gentleness, self-control, and joy. Those qualities are present and visible in our lives only to the extent that we walk with God. Furthermore, growth in Christlikeness is gradual; it takes time.

As with assurance and peace, joy also is dependent on knowledge of God's Word. Joy, in fact, is dependent on having assurance and peace of mind and conscience. Uncertainty and guilt are the greatest enemies of joy. How can a person be joyful if he is not assured of salvation or if he is plagued by a guilty consicence? It is a psychological impossibility.

It is the will of God that we rejoice in our salvation. Just before his death our Lord exhorted his followers to be joyful: "I have told you this so that my joy may be in you and that your joy may be complete."[32] Moments later he talked about his followers in prayer to the Father, saying, "I am coming to you now, but I say these things while I am still in the world, so that they may have the full measure of my joy within them."[33]

29

Present Blessings of Believers—Grace and Perseverance

Two additional blessings of salvation that we experience in this life are growth in grace and perseverance.

Growth in Grace

Though mercy and grace are closely related, and sometimes are used almost interchangeably, they are not exactly the same. In mercy God withholds his wrath, which we deserve; in grace he gives us salvation, which we do not deserve. In mercy he spares us; in grace he saves us.

Following are several good definitions of biblical grace:

> The grace of God is His free love and unmerited favor, imparted to men through Christ. (F. F. Bruce)[1]
>
> The idea is that of a gift which a man never deserved and could never earn, and which is given to him in the generous goodness and love of the heart of God. (William Barclay)[2]
>
> Grace is love which passes beyond all claims to love. It is love which after fulfilling the obligations imposed by law, has an inexhaustible wealth of kindness. (Robert Dale)[3]

Those definitions, which say more or less the same thing, combine several ideas: the grace of God is his love, kindness, or favor; it is freely given; and it is totally undeserved.

Following are three texts from the New Testament. They do not give definitions of grace, but they tell us a great deal about grace and about what grace does.

> For you know the grace of our Lord Jesus Christ, that though he was rich, yet for your sakes he became poor, so that you through his poverty might become rich.[4]

> For it is by grace you have been saved, through faith—and this is not from yourselves, it is the gift of God—not by works, so that no one can boast.[5]

> For the grace of God that brings salvation has appeared to all men.[6]

A New Testament definition of grace, derived from a combined summary of those passages, could be: Grace is the working of God's love, goodness, and kindness (actually, all of those and more) that brings salvation to undeserving sinners.

God's grace increases from the moment we first trust Christ for salvation until our salvation is completed and perfected.[7] No Christian can live a godly life without continuous help from God. It is God's grace that brings salvation, and it is his grace that keeps us on the track. Both of those aspects of grace are indicated in the tenth of the Thirty-nine Articles of the Church of England. After pointing to man's moral helplessness after the Fall, it says: "Wherefore we have no power to do good works pleasant and acceptable to God, without the grace of God by Christ preventing us, that we may have a good will, and working with us, when we have that good will."

Since that statement of faith is about four hundred years old, the wording is a bit archaic. "Preventing" does not here mean hindering; it means "prevenient," that is, to come before, to precede. God's grace operates on the will *before* a person turns to Christ—before a person *can* come to Christ. Otherwise no one could be saved. God's grace is more than an attitude of goodwill toward us; it is his love in action. He helps us in a way—and after that in many ways—in which we could never help ourselves.

Growing in grace is one of the beautiful blessings that accompany salvation. God's grace brings us *to* Christ, places us *in* Christ through our faith, and enables us then to live *for* Christ. That seems to be what Paul expresses to his friends in Philippi: "He who began a good work in you will carry it on to completion until the day of Christ Jesus."[8] In the same letter Paul exhorts his friends to "work out your salvation with fear and trembling, for it is God who works in you to will and to act according to his good purpose."[9]

God's grace carries to completion the work he began in us even before conversion. That is the continuous working of divine grace. Our growth in grace is no more our own doing than was our salvation in the first place. Growing in grace is "that indwelling and assistance of the Holy Spirit whereby all that has been attained in grace is secured, and new progress is made from grace to grace."[10]

Sinful people, even saved sinful people, cannot please God unless he himself enables them to do so. That he does enable sinful people to please him is one of the New Testament's most reassuring truths. He does this as the God of all grace, who gives us grace to do what we ought to do.

Commenting on that truth, W. H. Griffith Thomas explains that,

> To speak of grace is only another way of saying that we receive the Lord Jesus Christ in all the glory of His presence and power as the indwelling energy for holiness and obedience. The Holy Spirit applies with power to our inner being the life of our Lord Jesus, and in this is "grace to help in time of need" (Hebrews 4:16). . . . God's divine power has provided "all things that pertain unto life and godliness" (2 Peter 1:3), and no heart need be discouraged or cast down with the thought of life's difficulties and perplexities in view of the marvelous and bountiful provision of grace to meet every possible contingency, and to guarantee a strong, growing, vigorous life.[11]

"With God all things are possible," Jesus replied to some followers who asked him, "Who then can be saved?"[12] To a man who was not quite sure Jesus could help him, Jesus said, "Everything is possible for him who believes."[13] If we combine those two statements of Jesus, we have a concise but comprehensive picture of grace. God's power is ready to help at all times, but it must be accepted and used. With God all things are possible. God can do anything and will do anything for those who believe.

Means of Grace A means to an end is that by which, or through the help of which, an end is achieved. If our end or objective is a good job, a university degree is a useful means to that end. If our objective is winning the Boston Marathon, training hard is a means to that end. But what do theologians and preachers mean when they talk about various "means of grace"?

There is, of course, no specified number of the means of grace that are available. Since the Lord tells us that "everything is possible for him who believes," we know that every means necessary for growing in grace is available to us. In one sense the means are limitless. But in discussions of the means of growing in grace the following are nearly always included: the Bible; prayer; worship; and the ordinances or sacraments.

It goes without saying that believers who neither study the Bible nor pray cannot experience growth in God's grace. They have no nourishment to give them growth. Peter says, "Like newborn babies, crave pure spiritual milk, so that by it you may grow up in your salvation."[14] He is calling for Bible study. Jude says, "Build yourselves up in your most holy faith and pray in the Holy Spirit."[15] He obviously is calling for prayer.

Bible study, by which we learn what God has to say to us, and prayer, by which we open our hearts to God, are vital to Christian living. Some believers tend to regard them as spiritual obligations they must meet in order to keep in good with God. The truth is, prayer and Bible study are two vital means of our spiritual growth. They are channels through which God continues to send us his grace. In neglecting them we lose a great deal. We lose the full measure of grace God wants all of his children to have—which they *must* have if they are to live triumphantly in the world.

Regular worship with God's people is also a means of growing in grace. It helps us grow spiritually, and it helps us live more faithfully as Christians. We worship together because we need each other. "And let us consider how we may spur one another on toward love and good deeds. Let us not give up meeting together, as some are in the habit of doing, but let us encourage one another—and all the more as you see the Day approaching."[16]

God's continuing grace, to live faithfully as his children, comes through our brothers and sisters in Christ. If we avoid regular worship with them, we forfeit the wonderful blessings of God's grace that come with that worship.

The same is true with the sacraments or ordinances. We go to the Communion service because Jesus commanded that we should and because, when participated in with the right spirit, it builds us up in the Lord, which is to say in grace. The sacraments, or ordinances, are ceremonies instituted by Christ. Many, if not most, evangelicals believe there are only two: baptism and the Lord's Supper, which some call Communion, or the Eucharist.

For the sake of our discussion here, I will comment only on the Lord's Supper—partly because it is a repeated observance in which most believers participate many times during their Christian lives. We observe the Lord's Supper first of all because the Lord commanded us to do so. "Do this in remembrance of me," Jesus said.[17] Why did he want to be remembered in this way? For *our* sakes as well as his own. Remembering his suffering and death on our behalf is a means of growing in grace. It is also, of course, an act of worship. In the very act of worshiping him, we experience an inflowing of the continuing grace of God. The cup—that symbol of his sorrows—is for us a "cup of blessing."[18]

Perseverance

As discussed earlier, the Bible teaches that a saved person cannot be lost. One who is born again cannot revert to his unregenerate state. As we saw, the doctrine of assurance is closely linked to the doctrine of eternal security. Also closely linked with eternal security is the doctrine of perseverance. If a saved person cannot become lost, then obviously he is somehow enabled to persevere in the faith to the end. He *will* reach his heavenly home.

The doctrine of perseverance is therefore really an aspect of eternal security. Jesus said, "My sheep listen to my voice; I know them, and they follow me. I give them eternal life, and they shall never perish; no one can snatch them out of my hand."[19]

The terms *final perseverance* and *eternal security* have been used in the Church for a long time, and are often used interchangeably. They are not exactly synonymous, but their intent is the same: expressing the truth that Christ's people cannot lose their salvation. Having trusted Christ for salvation, they are secure. Their security is God's responsibility, which is the gist of the text just quoted. Christ gives his sheep eternal life, and no one can snatch them out of his hand.

Many forces try to snatch Christ's sheep out of his hand. Says John Ryle: "To feel that something is always 'plucking' and 'pulling' at us must never surprise believers. There is a devil, and saints will always feel and find his presence."[20] Yet Bishop Ryle has encouraging words for people who do not *feel* secure. "To *be* safe in Christ's hand, and so never to perish, is one thing; but to *feel* that we are safe is quite another. Many true believers *are* safe, who do not realize and *feel* it."[21] Our salvation is not like an insurance policy that can expire or be canceled; it is eternal, irrevocable. We *will* persevere to the end.

Just as perseverance is inextricably related to eternal security, it is also inextricably related to election and predestination. Though very close in meaning, election refers to God's determining those whom he saves—who are, of course, believers. Predestination, on the other hand, refers to God's determining the goal to which he leads his people—what happens to the elect, the saved. God chooses (elects) those who are saved, and he also determines (predestines) the nature of the salvation given them.

Perhaps the clearest statement about the goal of salvation is found in the Book of Romans. "For those God foreknew he also predestined to be conformed to the likeness of his Son," Paul says. The chapter concludes with these well-known lines:

> For I am convinced that neither death nor life, neither angels nor demons, neither the present nor the future, nor any powers, neither height nor depth, nor anything else in all creation, will be able to separate us from the love of God that is in Christ Jesus our Lord.[22]

The link between predestination and perseverance is obvious. God has predestined us to eternal life, and he has pledged himself to keep us safe. Predestination is the divine side of perseverance. God's predestination makes our perseverance possible. It emphasizes God's work in preserving us. *Our* perseverance is really *his* work. Our perseverance is God's preservation.

Doesn't that truth make Christians careless? It can, of course, but it should not. Says W. H. Griffith Thomas,

> It humbles man's pride by putting God first as the source of all grace; it encourages our trust by assuring us that grace is a reality. . . . It elicits our earnestness, for it reminds us that we are in God's thought, and that we are intended to live to the praise of the glory of His grace.[23]

Occasionally it is necessary to have the wheels balanced on our automobiles. Balanced wheels are necessary for smooth, safe driving and to prevent excessive wear on the tires. Balanced biblical teaching is important to prevent theological and practical problems of a much more serious nature.

Some doctrines lend themselves to mistreatment. Among them is the doctrine of perseverance of the saints. So far we have emphasized the divine side of this truth. God gives his people *eternal* life—not something provisional, temporary, or renewable—and he preserves them in that life. In the interests of balance and completeness, however, something must also be said about the human side of perseverance.

Jesus says he gives his sheep eternal life and they shall never perish. But let it be remembered, Bishop Ryle warns, that

> the character of those who shall never perish is most distinctly and carefully laid down. . . . It is those who hear Christ's voice and follow Him who alone are "sheep"; it is his sheep and his sheep alone who shall never perish. . . . The man who boasts that he shall never be cast away and never perish, while he is living in sin, is a miserable self-deceiver. It is the perseverance of *saints,* and not of sinners and wicked people, that is promised here.[24]

The truth that God preserves his people must be balanced by the truth that God's people are those who persevere. Terms such as *election, predestination,* and *eternal security* emphasize the divine aspect of the truth. The saints who really are saints persevere. As Jesus says, "My sheep listen to my voice. . . and they follow me."[25] Expressing the same basic truth, Paul says, "Everyone who confesses the name of the Lord must turn away from wickedness."[26]

Balance between the divine and human sides of perseverance is clearly seen by comparing 1 Peter 1:5 and Jude 21. Peter says, "[You are] shielded by God's power until the coming of the salvation that is ready to be revealed in the last time," while Jude, who shared Peter's God-given understanding of truth, nevertheless exhorts believers to "Keep yourselves in God's love as you wait for the mercy of our Lord Jesus Christ to bring you to eternal life."

God preserves his people, and his people persevere. The divine side of the truth emphasizes eternal security. The human side emphasizes constancy in following Christ. If somehow it could be shown that a believer *could* fall away, it can also be shown that he *will not* fall away. A true believer *will* persevere to the end, because God *will* preserve him.

Why, we may then wonder, are so many Christians found in psychiatric hospitals? By "Christian" I do not mean a broad religious designation, such as Christian contrasted with Jewish, Muslim, or Buddhist. I mean people who are born again and who are serious about their relationhip with Christ, who recall an occasion when they turned to Christ for forgiveness of sins and the promise of eternal life. In some cases there was a radical change in their manner of life, and they were filled with the joy of the Lord. Why, then, are they now in a psychiatric ward or under the regular care of a psychologist, psychiatrist, or professional counselor? What happened?

Obviously no general diagnosis is possible. I suspect, however, that whatever additional factors may be present, in every case there is failure to contemplate and rejoice in the benefits that accompany salvation. How else can we explain chronic depression and other such psychological and emotional afflictions that beset Christians?

Every Christian should commit to memory part of the eighth chapter of Nehemiah. As the people of God listened to public reading of the Scriptures, they began to mourn and weep. No doubt they felt that the Word of God rebuked them. But Ezra the scribe said, "This day is sacred to the Lord your God. Do not mourn or weep."[27] Then he told them to show their response to the Word in practical ways, not by wringing their hands. "Do not grieve, for the joy of the Lord is your strength."[28]

The joy of the Lord is our strength. Believers who use the Word of God to torture their consciences are headed for trouble. Mourning has its place. Our Lord said, "Blessed are those who mourn." But he added that they would be comforted.[29] Mourning is temporary; it will end. Joyfulness, on the other hand, should be the habitual frame of mind of God's people. I do not mean careless frivolity, but the joy of the Lord. That, Ezra says, is our strength. It is what enables us to live triumphantly and to endure.

David understood this truth. In his great penitential Psalm (51), he asks God to give him back his lost joy.

> Restore to me the joy of your salvation
>   and grant me a willing spirit, to sustain me.

What would be the effect of recovered joy? David continues,

> Then I will teach transgressors your ways,
>   and sinners will turn back to you.[30]

There are many reasons why Christians become unhappy and depressed. But they would all be happier and more stable if they heeded Paul's call to rejoice in the Lord.[31] That is the Lord's *command*—having as much authority as his command to be truthful or to attend church faithfully or to support the work of the Lord. It is not an option. Faithful Christians *must* "rejoice in the Lord."

30

Future Blessings of Believers

Just as some blessings (such as justification and adoption) come to us the moment we accept Christ as Lord and Savior, and some (such as assurance of salvation and perseverance) come during the remainder of our lives on earth, still other blessings will not be ours until after we leave our present earthly life. Future blessings will be in two categories: those received at death and those received at the resurrection.

Death is the separation of the soul from the body, the separation of the immaterial part of us from the material part. At death, something happens to the soul, and something happens to the body. What happens to the body is obvious; it begins to decay. What happens to the soul is not obvious. For that information we must depend entirely on God's Word. Apart from the Bible, we have nothing but speculation, which is *only speculation,* whether expressed as philosophy or framed in myths, legends, and superstitions.

The Bible teaches the survival of all souls, of believer and unbeliever, after death. When his opponents told a silly story designed to ridicule the idea of resurrection, Jesus told them they were in error because they did not know either the Scriptures or the power of God. He then quoted Exodus 3:6, where God reveals himself to Moses as "the God of Abraham, the God of Isaac and the God of Jacob." God did not mean just that all three men had once worshiped him, but that they were *still* living and that he was *still* their God. As Jesus explained, "He is not the God of the dead but of the living."[1] By calling himself the God of those three patriarchs, the Lord asserted that they had survived death; they were still living.

It is not necessary to pile up texts that teach the survival of the soul. Where the Bible does not state the truth as fact, it assumes it.

The question is not whether we will continue to exist, but where and how. What happens to our soul when we die depends on our relationship with God at the moment of death. If we do not know God and persist in unbelief up to that fateful moment, our soul will survive, but not in a state that we will enjoy. The cowardly, with the unbelieving, the vile, the murderers, the sexually immoral, those who practice magic arts, the idolaters, and all liars are not admitted to the Holy City above. "Their place will be in the fiery lake of burning sulphur. This is the second death."[2]

The Westminster Confession of Faith, published in 1647, comments:

> The bodies of men after death return to dust, and see corruption; but their souls (which neither die nor sleep), having an immortal subsistence, immediately return to God who made them. The souls of the righteous, being then made perfect in holiness, are received into the highest heavens, where they behold the face of God in light and glory, waiting for the full redemption of their bodies; and the souls of the wicked are cast into hell, where they remain in torments and utter darkness, reserved to the judgment of the great day. Besides these two places for souls separated from their bodies, the scripture acknowledges none.

The paragraph just quoted sets forth three biblical truths: first, the survival of the soul, as opposed to the idea of annihilation; second, a difference in destinations, with bliss for some and agony for others, corresponding to heaven and hell, and contradicting the idea of universal salvation; third, immediate arrival into one place or the other, as opposed to the idea of an intermediate state such as purgatory.

The Lord's words prove that for some, death is a door to heaven, for others a door to hell. In the story of the rich man and Lazarus, Jesus said that Lazarus, though destitute and diseased in this life, went to be with the Lord when he died. He was, in fact, carried by angels to Abraham's side and was comforted. A certain rich man, however, died and went to hell, where he suffered in torment. As Abraham explained to that rich man, "Between us and you a great chasm has been fixed, so that those who want to go from here to you cannot, nor can anyone cross over from there to us."[3] On another occasion Jesus said, "Whoever believes in the Son has eternal life, but whoever rejects the Son will not see life, for God's wrath remains on him."[4]

The Scripture does not teach, and does not make any allowance for, an intermediate state such as purgatory. Consequently there can be no benefit in praying for the dead. Their eternal destiny was sealed by their own choice before they died. Our prayers can neither add to the blessings of the saved dead nor diminish the punishment of the unsaved dead. The issue of eternal destiny is settled in this life, and how it has been settled determines the dying person's *immediate and eternal* destination.

Blessings Received at Death

We will here be focusing on the destiny of those who belong to Christ. If we know him, our souls not only will survive the passage from life to death, but will experience two magnificent changes. The first is freedom from sin, perfection in holiness. The second is immediate entrance into glory, into God's very presence.

Perfection in Holiness For Christians, death means instant holiness. The sinful nature will be sloughed off—to be gone forever, with all its evil thoughts and deeds. "But you have come to Mount Zion, to the heavenly Jerusalem, the city of the living God," the writer of Hebrews assures us. "You have come to thousands upon thousands of angels in joyful assembly, to the church of the firstborn, whose names are written in heaven. You have come to God, the judge of all men, to the spirits of righteous men made perfect."[5] John tells believers: "Dear friends, now we are children of God, and what we will be has not yet been made known. But we know that when he appears, we shall be like him, for we shall see him as he is."[6] A third text is also from John. "[God] will wipe every tear from their eyes. There will be no more death or mourning or crying or pain, for the old order of things has passed away."[7]

Many other texts indicate the immediate and marvelous change of believers. These texts do not indicate a static condition in heaven, as if "righteous men made perfect" were incapable of learning or doing anything more. What they teach is complete freedom from sin. Freed from sin, those who die in the Lord are fit for the presence and the perfect service of God. Those who know Christ shall be like him. At death, the change that begins at conversion will be instantly completed. Even death, though an enemy, is made to play its divine part in the redemption that is in Christ Jesus.

Entrance into God's Presence Paul looked forward to death not as extinction but as a departure. He said, "The time has come for my departure. . . . Now there is in store for me the crown of righteousness, which the Lord, the righteous Judge, will award to me on that day."[8] As mentioned above, God told Moses that he was the God of Abraham, Isaac, and Jacob. Jesus interpreted that statement as proof that those three men were still living at the time that he was speaking. They had died and their tombs could be found, but they were still living.[9] Those who are alive in God will remain alive as long as God lives.

Blessings Received at the Resurrection

Some people wonder what happens to the bodies of those who are eaten by a shark or blown to pieces in an explosion. Biologically speaking, the same thing happens to bodies that suffer violence of that sort as to bodies laid gently to rest in a coffin. They disintegrate and pass into the ecosystem. But theologically speaking, every dead body, whether intact or not, rests in its "grave" (whatever and wherever that might be) until the resurrection.

Though the souls of believers pass immediately into heaven, their bodies do not receive any immediate benefits. Whether eaten by sharks, blown to pieces, or left to decompose quietly in a grave, all bodies return to dust.

Our Bodies Made Like Christ's But the bodies of believers are not lost. The Bible teaches that Christ's redemption includes the body as well as the soul. Paul says that even in this life our bodies are "members of Christ himself."[10] We therefore are obligated to take care of our bodies, remembering Paul's prayer for the "whole spirit, soul and body."[11] But our bodies eventually die and decompose. Nevertheless, Christ will redeem them from the bondage of decay. Paul explains: "But our citizenship is in heaven. And we eagerly await a Savior from there, the Lord Jesus Christ, who, by the power that enables him to bring everything under his control, will transform our lowly bodies so that they will be like his glorious body."[12] "The body that is sown is perishable, it is raised imperishable; it is sown in dishonor, it is raised in glory."[13]

Our bodies will disintegrate when we die, but they will not be lost. The Savior will raise them up in glory. They are part of us now, and after being vastly improved they will be part of us forever. Our bodies may rest in the grave or be scattered to the winds. But at the resurrection God will transform our once lowly bodies into bodies like Christ's own body of glory. It is something to look forward to with great expectation, joy, and thanksgiving.

We cannot perform an experiment to demonstrate the resurrection of the body. We know the doctrine is true because of our trust in God and in his Word. Similarly, we know by faith that the universe was formed at God's command, and we know by faith that God will create a new heaven and a new earth, the home of righteousness—because the Bible teaches those things.[14] In the same way, we *know* that our bodies will be raised up in glory.[15] We know because we believe the Bible.

We know by faith, but there is also substantial backing for our faith. If he had wanted to use philosophical terms, Paul might have said that there is empirical evidence for resurrection. In fact, he begins a discourse on Christ's resurrection by listing the names of reliable witnesses. By accepted rules of evidence, Christ's resurrection was proven. By the testimony of Peter, of the Twelve, of James and Paul, and of more than five hundred others, Jesus had appeared to them bodily after his death and burial.[16]

There could not, of course, be such evidence for our own resurrection. That one day we will be raised to be like Christ we accept by faith, not by sight or empirical proof. The belief that Christ's resurrection guarantees ours cannot be tested or demonstrated. But Paul himself was so convinced of its inevitability that he bases an appeal for spiritual stability on the certainty of the resurrection. "Stand firm," he says. "Always give yourselves fully to the work of the Lord, because you *know* that your labor in the Lord is not in vain."[17] Faith in the prospect of our bodies being raised up in glory is based on two proven facts: Christ's own resurrection, and the reliabilty of Holy Scripture.

Heavenly Acknowledgment by God At the resurrection of our bodies we will be openly acknowledged by God. Jesus said, "Whoever acknowledges me before men, I will also acknowledge him before my Father in heaven."[18] He also said that he would acknowledge us before the angels of God.[19] Christ already acknowledges believers as being his children and his friends.[20] God the Father also acknowledges us as those whom he foreknew and predestined to be like his Son.[21]

The world does not know about that acknowledgment, or accept it. To the world, the very idea is foolishness. The world will not listen to us anymore than it listened to the prophets or apostles. Jesus said: "They [people of the world] will persecute you. . . . They will treat you this way because of my name, for they do not know the One who sent me."[22] Later in the same discourse the Lord said, "They will put you out of the synagogue; in fact, a time is coming when anyone who kills you will think he is offering a service to God. They will do such things because they have not known the Father or me."[23] The world does not recognize or accept God's people or spokesmen because it does not recognize or accept the true God.

Remembering these words, the Apostle John was able to understand his circumstances half a century later, when opposition to his preaching was fierce. Speaking of false prophets, who *were* accepted by the world, he said, "They are from the world and therefore speak from the viewpoint of the world, and the world listens to them. We are from God, and whoever knows God listens to us; but whoever is not from God does not listen to us."[24]

But at the resurrection, *every one* of God's people will be openly acknowledged by the Lord himself. Lost souls will not be present to see it, but the angels of God will be there. Christ will openly acknowledge his people before God and the holy angels. Then God's people will have the recognition denied them on earth. Then they will be recognized as the servants of God and the friends of Jesus, whom they call Lord.

That day is so momentous that Paul says, "The creation waits in eager expectation for the sons of God to be revealed."[25] His statement in Colossians 3:4 is even clearer: "When Christ, who is your life, appears, then you also will appear with him in glory."

Not only will we be identified as God's people, but the quality of our lives as his people will be revealed. Referring to that day, Paul says that each man's "work will be shown for what it is."[26] He explains that the Lord "will bring to light what is hidden in darkness and will expose the motives of men's hearts."[27]

At first glance that seems intimidating. Is God going to expose all our sin and folly? Probably, but that is not the primary point Paul is making. His point is that *then,* when God reveals the true character of our lives as believers, we will get our due praise from him.

In that coming day we will get an accurate appraisal of our lives as Christians. Then we will know what kind of Christians we really were. We will begin eternity with no illusions about the quality of our life and service in the Lord. Some of us, who have had much praise from men, will discover that we were not as spiritual, not as noble, not as effective—in short, not as praiseworthy—as we were led to believe. Popularity and pride deceived us. Others, obscure for the most part, will learn that their lives were more precious in God's sight than the lives of many prominent Christians. At that time, Jesus promises, many who were first will be last, and many who were last will be first.[28]

Enjoyment of God Forever As long as we are in the flesh, there are many hindrances to perfect, uninterrupted enjoyment of God. Our intellectual, emotional, and spiritual limitations impede us. At the resurrection, however, those impediments will be removed. We will be made *perfectly* blessed in the *full* enjoying of God for all eternity.

Even Old Testament believers knew that truth. David said, "You [God] will fill me with joy in your presence, with eternal pleasures at your right hand."[29] Asaph, another psalm-writer, testified, "My flesh and my heart may fail, but God is the strength of my heart and my portion forever."[30]

It is not possible now to know *how* we will enjoy God eternally. Our present experiences and understanding are too limited. Paul says, however, that then—in eternity—we will see face to face, and will know fully, even as we are fully known.[31] Seeing God, and knowing him more and more, will surely contribute greatly to our enjoying him. The last chapter in the Bible says we shall see his face, and we shall reign forever and ever. Who, then, does not long for the day? Who, then, can keep from crying out, "Amen. Come, Lord Jesus"?[32]

Notes

Chapter 1 / The Purpose of Man

1. Alexander Whyte, *The Shorter Catechism* (Edinburgh: T. & T. Clark, 1949), p. 1.
2. 1 Thess. 4:11, 12; cf. 1 Tim. 5:8.
3. *Webster's Collegiate Dictionary*, 5th ed., 1946.
4. Ex. 3:14.
5. John 1:14.
6. 1 Chron. 16:23, 24.
7. Ps. 96:7.
8. Isa. 43:7.
9. TEV.
10. Cf. Ps. 8.
11. John 17:4
12. John 1:18.
13. 1 Cor. 6:18-20; cf. 1 Pet. 1:17-19.
14. 2 Cor. 11:3.
15. 1 Tim. 2:14, NASB.
16. John 15:11.
17. John 17:13.
18. Phil. 4:4.
19. Isa. 59:2.
20. Col. 1:21, 22.
21. Rom. 5:10; 2 Cor. 5:18; Eph. 2:1ff.
22. Rom. 5:11.
23. John 3:36.
24. John 5:24.
25. John 10:27, 28.
26. 1 John 5:1.
27. 1 John 5:11-13.
28. See 1 Pet. 1:13-21.
29. 2 Tim. 3:12.
30. Eccles. 3:11.
31. Rom. 2:14, 15, NASB.
32. Ps. 14:1.

33. Ps. 14:3.
34. Rom. 1:21-23.
35. Isa. 40:28.
36. Gen. 21:33.
37. Ps. 90:1, 2.
38. Ps. 102:24b-27.

Chapter 2 / The Bible and Its Authority

1. Eph. 4:17, 18.
2. Col. 1:13.
3. Rom. 1:19, 20.
4. Job 23:3.
5. Job 19:25-27.
6. Heb. 1:1.
7. John 1:1, 14; cf. Rev. 19:13.
8. 2 Tim. 3:16.
9. 2 Tim. 3:15.
10. Heb. 9:16, 17.
11. James Fisher, *Fisher's Catechism* (Philadelphia: n.p., 1916), p. 17.
12. 2 Tim. 3:16, 17.
13. Deut. 4:2; cf. 12:32.
14. Matt. 15:3.
15. Matt. 23:16; cf. vv. 17, 19, 24, 26.
16. Matt. 23:15.
17. Isa. 8:19, 20.
18. John 5:38-40.
19. John 1:18.
20. Gen. 36:40, 41; Rom. 5:6.
21. *Webster's Collegiate Dictionary*, 5th ed., 1946.
22. John 2:23-25.
23. Gal. 4:11; cf. Heb. 6:4-6; 10:26-31.
24. Acts 1:3.
25. *The Authority of the Bible* by John R. W. Stott is an excellent forty-one-page booklet. A more ambitious work is F. F. Bruce's *The New Testament Documents: Are They Reliable?* Paul E. Little's *Know Why You Believe* is another useful book that discusses reasons for believing the Bible.
26. "We Believe . . ." (the doctrinal statement of Dallas Theological Seminary).
27. John 20:30, 31.
28. 1 John 5:9, 10.
29. Ex. 20:1, 2.
30. Eph. 2:8-10.
31. James 2:17, 20.

Chapter 3 / Knowing God

1. James W. Sire, *The Universe Next Door* (Downers Grove, Ill.: InterVarsity Press, 1977).
2. John 4:25.
3. Luke 23:46.
4. Luke 24:39.

5. Ps. 27:8, 9.
6. Deut. 4:12, 15-19; cf. 5:8, 9; Rom. 1:23.
7. John 1:18.
8. John 14:9.
9. John 4:20.
10. Acts 17:24, 25, 29.
11. John 4:24.
12. John 17:3.
13. John 1:18.
14. Isa. 7:14; Matt. 1:23.
15. John 14:9.

Chapter 4 / What God Is Like—His Attributes

1. 1 Chron. 29:11.
2. 1 Pet. 1:15, 16.
3. Job 11:7-9.
4. 1 Kings 8:27; cf. 2 Chron. 6:18.
5. Heb. 13:5.
6. Matt. 18:20.
7. Isa. 43:2, 3.
8. *Webster's Collegiate Dictionary*, 5th ed., 1946.
9. Ps. 90:1, 2.
10. 2 Thess. 1:8, 9.
11. Deut. 31:6; cf. Heb. 13:5.
12. Ps. 73:26.
13. Ps. 102:25-27.
14. Mal. 3:6.
15. James 1:17.
16. Jonah 3:10.
17. Mic. 7:18, NASB.

Chapter 5 / What God Is Like—His Being

1. Alexander Whyte, *The Shorter Catechism* (Edinburgh: T. & T. Clark, 1949), p. 10.
2. Ps. 106:19-43.
3. Eph. 1:9-12, *Phillips*.
4. 1 Sam. 2:3.
5. 1 Cor. 4:4, 5; cf. Heb. 4:13.
6. Ps. 139:1-6.
7. Matt. 10:29, 30.
8. 1 John 3:20.
9. Ps. 2:6.
10. James Fisher, *Fisher's Catechism* (Philadelphia: n.p., 1916), p. 33.
11. Rom. 5:20, 21.
12. Rom. 8:28.
13. Rom. 11:33-36.
14. Rom. 16:27.
15. Ps. 14:1.

16. Ps. 119:98-100.
17. Prov. 2:4.
18. Prov. 2:6; James 1:5a.
19. Job 38:4-7.
20. Ps. 8:3.
21. Gen. 18:14; 21:2.
22. Jer. 32:17-25.
23. Luke 1:37.
24. Zech. 8:6.
25. Matt. 16:18.
26. 1 Tim. 1:17.
27. Ex. 15:11.
28. *The Book of Common Prayer* (New York: Harper & Brothers, 1952), p. 6.
29. Rev. 4.
30. Ps. 5:4-6.
31. Jer. 16:18.
32. Jer. 44:4.
33. Heb. 1:8, 9; cf. Ps. 45:6, 7.
34. 2 Pet. 2:4-7, 9.
35. 2 Pet. 2:6.
36. 2 Pet. 3:3-7.
37. Matt. 27:46.
38. 2 Cor. 5:21.
39. 1 Pet. 1:14-16.
40. Heb. 12:10, 14.

Chapter 6 / What God Is Like—Just, Good, and True

1. *Webster's Collegiate Dictionary*, 5th ed., 1946.
2. *The New Combined Bible Dictionary and Concordance* (Grand Rapids: Baker, 1965), p. 359.
3. *Webster's Collegiate.*
4. Deut. 32:3, 4.
5. Cf. Ps. 82:2.
6. 1 Sam. 2:10; Ps. 96:13.
7. Alexander Whyte, *The Shorter Catechism* (Edinburgh: T. & T. Clark, 1949), p. 11.
8. Isa. 45:21, 22.
9. Rom. 2:5.
10. Mic. 4:1-3.
11. Isa. 32:1, 16.
12. Gal. 2:20.
13. 1 Pet. 2:24.
14. 1 Pet. 3:18.
15. Gal. 3:13.
16. Rom. 5:8.
17. Rom. 3:26.
18. 1 John 4:14.

19. 1 John 2:2.
20. Heb. 2:3.
21. Heb. 10:28, 29, 31.
22. Ps. 86:5.
23. Ps. 25:8.
24. Ps. 119:68.
25. Gal. 5:22
26. John 18:37, 38.
27. John 14:6.
28. Matt. 17:5.
29. John 8:44.
30. Cf. Gen. 3:4, 5.
31. 1 Tim. 4:1-3.
32. Col. 2:23.
33. John 8:31, 32.
34. Col. 2:8.
35. Col. 2:2, 3.
36. Whyte, *Catechism*, p. 12.
37. 1 John 5:10, 11.
38. 3 John 4.
39. Heb. 10:23, 24.

Chapter 7 / The Trinity

1. Deut. 6:4.
2. Deut. 5:7, 8; cf. Ex. 20:3, 4.
3. J. A. Thompson, *Deuteronomy*, Tyndale Old Testament Commentaries (Downers Grove, Ill.: InterVarsity Press, 1978), pp. 121, 122.
4. *Ibid.*, p. 122.
5. Rev. 4:10, 11.
6. Acts 17:24, 25.
7. John 14:6.
8. 1 John 2:25.
9. 1 Cor. 8:5, 6.
10. Stephen Neill, *The Christian's God* (London: Oxford University Press, 1963), p. 82.
11. 2 Cor. 13:14.
12. J. H. Large, "The Holy Trinity," in *Treasury of Bible Doctrine*, edited by John Heading and Cyril Hocking (Calne, Wiltahire: Precious Seed, 1977), p. 47.
13. Cf. *Notes on the Heidleberg Confession* (Lancaster, Penn.: n.p., 1887), p. 57.
14. Frank Colquhoun, *The Cathechism and the Order of Confirmation* (London: Hodder and Stoughton, 1963), p. 53.
15. *Ibid.*
16. Alexander Whyte, *The Shorter Catechism* (Edinburgh: T. & T. Clark, 1949), p. 15.
17. Quoted in *ibid*, p. 15.
18. Rom. 1:13; 11:25; etc.
19. Whyte, *Catechism*, p. 15; cf. Heb. 1:5; John 1:14; 15:26; Gal. 4:6.
20. Neill, *The Christian's God*, p. 83.

21. Rom. 15:6; cf. John 17:1; etc.
22. Eph. 1:17.
23. Matt. 6:8-15; cf. Gal. 1:4.
24. Acts 17:28, 29.
25. John 3:16.
26. 1 John 4:15; 5:5.
27. Mark 4:41.
28. Rom. 10:9.
29. John 10:30-33.
30. John 5:20, 23; 6:46, 57; 8:16, 55, 58; 14:9.
31. John 8:58; cf. 4:26; 6:20; 8:24, 28; 13:19; 18:5-8.
32. Ex. 3:13, 14.
33. Isa. 44:6; Rev. 1:17.
34. John 14:16, 17.
35. John 14:26.
36. 1 John 2:1.
37. Acts 5:3, 4, 9.
38. Acts 13:2.
39. Gal. 1:1; etc.
40. Matt. 28:19.
41. 2 Cor. 13:14.
42. Martin Luther, *Luther's Small Catechism* (St. Louis: Concordia, 1943), p. 51.
43. *Webster's Collegiate Dictionary*, 5th. ed., 1946.
44. John 14:2, 23; cf. 2 Cor. 5:8.

Chapter 8 / The Eternal Purpose of God

1. Eph. 1:3-14, emphasis added.
2. Dora Greenwell, "I Am Not Skilled to Understand."
3. Gen. 1:1.
4. Joseph Parker, quoted by Alexander Whyte, *The Shorter Catechism* (Edinburgh: T. & T. Clark, 1949), p. 21.
5. Quoted in *ibid.*
6. 1 Cor. 15:27.

Chapter 9 / The Work of Creation

1. Gen. 1:1.
2. Isa. 42:5.
3. Isa. 45:18.
4. Gen. 1:4, 10, 12, etc.
5. Rom. 1:25.
6. James S. Candlish, *The Christian Doctrine of God* (Edinburgh: T. & T. Clark, n.d.), p. 26.
7. *Ibid.*, p. 27.
8. *Ibid.*, p. 28.
9. 1 Cor. 8:5, 6.
10. Rev. 4:11.
11. T. C. Hammond, *In Understanding Be Men* (London: Inter-Varsity Fellowship of Evangelical Unions, 1936), p. 71.

12. Eph. 3:11, 12.
13. Quoted by Colin Chapman, *Christianity on Trial* (Wheaton, Ill.: Tyndale, 1975), p. 355.
14. Candlish, *Doctrine*, p. 25.
15. *Ibid.*, p. 28.
16. Heb. 11:3.
17. See, e.g., Isa. 42:5-9; 54:4-11.
18. Ps. 121:1, 2.
19. Henry M. Morris, *The Bible Has the Answer* (Nutley, N.J.: Craig Press, 1971), p. 94.
20. Ex. 20:9-11.
21. Derek Kidner, *Genesis* (Downers Grove, Ill.: InterVarsity Press, 1972), pp. 54, 55.
22. Gen. 1:31.
23. Phil. 4:8.
24. 1 Sam. 16:12; 25:3; 2 Sam. 11:2.
25. Ps. 90:17, KJV.
26. Gen. 2:15.
27. Rom. 8:20, 21.
28. 1 Pet. 3:4, 5.

Chapter 10 / The Creation of Man

1. Gen. 1:26-28.
2. Col. 3:10.
3. Eph. 4:24.
4. Alexander Whyte, *The Shorter Catechism* (Edinburgh: T. & T. Clark, 1949), p. 23.
5. Gen. 2:7.
6. 1 Pet. 3:7.
7. John 4:24.
8. Gordon R. Lewis, *Decide for Yourself: A Theological Workbook* (Downers Grove, Ill.: InterVarsity Press, 1971), pp. 79, 80.
9. 1 Cor. 2:11, *Phillips*.
10. Rom. 6:12; cf. 1 Cor. 9:27.
11. Rom. 14:12.
12. 1 Cor. 2:11, 12, *Phillips*.
13. T. C. Hammond, *In Understanding Be Men* (London: Inter-Varsity Fellowship of Evangelical Unions, 1936), p. 88.
14. Erich Sauer, *The Dawn of World Redemption* (Grand Rapids: Eerdmans, 1953), p. 41 emphasis his.
15. *Ibid.*, p. 42.
16. *Ibid.*
17. 2 Cor. 3:18.
18. Ps. 8:4.
19. Gen. 3:8, 10.
20. 2 Tim. 3:7.
21. Cf. Rom. 2:14.
22. Ps. 8:6-8.
23. Gen. 1:30.

24. Gen. 2:19.
25. Isa. 11:6.
26. Heb. 2:9.

Chapter 11 / God's Providence

1. *Webster's New Collegiate Dictionary*, 7th ed., 1969.
2. 2 Pet. 3:10.
3. 1 Kings 13.
4. 1 Kings 19:9, 13.
5. Gen. 12:10-20.
6. James 1:13.
7. 1 John 5:19.
8. Eph. 2:2.
9. Gen. 1:28-30; 2:15-17.
10. Derek Kidner, *Genesis* (Downers Grove, Ill.: InterVarsity Press, 1972), p. 63.
11. *Ibid.*, p. 62.
12. Alexander Whyte, *The Shorter Catechism* (Edinburgh: T. & T. Clark, 1949), p. 31.
13. Quoted in *ibid.*
14. Rev. 22:1, 2.

Chapter 12 / What Caused the Fall?

1. Quoted by Alexander Whyte, *The Shorter Catechism* (Edinburgh: T. & T. Clark, 1949), p. 32.
2. James Fisher, *Fisher's Catechism* (Philadelphia: n.p., 1916), p. 78.
3. *Ibid.*; cf. Mal. 3:6; James 1:17.
4. *Paradise Lost.*
5. Ps. 51:4.
6. John 8:44; cf. 1 Tim. 3:6, 7.
7. 1 Cor. 10:12.
8. Heb. 4:11.
9. Heb. 6:6.
10. 2 Pet. 3:17.
11. James 4:17.
12. Matt. 23:23.
13. 1 John 3:4.
14. 1 John 5:17.
15. Ps. 32:1, 2, 5.
16. M. Goodwin; quoted by Alexander Whyte, *Catechism*, p. 35.
17. Eph. 4:18.
18. Rom. 5:19.
19. Ps. 51:1-4.
20. Rom. 7:7, 8.
21. Rom. 5:14ff.
22. 1 John 3:4.
23. Rom. 5:19.
24. Rom. 5:20.
25. Rom. 5:12.
26. 1 Cor. 15:22.

27. Cf. Heb. 7:9, 10.
28. 1 Cor. 15:45.
29. Cf. Heb. 7:9, 10.
30. 1 Cor. 15:49.
31. Whyte, *Catechism,* pp. 36, 37.
32. T. C. Hammond, *In Understanding Be Men* (London: Inter-Varsity Fellowship of Evangelical Unions, 1936), p. 89.
33. *Ibid.*
34. 1 Pet. 2:24.

Chapter 13 / The Consequences of the Fall—Corruption and Depravity

1. William Dyrness, *Themes in Old Testament Theology* (Downers Grove, Ill.: InterVarsity Press, 1979), p. 110.
2. Alexander Whyte, *The Shorter Catechism* (Edinburgh: T. & T. Clark, 1949), p. 39.
3. Job 4:17-19.
4. Quoted in Whyte, *Catechism,* p. 40.
5. Rom. 3:23.
6. Rom. 5:8.
7. Eph. 2:1-3, NASB.
8. Eph. 2:8-10, NASB.
9. Quoted in Whyte, *Catechism,* p. 40.
10. 2 Cor. 3:18.
11. J. P. Lilley, *The Principles of Protestantism* (Edinburgh: T. T. Clark, 1911), p. 17.
12. In A. C. Whitmer, *Notes on the Heidelberg Confession* (Lancaster, Pa.: n.p., 1887).
13. Article II. Cf. Henry Bettensen, *Documents of the Christian Church* (London: Oxford University Press, 1947), p. 297.
14. *The Encyclopedia of Philosophy* (New York: Macmillan, 1967), Vol. 6.
15. Mark 7:20-23.
16. Jer. 17:9.
17. Gal. 5:19-21.
18. Quoted in Whyte, *Catechism,* pp. 42, 43.

Chapter 14 / The Consequences of the Fall—Cursed in Death

1. See Acts 2:42; 1 Cor. 1:9; 10:16, AV; 2 Cor. 6:14, 13:14; Phil. 1:5; etc.
2. E. M. Blaiklock, *Letter to Children of Life* (Glendale, Cal.: Regal, 1975), pp. 18, 19.
3. Gen. 1:28.
4. Gen. 4:6ff.
5. Eph. 4:17-19.
6. Ps. 5:5; 11:5.
7. Rom. 1:32.
8. Eph. 5:6.
9. Col. 3:5, 6.
10. See *The Believers Hymnbook* (London: Pickering & Inglis, Ltd., n.d.).
11. Gen. 3:14, 17; 4:11, 12.

12. Gal. 3:10, 13.
13. Gal. 3:14.
14. Rom. 1:28.
15. 1 John 5:19.
16. Job 1:8-19.
17. Rom. 8:28ff.
18. Rom. 5:12.
19. Rom. 6:23.
20. 1 Cor. 15:56.
21. Heb. 9:27.
22. 1 Cor. 15:50ff.
23. James Fisher, *Fisher's Catechism* (Philadelphia: n.p., 1916), p. 98; cf. Matt. 25:21; 1 Cor. 3:22.
24. 1 Cor. 15:55.
25. Matt. 25:41, 46.
26. John 3:36.
27. 2 Thess. 1:7-10.
28. 2 Thess. 1:8, 9.
29. Jude 7.
30. John 3:16-18a.

Chapter 15 / God's Gracious Provision

1. 1 John 4:10, 14.
2. Matt. 11:26.
3. Eph. 1:5.
4. J. S. Candlish, *Ephesians* (Edinburgh: T. & T. Clark, 1901), p. 35.
5. *Ibid.*
6. Eph. 1:13.
7. Francis Foulkes, *Ephesians* (London: Tyndale Press, 1963), p. 46, emphasis his.
8. 1 Thess. 1:6, 9, 10.
9. Acts 17:24, 26, 27.
10. Acts 15:16-18, emphasis added.
11. Rom. 1:16.
12. 1 Cor. 1:21.
13. E. A. Litton, *Introduction to Dogmatic Theology* (London: James Clark and Co., 1912), pp. 349, 350.
14. J. A. Beet, *Commentary on Romans* (London: Whitaker, 1878), p. 279.
15. Rom. 8:29, 30, 38, 39.
16. Quoted by Alexander Whyte, *The Shorter Catechism* (Edinburgh: T. & T. Clark, 1949), p. 30.
17. *Ibid.*, pp. 46, 47, emphasis his.
18. Eph. 2:8, 9.
19. Quoted in Whyte, *Catechism*, p. 47.
20. George Smeaton, *The Doctrine of the Atonement as Taught by Christ Himself* (Edinburgh: T. & T. Clark, 1871), p. 66.
21. Lewis Sperry Chafer, *Systematic Theology* (Dallas: Dallas Seminary Press, 1948), Vol. VIII, p. 67.

22. Charles C. Ryrie, *Dispensationalism Today* (Chicago: Moody Press, 1965), pp. 183, 184.
23. John 3:16.
24. 1 John 4:14.
25. 2 Pet. 3:9.
26. Titus 2:11-13.

Chapter 16 / The Person of Jesus Christ

1. See Acts 7:45; Heb. 4:8.
2. Josh. 1:1; 1 Sam. 6:14; 2 Kings 23:8; Zech. 3:1; Col. 4:11.
3. Matt. 1:21.
4. John Newton, "How Sweet the Name of Jesus Sounds."
5. Matt. 16:16.
6. Matt. 26:63.
7. Ps. 2:2.
8. John 4:25, 26.
9. John 1:41.
10. John 4:29, 42; cf. Acts 10:38-43.
11. Rom. 10:9.
12. Matt. 16:16.
13. James 2:1.
14. *Webster's Collegiate Dictionary*, 5th ed., 1946.
15. Alexander Whyte, *The Shorter Catechism* (Edinburgh: T. & T. Clark, 1949), p. 49.
16. *The Jerusalem Bible* (New York: Doubleday, 1966).
17. Acts 13:32, 33.
18. Gal. 4:4.
19. John 16:28.
20. 1 John 1:2.
21. W. E. Vine, *The First and the Last* (London: Pickering & Inglis, n.d.), pp. 10, 11.
22. Col. 2:9.
23. Heb. 9:14.
24. W. H. Griffith Thomas, *The Principles of Theology* (London: Longmans, Green, 1930), pp. 38, 39.

Chapter 17 / The Incarnation—God and Man

1. John 1:14.
2. 1 Tim. 3:16.
3. *Webster's Collegiate Dictionary*, 5th ed, 1946.
4. Gal. 4:4.
5. Alexander Whyte, *The Shorter Catechism* (Edinburgh: T. & T. Clark, 1949), p. 51.
6. Heb. 2:17, 18; cf. 4:14-16.
7. In John Macpherson, *The Confession of Faith* (Edinburgh: T. & T. Clark, 1882), p. 71.
8. In E. A. Litton, *Introduction to Dogmatic Theology* (London: James Clark and Co., 1912), p. 192.
9. Acts 20:30.

10. 2 Pet. 2:1.
11. W. H. Griffith Thomas, *The Principles of Theology* (London: Longmans, Green, 1930), p. 40.
12. *Ibid.*
13. Thomas Hooker, *Ecclesiastical Polity*, Bk. V, Ch. 53, Section 4; cf. Thomas, *Principles,* pp. 41, 42.
14. *Ibid.*
15. Gal. 2:5.
16. Jude 3.
17. Heb. 13:8.
18. Heb. 7:24, 25.
19. John 14:19.

Chapter 18 / The Incarnation—Truly Man, Without Sin

1. Heb. 2:14.
2. Alexander Whyte, *The Shorter Catechism* (Edinburgh: T. & T. Clark, 1949), p. 53.
3. *Webster's New Twentieth Century Dictionary*, 1967.
4. Paul Johnson, *A History of Christianity* (New York: Atheneum, 1977), p. 45.
5. *Ibid.*
6. 1 Cor. 15:3, 17.
7. Whyte, *Catechism,* p. 54.
8. Heb. 5:7-9.
9. Luke 1:34, 35.
10. Matt. 1:20.
11. Matt. 1:22, 23; cf. Isa. 7:14.
12. James Orr, *The Virgin Birth of Christ* (London: n.p., 1907), pp. 228, 229.
13. W. H. Griffith Thomas, *The Principles of Theology* (London: Longmans, Green, 1930), pp. 47-49.
14. *Ibid.,* p. 48.
15. Orr, *Virgin Birth,* p. 229.
16. Marcus Dods, *Christian Instructor,* 1830; quoted in Whyte, *Catechism,* p. 54.
17. Luke 1:35, NASB.
18. Whyte, *Catechism,* p. 55.

Chapter 19 / Jesus Christ as Prophet

1. Deut. 18:18.
2. Acts 3:17-24.
3. Luke 24:25-27.
4. 1 Pet. 1:10-12.
5. John 1:18.
6. John 15:15.
7. Matt. 11:25-27.
8. Erich Sauer, *The Triumph of the Crucified* (Grand Rapids: Eerdmans, 1952), p. 47.
9. Col. 3:10.

10. John 14:10, 23, 24.
11. Sauer, *Triumph,* pp. 47, 48.

Chapter 20 / Jesus Christ as Priest

1. Ps. 110:1, 4.
2. Heb. 5:5, 6.
3. Heb. 5:1, 4.
4. See Ex. 28:15-30.
5. Heb. 10:5-7, 10.
6. Gal. 2:20.
7. Heb. 9:14.
8. Heb. 10:7; cf. John 4:34.
9. A. M. Toplady, "From Whence This Fear."
10. Horatius Bonar, "I Hear the Words of Love."
11. Alexander Whyte, *The Shorter Catechism* (Edinburgh: T. & T. Clark, 1949), p. 60.
12. See E. A. Litton, *Introduction to Dogmatic Theology* (London: James Clark and Co., 1912), p. 223.
13. *Ibid.,* p. 224.
14. Paraphrased in *ibid.*
15. Rom. 8:31-33.
16. *Webster's Collegiate Dictionary,* 5th ed., 1946.
17. 2 Cor. 5:17-20.
18. Rom. 5:10.
19. Eph. 2:14-16.
20. Lewis Sperry Chafer, *Systematic Theology* (Dallas: Dallas Seminary Press, 1948), Vol. III, p. 93.
21. *Ibid.*
22. R. C. Trench, *Synonyms of the New Testament* (London: Kegan Paul, 1892), p. 292.
23. *Ibid.*
24. Matt. 11:28.
25. Rom. 5:8.
26. Quoted in Whyte, *Catechism,* p. 61.
27. Chafer, *Theology,* Vol. III, p. 93.
28. *Ibid.*
29. *Ibid.*
30. 2 Sam. 14:14.
31. Heb. 7:24, 25.
32. Chafer, *Theology,* Vol. V, p. 276.
33. Heb. 1:3; 8:1; 10:12.
34. *The Ascended Christ,* p. 95, quoted in Thomas, *Principles,* p. 85.
35. *Ibid.*

Chapter 21 / Jesus Christ as King

1. Matt. 21:4, 5.
2. Matt. 2:1, 2.
3. Rom. 10:9.
4. Col. 1:13.

5. Alexander Whyte, *The Shorter Catechism* (Edinburgh: T. & T. Clark, 1949), pp. 63, 64.
6. John 14:21.
7. 1 John 4:4, cf. vv. 1-3.
8. Jude 24.
9. See Job 1:12; 2:6.
10. 1 John 3:8.
11. Rom. 16:20.
12. 1 Cor. 15:25, 26.
13. Rev. 11:15.

Chapter 22 / Christ's Humiliation

1. Acts 8:33-35.
2. Edward Caswall, "See Amid the Winter's Snow."
3. Ann Gilbert, "What Led the Son of God?"
4. Luke 2:7.
5. Lev. 12:8.
6. Luke 2:22-24.
7. John 1:29, 36.
8. Luke 9:58.
9. Matt. 17:24-27.
10. 2 Cor. 8:9.
11. Gal. 4:4.
12. Matt. 1:1-17.
13. Rom. 1:3.
14. Rom. 9:4, 5.
15. 1 Cor. 3:22, 23, NASB.
16. Gal. 3:13.
17. 1 Pet. 2:24.
18. Author unknown, "Behold a Spotless Victim Dies."
19. Matt. 9:36; cf. 14:14; 18:27; Mark 1:41; 6:34.
20. John 11:35; Luke 19:41.
21. John 2:17; cf. Mark 8:11; Matt. 23:33.
22. Isa. 53:3.
23. 1 Pet. 2:21.
24. *Webster's Seventh New Collegiate Dictionary*, 1969.
25. Isa. 28:21.
26. W. E. Vine, *Expository Dictionary of New Testament Words* (Westwood, N.J.: Revell, 1956), n.p.
27. John 3:36.
28. Col. 3:5, 6.
29. 1 Thess. 1:10.
30. Rom. 8:1, *Phillips*.
31. 2 Cor. 5:21.
32. Quoted by Alexander Whyte, *The Shorter Catechism* (Edinburgh: T. & T. Clark, 1949), p. 66.
33. Isa. 53:10.
34. Gal. 3:10, 13; cf. Deut. 21:23; 1 Pet. 2:24.
35. Source unknown.

36. Acts 2:24.
37. Matt. 12:40.
38. See Acts 3:15.
39. John 19:30.
40. Acts 2:26.

Chapter 23 / Christ's Exaltation

1. Alexander Whyte, *The Shorter Catechism* (Edinburgh: T. & T. Clark, 1949), p. 68.
2. 1 Cor. 15:14, 15, 17.
3. Mark 16:19.
4. Luke 24:51.
5. Acts 1:9-11; cf. v. 2.
6. E. A. Litton, *Introduction to Dogmatic Theology* (London: James Clark and Co., 1912), p. 192.
7. John 16:28.
8. Matt. 28:18-20.
9. Ps. 68:18.
10. Eph. 4:9-12.
11. Heb. 4:14.
12. Heb. 6:20.
13. Heb. 7:26.
14. Heb. 9:24.
15. Mark 16:19; Acts 2:33; Rom. 8:34; Col. 3:1; etc.
16. In Whyte, *Catechism*, p. 68.
17. See W. H. Griffith Thomas, *The Principles of Theology* (London: Longmans, Green, 1930), p. 83.
18. 1 John 2:1, 2.
19. Thomas, *Principles*, p. 85.
20. Acts 1:11.
21. 1 Thess. 1:10.
22. Titus 2:13.
23. Thomas, *Principles*, p. 87.
24. John 5:22-24.
25. Rom. 8:1.
26. 1 Cor. 3:10-15.
27. John 5:22-24.
28. Acts 17:31.
29. Rom 3:5, 6.
30. 2 Thess. 1:5-9.

Chapter 24 / The Holy Spirit's Work in Redemption

1. Titus 3:5-7, TEV.
2. Matt. 20:28.
3. 1 Cor. 6:19, 20.
4. 1 Pet. 1:18, 19.
5. Titus 3:5, 6.
6. Jer. 17:9.
7. Rom. 7:18.

8. Acts 16:31.
9. 1 Cor. 12:3.
10. 1 Thess. 1:4, 5.
11. Acts 16:14.
12. 2 Cor. 5:17.
13. Col. 1:27.
14. Titus 3:5, 6.
15. Eph. 1:13, 14.
16. John 15:1-8.
17. 1 Cor. 12:27; Col. 1:18.
18. I. Howard Marshall, *Christian Beliefs* (Downers Grove, Ill.: InterVarsity Press, 1978), p. 96.
19. *Ibid.*
20. 2 Tim. 1:9.
21. 2 Thess. 2:13, 14.
22. John 16:7-11.
23. Heb. 4:1, 2.
24. Alexander Whyte, *The Shorter Catechism* (Edinburgh: T. & T. Clark, 1949), p. 74.
25. John 7:17.
26. John 9:39.
27. 2 Cor. 4:3, 4.
28. Eph. 4:18.
29. Whyte, *Catechism,* p. 75.
30. Eph. 4:18.
31. Rom. 3:20.
32. See Deut. 4:13; 10:4.
33. Rom. 10:17.
34. Eph. 1:13.
35. 1 Thess. 1:4, 5.
36. W. H. Griffith Thomas, *The Principles of Theology* (London: Longmans, Green, 1930), pp. 165, 166.
37. Whyte, *Catechism,* pp. 75, 76.
38. *Ibid.*, p. 76.
39. John 5:40.
40. "Of Free-Will," Section IV.
41. Rom. 7:21.
42. "Of Free Will," Section V.
43. John Macpherson, *The Confession of Faith* (Edinburgh: T & T Clark, 1882), p. 82.
44. Acts 16:14.
45. John 15:26.
46. Charles Hodge, quoted in Whyte, *Catechism,* p. 77.

Chapter 25 / Justification

1. *Webster's Seventh New Collegiate Dictionary,* 1969.
2. Rom. 4:5.
3. Rom. 4:7, 8.
4. Civilla D. Martin, "Accepted in the Beloved."

5. Rom. 4:5, 6, 11, 22, 23, 24; 5:13; 2 Cor. 5:19; etc.
6. Alexander Whyte, *The Shorter Catechism* (Edinburgh: T. & T. Clark, 1949), p. 83.
7. Eph. 2:8, 9.
8. Rom. 4:4, 5.
9. Rom. 3:8.
10. James 2:14.
11. James 2:24.

Chapter 26 / Adoption

1. Rom. 8:15.
2. Rom. 8:23.
3. Eph. 1:4, 5.
4. Eph. 1:13, 14.
5. Compare, e.g., John 1:12, 13 and 1 John 3:1, 2 with Rom. 8:15, 23; Gal. 4:5; Eph. 1:5.
6. Gal. 3:26.

Chapter 27 / Sanctification

1. *Webster's Collegiate Dictionary,* 5th ed, 1946.
2. 1 Thess. 4:3.
3. Ex. 19:22, 23; 29:44; Lev. 27:14ff.; Isa. 8:13; 1 Pet. 3:15; etc.
4. 1 Pet. 1:2, 18, 19.
5. Heb. 10:14; 1 Cor. 1:2.
6. 1 Cor. 1:2, emphasis added.
7. Rom. 6:19, 22.
8. 1 Thess. 4:3, 7.
9. Heb. 12:14.
10. 1 Cor. 3:1-4.
11. Heb. 5:11-14; 6:1, 2, 12.
12. 1 John 3:2.
13. Rom. 12:2.
14. Col. 3:9, 10.
15. John 17:17.
16. 1 John 1:9.
17. Rom. 6:2.
18. Rom. 6:6.
19. Rom. 6:10, 11.
20. 2 Cor. 5:14.
21. Rom. 6:11, 13.
22. Gal. 5:24.
23. Col. 3:5, 8-10; cf. Eph. 4—6.

Chapter 28 / Present Blessings of Believers—Assurance, Peace, Joy

1. John 7:34.
2. John 3:14, 15.
3. Rom. 6:23.
4. John 5:24.
5. John 10:27, 28.

6. Rom. 8:38, 39.
7. Phil. 1:6.
8. Heb. 7:25, NASB.
9. John 5:24.
10. Col. 1:13.
11. Eph. 1:13, 14.
12. Heb. 6:4-6.
13. William Evans, *The Great Doctrines of the Bible* (Chicago: Moody Press, 1974), p. 315.
14. 1 John 1:9; 2:1.
15. Rom. 8:31, 33.
16. 1 John 5:11-13.
17. Rom. 5:1.
18. Phil. 4:6, 7.
19. Gal. 4:6.
20. Rom. 5:1.
21. Acts 24:16.
22. Edward H. Bickersteth, "Peace, Perfect Peace."
23. John 14:27.
24. Rom. 1:7; cf. 1 Cor. 1:3; 2 Cor. 1:2; Gal. 1:3; etc.
25. W. E. Vine, *Expository Dictionary of New Testament Words* (Westwood, N.J.: Revell, 1956). See also *The New International Dictionary of New Testament Theology* (Grand Rapids: Zondervan, 1979).
26. Eph. 2:17.
27. Rom. 14:17.
28. Phil. 4:4.
29. *New International Dictionary*, Vol. 2., p. 359.
30. Gal. 5:22.
31. 1 Thess. 1:6.
32. John 15:11.
33. John 17:13.

Chapter 29 / Present Blessings of Believers—Grace and Perseverance

1. Quoted by Bernard Osborne, in *Treasury of Bible Doctrine*, ed. by J. Heading and C. E. Hocking (Calne, Wiltahire: Precious Seed, 1977), pp. 285, 286.
2. *Ibid.*
3. *Ibid.*
4. 2 Cor. 8:9.
5. Eph. 2:8.
6. Titus 2:11.
7. 1 Pet. 1:13.
8. Phil. 1:6.
9. Phil. 2:12, 13.
10. Alexander Whyte, *The Shorter Catechism* (Edinburgh: T. & T. Clark, 1949), p. 94.
11. W. H. Griffith Thomas, *The Catholic Faith* (London: n.p., 1947), p. 133.
12. Matt. 19:26; cf. Mark 10:27; 14:36.

13. Mark 9:23.
14. 1 Pet. 2:2.
15. Jude 20.
16. Heb. 10:24, 25.
17. 1 Cor. 11:24.
18. 1 Cor. 10:16, NASB.
19. John 10:27, 28.
20. John C. Ryle, *Expository Thoughts on the Gospels, St. John,* Vol. II (New York: Carter & Bros., 2nd. ed., 1869), p. 212.
21. *Ibid.*
22. Rom. 8:29, 38, 39.
23. Thomas, *Catholic Faith,* p. 107.
24. Ryle, *St. John,* Vol. II, p. 212.
25. John 10:27.
26. 2 Tim. 2:19.
27. Neh. 8:9.
28. Neh. 8:10.
29. Matt. 5:4.
30. Ps. 51:12, 13.
31. Phil. 4:4.

Chapter 30 / Future Blessings of Believers

1. Matt. 22:32.
2. Rev. 21:8.
3. Luke 16:19-31.
4. John 3:36.
5. Heb. 12:22, 23.
6. 1 John 3:2.
7. Rev. 21:4.
8. 2 Tim. 4:6, 8; cf. 2 Cor. 5:5.
9. Matt. 22:31, 32.
10. 1 Cor. 6:15.
11. 1 Thess. 5:23.
12. Phil. 3:20, 21.
13. 1 Cor. 15:42, 43.
14. 2 Pet. 3:13.
15. 1 Cor. 15:43.
16. 1 Cor. 15:5-8.
17. 1 Cor. 15:58.
18. Matt. 10:32.
19. Luke 12:8; Rev. 3:5.
20. John 13.33; 15:14, 15.
21. Rom. 8:29, 30.
22. John 15:20, 21.
23. John 16:2, 3.
24. 1 John 4:5, 6.
25. Rom. 8:19.
26. 1 Cor. 3:13.

27. 1 Cor. 4:5.
28. Matt. 19:30.
29. Ps. 16:11.
30. Ps. 73:26.
31. 1 Cor. 13:12.
32. Rev. 22:4, 5, 20.